NO MORE DEATHS BY WELFARE

'An enraging and energising call to action against the many murderous continuities between state violence and state neglect and the wilful construction of conditions of death in the name of "welfare". Abolition means building something different and better together, this work helps us to think how.'

—**Gargi Bhattacharyya,**
author of *Rethinking Racial Capitalism*

'This brilliant and essential book exposes how stigma and violence have been designed into the UK welfare state and demonstrates how we can and must abolish the current system and build life-affirming alternatives.'

—**Imogen Tyler,**
author of *Stigma: The Machinery of Inequality*

'This hugely important book needed to be written, and there was no-one better qualified to write it than China Mills, who has been at the heart of investigating and researching these deaths for two decades and – perhaps most importantly – has spent years building powerful relationships with those whose lives have been shattered by the Department for Work and Pensions. Somehow, she finds a way to combine searing anger at the deaths inflicted on so many people with the empathy and generosity that will be needed to destroy this oppressive panopticon and find a path towards a kinder, gentler future.'

—**John Pring, author of *The Department: How a Violent Government Bureaucracy Killed Hundreds and Hid the Evidence***

'Mills offers an erudite critique of the life-denying logics embedded within our social assistance systems and a compelling vision for a new welfare architecture grounded in the affirmation of all human life. A powerful corrective to both the anti-welfare common sense that dominates contemporary political imagination and the state-perpetrated violence rampant in contemporary policy, we should read this book – and especially the voices of lived experience it amplifies – with great care.'

—Jamie Redman, Research Associate at the Centre for Regional Economic and Social Research, Sheffield Hallam University

'A necessary book and a testament to what research can look like when it's actually led by disabled and minoritised activists and when it opts out of just urging "leaders" to improve systems, delivering instead a devastating analysis of how such systems are in need of dismantling. It is not easy to stay attuned to writing this and see it through nor should it be easy to read. But read we must, especially now as this violence accelerates.'

—Stan Papoulias, Institute of Psychiatry, Psychology & Neuroscience, King's College London

No More Deaths by Welfare

CHINA MILLS

PLUTO PRESS

First published 2026 by Pluto Press
New Wing, Somerset House, Strand, London WC2R 1LA
and Pluto Press, Inc.
1930 Village Center Circle, 3-834, Las Vegas, NV 89134
www.plutobooks.com

A CIP catalogue record for this book is available from the British Library

978-0-7453-5228-2 (paperback)
978-0-7453-5230-5 (.epub)
978-0-7453-5229-9 (.pdf)

Typeset by Tetragon, London
Cover design by Keith Dodds
Printed in the United Kingdom

EU GPSR Authorised Representative
LOGOS EUROPE, 9 rue Nicolas Poussin, 17000, LA ROCHELLE, France
Email: contact@logoseurope.eu

This book is dedicated to all people harmed or killed by the welfare system, and all of its connecting threads of state violence. We hold you all in spirit as we continue to fight for and dream of justice, and while we co-create worlds designed to honour all of our inherent dignity, where no one is a burden, where you will be valued, in life and death, no matter what.

CONTENTS

PREFACE

Creating the Deaths by Welfare Project

It was almost 20 years ago when disabled people started telling me that the welfare system was killing them. I was meeting people who were terrified of the Department for Work and Pensions[1] (often referred to by the abbreviation 'DWP'). Then I heard from welfare advisers whose clients were dying, and from families, grieving for loved ones killed by the welfare system.

During 2007–08, the British Labour government ramped up reforms that claimed to be about providing incentives into work for disabled people and others claiming long-term benefits. The new regulations intensified policies of conditionality, sanctions and disability assessments that would come to be life threatening. A key part of this was the introduction of the Work Capability Assessment – an assessment outsourced to private companies which determines how a health condition or disability affects your ability to work.

I watched my own family members unravel in trying to navigate these reforms – how they played into and worsened their existing mental distress. These 'reforms', rooted in austerity, dehumanisation and punishment, make people on welfare out to be undeserving, prioritise work at any cost, and make life, for many, unliveable. And all have become synonymous with disabled people's deaths. Or to put it another way, they have killed, and continue to kill, disabled people. People have died through destitution, they have starved to death, they have been killed by anxiety, stress and fear, and people have died by suicide. We write 'Cuts Kill' on our placards, because they do. One study found that austerity policies, including spending cuts to public services, led to over 330,000 excess deaths in Great Britain between 2012 and 2019.[2]

Protesting these reforms, I could never have predicted or comprehended (unlike many disabled people who warned us) the harm that was to come. I would not have believed you if you told me this would begin my own personal journey researching welfare state violence spanning two decades. As a researcher, I started investigating – looking for more evidence, scouring policy documents, newspaper coverage. I felt sure that if we could find the evidence showing that welfare policy is causing harm and make it public, then it would stop. And that's what I have done for years, and the harm hasn't stopped. This journey has also taught me that the harms of the welfare system go much deeper than cuts. Nor could I have predicted that almost 20 years later I would write a book about just some of the many disabled people who have been killed by a violence innocuously named a 'reform'. A book that can never be complete because we will never know the names of everyone who has died. It's from this place of grief and rage that I write this book. And I also write it grounded in the belief that we can collectively build power towards something radically different – something life-affirming and dignifying.

Protests, direct action, chats with activists on the streets, on Zoom – disabled activists wanting documentation of harms – a database, an archive, a timeline of evidence. The Deaths by Welfare project was created to document evidence of harm; a way of honouring, uplifting and learning from disabled people's and bereaved families' lived experience, labour, resistance, defiance, grief, creativity and solidarity; and also a way of remembering and memorialising those who have died and been killed. It helped a lot that at this time I was exhausted and angry from working in academia for a decade and had found a new home – the soil from which the Deaths by Welfare project grew – at Healing Justice Ldn, an organisation building the capacities, skills, and infrastructures we need to support abundant and accessible community-led health and healing.

Disabled people's activism, whether from bed or on the streets, is where I come across the sharpest analysis, where people honour those who have died and fight like hell for those still alive, where I witness rage and love, where I see people rehearsing the worlds they dream of, doing collective access, leaving no one behind, where I see exhaustion, burnout, where I listen as people skilfully navigate complicated forms of justice, and where I learn about naming state violence as a killer while holding space for joy. Doing justice together in a context that systemically devalues certain people is messy. There are also times when people piss each other off; when people want to talk about their grief and then other people get triggered; when disability activism reproduces racism and ableism; when everyone's knackered and not well resourced to hold complexity and nuance; when we slip into old shapes and binary thinking and we pit ourselves against each other, tear each other apart because tearing down the systems that harm us feels impossible; when we forget that we don't have to like each other to move together.

Long-time involvement in disabled people's and Mad activism taught me that disabled people were doing a huge amount of the labour of documenting the mountains of evidence we have that the welfare system kills people. This labour looks like submitting freedom of information requests, waiting, following up on responses, submitting appeals, late nights trawling the internet, documenting evidence of harm through collecting people's stories, creating lists of people who have died, supporting others to navigate the welfare system so they can stay alive, organising protests on the streets, finding allies, lobbying the United Nations, and on and on. This labour tells us so much about the design of the welfare system – its opacity and intentional complexity.

One of the people doing this work was John Pring – the editor of Disability News Service. I'd been reading his articles for a long time – I wouldn't know even half as much as I do about welfare state violence if it wasn't for John. On 4 January 2021, I (nervously) emailed John to ask if he'd like to work together to create a tool showing the links between the UK welfare system and disabled people's deaths. John replied the same day and said yes. We have been friends ever since.

John and I wanted to document the cumulative build-up of harms, the patterns and wider context of welfare deaths. We decided to create a timeline as a counter-history and a living document (always partial, never finished).[3] We did this in the way a journalist and a researcher know how – by piecing together evidence in the form of publicly available documents that relate to the deaths of disabled people claiming benefits (such as safeguarding reports and Prevention of Future Death reports). Pulling (sometimes wrenching) this evidence together helped us to expose patterns dispersed across time – connections across people's lives and deaths, and the strategies used over time by the DWP to deny accountability for people's deaths. We did this with help from three disabled activists and artists involved in significant campaigning around benefits-related deaths – Ellen Clifford, Dolly Sen and Rick Burgess – and from Nick Dilworth, who had decades of experience as a welfare adviser. We reworked the timeline and made it publicly available online as part of a public consultation for people to give feedback, then reworked it again before launching it.

We knew that one of the ways the welfare system is violent is through bureaucracy and we didn't want the Deaths by Welfare project to reproduce this. This meant practical things like making sure we found ways to pay disabled people for their expertise, and that payment was straightforward and speedy. Almost every single person was amazed that we had a budget and could pay them for the time and expertise that they are so often asked for and expected to give for free – in a climate that tarnishes disabled people as 'scroungers'. This told me everything about the devaluing of disabled people's labour and knowledge in research. The timeline also had to be accessible, and not as an afterthought or retrofit – accessible by design – because we wanted it to be used first and foremost by our people – people navigating, impacted and harmed by the welfare system. We wanted lived experience to shape the design of the timeline – just as it had shaped the demand for it – and for it to practise radical accessibility. That's how we found and started working with Access Power Visibility collective.[4]

We had long chats about when the timeline should begin. We knew we wanted to show how 'welfare reform' had a history going way back before 2007–08, but how would we choose how far back? We chose the 1940s, for now, because it's a significant time for the creation of the welfare state, but always knowing that we could have chosen centuries back – back to the Poor Laws and earlier (as we'll explore in this book). We talked a lot about naming – people, and what kills them. For a long time, John and I have struggled with the discomfort of wanting to name as many people as possible, while holding that some families don't agree about naming the welfare system as a cause of death, maybe some don't want their loved one associated with something so dehumanising. And many people I spoke to as part of the project also can't be named – need to remain anonymous – because of DWP surveillance and the very real fear of having their benefits stopped. John and I also struggled with another naming – whether we should say how people die when they die by suicide. We decided not to name methods of suicide – 'methods' sounds so cold and technical, these ways of describing how people choose to end their lives. Ultimately, why does it matter? They were made to feel awful and they died. We shouldn't need details to make us more sympathetic – we shouldn't need persuading to grieve.

I wanted to document evidence of what I started to understand as welfare state violence because I feel so angry about what's happening. I am not objective or dispassionate – how could I be when so many people are being killed? I am enraged. But my rage is rigorous. If there is a method to this research then it is rigorous rage. Part of that rigour lies in centring disabled people's creativity, resistance and expertise in demanding accountability for the ways the welfare system is killing people, while moving away from single-issue organising into the connection of different struggles; in holding and honouring people's creative, messy, imperfect and brilliant fights for justice; and honouring the way disabled people and bereaved families find each other, build solidarity and prefigure the world they want to live in against a context of engineered shame and isolation. Alongside the timeline sit over 50 conversations with disabled activists and bereaved families, some of which were part of a series of podcasts we produced at Healing Justice Ldn, centring disabled people's experience and analysis of the welfare system (and which make up a significant part of this book); archival work searching for lineages of resistance to welfare state violence; and an exhibition as part of a month-long festival, inviting people into conversation and connection to overturn state violence, and to repair and reimagine.[5]

HOW MANY TIMES DO WE NEED TO DESCRIBE HOW AWFUL THINGS ARE?

I have read (and written) so much academic research that repeats over and over again what the problem is – that people are dying because of the welfare system. Often these books and articles and blogs are an endless repetition of doom, with a few words of hope thrown in at the end. Ten chapters of how a system kills people, and then a few sentences in the conclusion on the need for hope. I didn't want the Deaths by Welfare project, or this book, to be like that – I wanted disabled people and others who claim welfare to be rooted in the analysis that I have learned on the streets and online, from those who know welfare state violence because they live and resist it daily.

If we know the welfare system kills people partly by demonising and dehumanising them, then I want the ways I document and talk about this to resist it on every page – to affirm people's inherent dignity and humanity in every word, every space, every full stop. If I think a powerful story – told by the powerful – about welfare is what keeps us small, pits us against each other, makes us feel undeserving, then how much should I repeat that story – even in critiquing it? I feel like this when I want to talk about the deep dehumanisation and engineered shame crafted by the government and media – should I repeat the words they use? How do we use evidence in ways that do not dehumanise disabled people and others who claim welfare?

I worried that my research, and a lot of the activism I was part of, was doing this – documenting the endless pain, repeating it on loop. I wondered:

> How many people have to die before people start listening and making change?
>
> Do we think that if we reach a certain number of deaths, people would suddenly start to care?
>
> Do we think those in power don't already know?
>
> Do we think they care?

The early days of the Deaths by Welfare project were about documenting harms in reference to the Department for Work and Pensions – even the name is a spin on DWP. The work felt needed. But then I started to feel stuck. I felt proud when we got coverage in newspapers, and the timeline was mentioned in Parliament – but then I started to wonder, why did I feel proud? Did I think change was going to come from Parliament, from an article in a prestigious journal, from a well-read left-leaning newspaper? In my life as an academic, I had been trained that I should write a report and make sure policymakers saw it, and then hopefully wait for them to implement the findings. I just had to make sure they saw the evidence. I just had to trust they'd do the right thing. But now I'm not so sure.

After ten years as an academic, I left. It was a slow departure. When I finally said goodbye, I felt a long period of grief at having stayed so long. I also felt a niggling loss of status which I hated, knowing it to be elitist rubbish. But still it was there. I got lucky because unlike so many of my beloved friends and colleagues, I wasn't pushed out as much as pulled away by something that I was longing for – to work somewhere that aligned with what I believed in, at Healing Justice Ldn. Still, it was hard. For me, academia was a place of critique – it taught me a lot about how to find out what is wrong with things but if you asked me to imagine something different I became unusually quiet.

I may not be the right person to do this work. I have lived experience of the mental health system, personally and through my family, and tend to think of myself as a system avoider – which for me, but not everyone who identifies like this, means I've leveraged privilege to avoid further contact with a system whose violence I have witnessed firsthand. Yet I know deep down that racial capitalism and neoliberalism disable and kill us all – it's just happening to some of us more slowly because of the differential distribution of privilege, power and wealth. It's partly because it's happening to me more slowly that gives me the space to write about it happening to other people, and that is extremely fucked up.

For years, when people ask me what I'm working on and I tell them, the conversation ends. It sounds too depressing and people don't want to hear about it. It's hard to explain that it is utterly horrendous and devastating and enraging, and also joyful, and that I have made wonderful friends along the way, and that the solidarity I have felt has made me realise this is what I've been longing for, for so long. Yes, there have been many moments when I've sat next to someone and felt a tightness in my chest; listened to people on a protest and burned with anger; moments when I've closed my laptop and sobbed; and a constant clenching of my jaw so bad I have a Post-it note stuck permanently to my laptop which says 'unclench your jaw'.

Being part of disabled people's anti-austerity activism and learning from people as part of the Deaths by Welfare project at Healing Justice Ldn has radicalised me. Don't get me wrong, I have never liked any of the governments I've seen in my lifetime. Yet for years, I took the government at its word, or at least vaguely trusted that when it talked of stigma and punishment, conditionality and sanctions, 'incentivising' people into work, it at least thought it was true. I thought that meant my job as a researcher was to show the government its evidence was not in fact true and that these processes are harmful – and ultimately kill people. I thought the more evidence we can document that proves the government's approach is not doing what it's intended to do, the better! The sooner the harm will end.

Over a decade later, and I've come to understand something different. The government knows that what it does under the name of 'welfare' is to punish, stigmatise, humiliate, gas-light and kill disabled people and many others claiming welfare. Not only does it know, but I can't shake off another suspicion – that welfare has been designed to harm people in order to get less people to claim, and ultimately to remove the social safety net of which welfare is a part. If I present my evidence that welfare reform worsens people's mental health, makes them feel ashamed or small, cultivates suicidality, does this give the government evidence that its policies are working? What if violence is a feature of the welfare state, and not a bug?

INTRODUCTION

Remembering the Dead and Fighting Like Hell for the Living

'We don't go a week on social media', Nila Gupta, a disabled, working-class Bengali writer and organiser, explains, 'without hearing about yet another death caused by the system we're reliant on. A system that is our right.' (I never got to meet Nila; they died in 2021.[1] But we'll hear from them throughout this book.) Disabled artist-activist Vince Laws told me something very similar: 'the system we rely on to keep us alive seems to want us dead'. Vince feels like he's 'one bad decision away from being one of the people who die'.[2] What 'system' are Nila and Vince talking about? The UK's welfare system.

What do you think of when you think of welfare? Something benevolent that needs protection, something broken in need of reform, or something violent right to the core? This book is about violence disguised as 'welfare', covered up by framing the people harmed and killed as economic 'burdens' and 'scroungers', people whose lives, we are told, don't matter and whose deaths are inevitable. Often we call this killing 'benefits deaths' or 'benefits-related deaths' instead of naming that people are killed by state violence enacted through the welfare system. This matters because if we say they died, then the next question might be 'how?' But if we name it as a killing, then the next question is 'who did it?' This cloaking of violence is also evident in the naming of life-saving entitlements as 'benefits', in a system where access to social goods is controlled through the idea of eligibility rather than inherent dignity. Disbelief is designed into this system, which asks us to prove that we're eligible and deserving, and often finds us not.

Disabled people, like Nila and Vince, have been telling us for over a decade that our welfare system is killing people. Paula Peters, who is a disabled activist and trade unionist, a member of Disabled People Against Cuts (DPAC), and a photographer of disabled people's protest, told me that we'll never know the full extent of the harm done, 'there will never, ever be any number, but one death is one too many. And there have been way too many.'

Remembering the dead and fighting like hell for the living is a big part of direct action against many forms of state violence; there's power in saying people's names together, remembering as a collective. Direct action led by disabled people against welfare cuts often remembers those who have been killed. I've been at many protests that start by speaking people's names – we remember you. Paula told me:

> We worked with Occupy and others to create the 10,000 Cuts and Counting memorial event, where we had thousands of white flowers which represented every person we've lost at the hands of Work Capability Assessments.

Naming those who have died is important to disabled people's documentation of evidence as part of a fight for justice. Created in 2011 by disabled campaigners as a memorial to those who have died because of welfare reform (though the website has since been taken over and changed), Calumn's List led me into researching how the welfare system harms and kills disabled people. The website was nothing fancy – it simply listed names, with links which took you to newspaper coverage (often local, sometimes national) about people who had died because of the welfare system. After knowing a few individual stories, there was something breathtaking about seeing such a long list of names. When I started reading these articles, a horrible pattern became visible. Yet this pattern often wasn't mentioned in the newspaper coverage of people's deaths – which tended to focus solely on individuals, and not on the systems which killed them. I felt bewildered. I guess if this were a crime novel – which in a way it is, except it's not a novel – this is when, after thinking there's a few disconnected murders, you come across the other bodies and realise the evidence is pointing to a serial killer. Except in this case the killer is a government department.

The Black Triangle Campaign seeks to 'galvanise opposition to the current vicious attack on the fundamental human rights of disabled people by the Government'. Their website also has a list of names, which artist-activist Vince Laws made into a film.[3] Lists of names and photos to show 'Deaths due to sanctions and benefits cuts' are stitched into the banner created by Maggie Zolobajluk, gripped tightly at so many protests. And list-making isn't confined to activists. In 2017, the Green Party created a dossier of 50 deaths of benefit claimants, for which it said, in an accompanying letter sent at the time to the Conservative government and reported in Disability News Service, there is 'good reason to believe their treatment at the hands of your department has been a factor in their deaths'.[4]

Some of these lists have made it into Parliament. In February 2020, it took MP Debbie Abrahams over three minutes to read a list, in an almost empty Commons, of 24 people whose deaths are linked to DWP policy:

> There are many, many more cases of DWP claimants dying, some of which I raised in last year's Westminster Hall debate. Jimmy Ballentine took his own life in 2018 after being found fit for work. Amy Nice also took her own life in 2018 after being found fit for work. Kevin Dooley committed suicide in 2018 after losing ESA. Brian Bailey died in July 2018, again taking his own life after being found fit for work. Elaine Morrall died in November 2017, taking her own life. Daniella Obeng died in December 2017, again taking her own life. Brian Sycamore died in September 2017, taking his own life after leaving a note blaming the DWP after failing his work

> capability assessment. Trevor Drakard took his own life in 2014. Shaun Pilkington … This is unforgivable. These are people's family members and we are failing them. We must not let this continue. Shaun Pilkington died in January 2014, and Terry McGarvey died in February 2014. This is not an exhaustive list, but it shames us all. This inaction shames the Government. I have raised this so many times over the past five years, and there has been no change whatsoever.[5]

After two minutes of reading names Debbie broke down, struggling to speak through her tears. There is something about seeing and reading these lists of names – something overwhelming in thinking about each person's life and holding this alongside the scale of harm. I can feel my body clench as I read these lists. And if there's something about the embodied experience of reading them, then what about the labour of making these lists, especially when we recognise the names we are listing, when these people are our friends and family?

Before lists of names made their way into Parliament, a small number of disabled people started documenting the harms they could see – pulling together the evidence that welfare reform was killing people. While 2010 was far from the beginning of the demonisation of welfare, it did signify a targeted attack on disabled people who claimed welfare and who had by then endured two years of austerity-driven welfare reform. It's no wonder then that 2010 also saw disabled people coming together in rage, fear and solidarity (building on decades of collective action) to form some of the activist and campaigning groups that would come to play such pivotal roles in the years to come. That government cuts and people's deaths birthed resistance is part of the origin stories of many groups, including Disabled People Against Cuts (DPAC). Black Activists Rising Against Cuts also came into being in 2010, as did the Black Triangle Campaign. Alongside this, the Mental Health Resistance Network was set up 'by people who live with mental distress in order to defend ourselves from the assault on us by a cruel government'. Naming and remembering those who have died has been an important tactic to many of these groups.

Before we created the Deaths by Welfare project, people had started showing me the lists of names they'd made of those who had died. In 2013, one disabled activist shared with me how they remembered starting a list of people who were dying but having to stop updating it 'because, you know, there were more and more deaths, and there's a point where you come and do that, you can't go on'. She felt the weight of this evidencing because at the time so few people knew about it. When she shared people's stories on social media, people would reply in shock, saying the 'DWP couldn't possibly have done that'. She explained:

> I kept seeing these, these, these stories about people who had died and it was just a name and their age. There was no story. It didn't explain who they were. I wanted to make them real people. So I'd see a story about somebody, and then I'd go and search around the internet to see who these people were, and even if it's just adding, you know, the fact that they are a dad or a mum or something like that. I mean, now they're big stories, but you know, they weren't in the national media. They were just little things, little stories in regional newspapers.

It was also around 2013/14, when this activist was digging around to find the people's lives behind the headlines of their deaths, that John Pring started to dig into these stories, chronicling deaths and resistance through Disability News Service. For John, as for me through Deaths by Welfare, these investigations have led to beautiful connections and friendships with bereaved families – some of whose stories John tells with depth and skill in his book, *The Department: How a Violent Government Bureaucracy Killed Hundreds and Hid the Evidence* (2024).

Remembering and naming, telling people's stories, takes so many forms in disabled people's activism and creative practice. DPAC member and artist-activist Vince Laws spray paints people's names and how they died onto bedsheets to create the *DWP Deaths Make*

Me Sick shrouds, which regularly travel around the UK and beyond – posted by Vince to protests and exhibitions.[6] I've held them tightly many times on demonstrations – engulfed by them in a gust of wind. Vince made the shrouds in memory of those who have died due to the 'hostile environment' for disabled people created by the DWP. Each shroud names an individual and how they died but when 'presented together … a second story begins to emerge, of a system that knowingly continues to fail the very people that it exists to support'.[7] Vince says he wants to

> get them seen. I feel the need to carry on screaming about the human rights abuses of the UK government … The shrouds are actually quite painful to make. I take breaks. They are very sad. But also very powerful, because they are the truth.

One shroud reads: 'Jodey Whiting. Missed a Work Capability Assessment while very ill. Disability benefits stopped. She took her own life.' Jodey Whiting died by suicide in 2017 after her benefits were wrongly cut by the DWP. She had missed a Work Capability Assessment because she'd been hospitalised for pneumonia and a cyst on her brain, and was found fit to work. Jodey's name is also written onto one of the red cardboard hearts that name people who have died 'due to DWP cuts', created by Mad artist-activist Dolly Sen, and held by family members and friends outside the DWP's headquarters, as part of a direct action and film *Broken Hearts for the DWP*.[8] Dolly stood beside Joy Dove, Jodey's mother, who has campaigned relentlessly for Justice for Jodey.

WELFARE STATE VIOLENCE

The violence disguised as welfare is part of a story we all know well – that paid work is the measure of human worth, where those who claim welfare, and welfare itself, are the baddies. Governments call this 'dependency' (as if we're not all interdependent) and 'eligibility' (as if we're not entitled to live and thrive); they name the people who need it as 'undeserving' (as if only some of us deserve support, love, life, as if anyone can decide who counts). You know they think it's bad from what they call the people whose lives are (or should be) sustained by welfare – 'drains on the state', 'burdens', 'scroungers'. Sometimes I dream of chopping up, letter by letter, these dehumanising words that make up the headlines – sticking them back together to make something new, something true that says: 'No one is a burden. Work does not equal worth. Our dignity and worth are non-negotiable.'

There is an incredible power to this story because in reality the number of people who fraudulently claim benefits is very small, while tax evasion by the rich is huge. According to the UK government, between 2024 and 2025, benefit fraud (which can mean a lot of different things) accounted for £6.5 billion.[9] This sounds a lot until we compare it to £24 billion in income-related benefits that goes unclaimed each year in the UK. Then compare that to the Tax Justice Network's estimated £388 billion that should have been paid in tax but disappears into tax havens.[10] Remind me again, who should we be mad at? And yet, who do we blame? Each other. Whether it's the racialised 'welfare queen', the so-called 'bogus asylum seeker', the 'benefits scrounger' or 'malingerer' – pretending to be ill or disabled in order to receive welfare – we are told, over and over again, that our welfare system is under attack from those committing benefit fraud. These ideas are in the design of the welfare system – written into the scripts of disability assessments, into the list of conditions we must meet in order to claim welfare and the sanctions and punishment we face if we do not, in the benefit fraud hotline number we are told to call to report each other, in the way we fear being a 'burden', and in the ways we feel ashamed.

But this is not just any story – scholar Jina B. Kim sees it as a cover story for global capitalism to justify dismantling social safety nets and diverting public resources away from poor people, especially racialised and disabled people – to make the rich richer.[11] It's a story that makes us feel small and undeserving, makes us surveil our neighbours, pits us against each other, and distracts our attention away from the real looters and hoarders of wealth – as they redistribute public money into private assets. What we're living now is a political choice that is fundamentally about distribution of wealth, life chances and premature death. This story also makes state violence seem necessary, legitimate, not like violence at all. Different people know this violence in different but interconnected ways: kids taken away by the state; assessments of your fitness for work; having no recourse to public funds because of your immigration status. Oppression operates through these connections. State violence hides and thrives, harms and disarms, because we're told it's for 'our own good'. The violent bureaucracy – assessments, waiting, being made to feel like you're undeserving, being told the problem is you and not the system – wears camouflage in the name of welfare. It passes under the radar for apprehending violence. But not for everyone. Not for those who experience it firsthand, full-on, every day, stitched onto skin and bone.

Welfare is much bigger than the DWP, which administers the UK's welfare 'benefits' system; it is a key material infrastructure that shapes everyday life. Yet it is the DWP which is often named as killing people. Richard Kitchen, previously chief investigation officer at the DWP and part of the DWP's deeply violent obsession with illness 'malingering', which we'll return to later, says the DWP's 'customers are, for all practical purposes, the total population of Great Britain; all of whom are at some time beneficiaries of income from the state, whether it be support while they are out of work or in relation to child benefit or pensions'.[12] That means all of us are under the purview of this government department, and it means for many people, the DWP basically determines whether they have enough money to eat, to heat their homes, to power medical equipment, to go to the toilet, to leave the house, to live. Currently, however, the UK welfare system destroys the basic structures for sustaining life and has become synonymous with the death of disabled people, especially since 2007.

From 2010 onwards, disabled people started to warn of the harms of the punitive 'welfare reform' regime and how it was already contributing to, and likely to cause, people's deaths. Welfare advisers started to talk about clients dying. Disabled people's groups started memorial websites, listing the names of those who had died, and protested, holding banners stitched with the photos of some of those lost. Families of those who had died started talking to the press – naming the government as responsible for their loved one's death. By 2010, coroner's reports started to name DWP policy as a 'trigger' in people's suicides, and about 'flaws' and 'mistakes' in the system. Such as the 28 'problems' with the DWP and its private sector contractor Capita (which carries out disability assessments), found by the coroner to have been 'the predominant factor and the only acute factor' that led Philippa Day to take her own life in 2019 after her disability benefits were stopped, and which it took a coroner two hours to read out during a nine-day inquest.[13] The coroner concluded that these problems were not individual errors but systemic flaws.[14] Philippa's sister, Imogen, who you will meet multiple times throughout this book, told me that Philippa knew what was happening to her was 'systemic' – she knew 'the DWP weren't treating disabled claimants with respect and people were losing their lives'. Before she died, she told her sister that she knew the assessment system was going to kill her: 'She felt that they were pressuring her to kill herself, she felt that she didn't matter because she was disabled.'[15] Exhaustive campaigning from Philippa's family and many disabled activists exposed these problems with the DWP and Capita, locating them as part of wider systemic neglect.

In understanding welfare as a site of state violence, we can trace its connections to other forms of state violence that are justified in the name of safety (such as policing, mental health, social care), and learn from how people resist. While some see the problem as flaws in a system that needs reform, others see this violence as a feature, not a bug. The framing and naming of welfare state violence invites us to grapple with violence as a feature of the welfare state, not a 'mistake', not a flaw, not something we fix. This is to take disabled people seriously when they say the welfare system is deadly by design, which means that the institutions we think of as – and are frequently told are – benevolent and good also surveil, regulate, criminalise, abandon and kill us. We'll trace what this framing does for welfare activism – how it invites us to spend less of our limited energy on reforms that tinker at the edges of a system that is deadly by design, and to resource our movements to imagine beyond the current welfare system, and perhaps beyond the state, towards life-affirming infrastructures grounded in our non-negotiable dignity and collective care.

THIS BOOK

If you read this book knowing the violence of the welfare system, I hope you will find validation and witnessing (not that you should need them – your feelings are valid without me writing about them). I also hope you will realise, if you don't already, that you're far from alone, and will take from this book a sense of how to deepen connection to other struggles, and reach into lineages of resistance against welfare state violence that are less explicit or missing from welfare activism. As much as it's about the violence of the current welfare system which tries to make us feel small and leave us dehumanised and undignified, these pages are a love letter to all of our inherent dignity and agency.

If welfare state violence is brand new to you, then I hope this book will help you to glimpse what welfare state violence feels like from the perspectives of those who live and resist it day by day and will make you angry but not defensive – open to noticing both how you might benefit, for now, from how things are, while at the same time being harmed, slowly. On reading this, I'd like you to feel ready not only to fight for change but also to be able to imagine what that change might be – what welfare could be beyond eligibility, deservingness, national borders, stigma, conditionality and punishment. If you struggle to imagine, then you're in good company – it's something we need to learn together, so that we can explore different practices of, and gestures and extensions towards, welfare justice and accountability. The book is written as an invitation towards us recognising and practising our connected liberations and solidarities. We may not always like each other, and we don't have to, but to riff off the famous message of civil rights leader Fannie Lou Hamer, we're not free until we're all free.

Disabled people do a lot of the work of evidencing the violence of welfare, and this mirrors the burden of proof they carry to prove that they are eligible and disabled in a welfare system designed on disbelief. Chapter 1 traces disabled people's and bereaved families' tactics of evidencing-making. It grapples with how cause, effect and time are weaponised, especially around deaths by suicide, in order for the DWP and the companies it contracts to deny accountability. It explores traps and tensions, and our longings to find proof of political intent to harm, even when we are surrounded by evidence of harmful impact, and how constant demands for more evidence might function as a distraction, another tool used by those in power to deny accountability. But evidence doesn't have to be only used to appeal to those in power, it can be for our communities, to inform radical action and build different futures.

Work-first approaches to welfare – making people look for work; finding people 'fit for work'; workfare (making people work as part of welfare conditionality); people struggling to find accessible, meaningful work – are a huge part of welfare state violence. Chapter 2 explores the history of how work has come to define our self-worth, and how ideas about 'malingering' (pretending to be ill) and 'benefit fraud' have enabled the private insurance industry to shape the design of UK welfare policy, including through the introduction of points-based disability assessments outsourced to private companies, and closely linked to suicide. We hear from people who have barely survived these assessments, and about people who have not, while tracing how this brutal bureaucracy that harms and kills so many disabled people is, by design and for profit, a form of extractive abandonment.

Closely tied to work defining our worth is the idea that some people, usually those who can't or won't work, are framed as economic burdens, as a cost to the state, and that this is key to the ways certain groups are devalued and made vulnerable to premature death. Chapter 3 shows how fear of being a burden shows up in people's suicide notes, and in the ways families speak about loved ones, in who can be mourned, whose lives we see as worth living, whose death is grievable, who we see as a victim and of what. We trace histories of how different groups over time have been seen as burdens, and how this has shaped anti-Black and anti-migrant welfare practices. These histories are full of resistance, whose lineages are sometimes missing from welfare activism, but which contain so many lessons for movements oriented towards welfare justice.

Chapter 4 delves into how the welfare system not only works *with* the police and the Home Office but also actively *polices* people, where the logic of 'benefit fraud' enabled the criminalisation of poverty and the policing of work under capitalism. We learn from disabled people's experiences of and resistance to welfare conditionality, sanctions and surveillance. Understanding welfare as policing shows the relevance of prison-industrial complex abolition to welfare, and how a future without policing would require radical transformation of our welfare system – helping us imagine welfare without conditionality and punishment, and stopping the policing of our imaginations.

Drawing on the longer lineages of welfare state violence from those who live the sharp edges of welfare shows us that welfare is deadly by design, and how state violence is a feature of the welfare system, not a bug. Chapter 5 explores how we all have different entry points to understanding welfare state violence – for some of us it's new, while some of us have lived it our whole lives. Post-2008 recession austerity is an entry point for many but one that sometimes overlooks how the welfare state was violent long before and keeps us focused on an opposition to 'cuts' rather than violent design. Entry points shape how we build movements against welfare state violence, and the kinds of solidarities we form. We hear about the solidarities formed between bereaved families, fuelled by a rebellious grief and a practice of witnessing.

Chapter 6 is about the complex and contradictory understandings of justice that we hold across welfare activism – from seeking justice through state machinery to practising justice in spite of and beyond the state. We recognise a deep longing to punish the architects of the policies that kill so many people, while questioning whether we would really find justice within the criminal justice system. This takes us into campaigning to change the system and prevent future deaths through the system, alongside what disability justice and reparative justice might offer us in understanding justice as a practice – something we *do* and not something we have.

The book ends with abolition – which is really a beginning. Chapter 7 roots our radical imaginations in everyday practices of mutual aid, interdependency and collective access that enable people to survive in the present while building towards worlds where we can all thrive. It grounds this vision in strategy – in the changes we can make now, the non-reformist reforms that build grassroots power towards larger radical transformation, while asking what we'd need to embody and who we'd need to be in order to inhabit these worlds. This means that abolition is also about embodied transformation, and about building welfare infrastructures that make stigma, shame and fear obsolete.

I

Evidence of Violence, and the Violence of Evidence

'Evidencing deaths doesn't curtail future deaths' (Anonymous disabled activist)

Another meeting, someone else, again, says we need more and better evidence. I can see the furrowed lines on my forehead in the little box on Zoom where my face lives. Is there some unknown amount and kind of evidence that if we produce it then suddenly things will change? What is this mythical evidence? Hidden behind my frown (god, the camera is unforgiving and I haven't drank enough coffee yet this morning), I wonder, what if . . .

> *We don't need more evidence?*
>
> *The government doesn't care when they see the evidence?*
>
> *The government doesn't need to see the evidence because they already know, they designed the system and don't want to change it?*
>
> *What if demands for more and more evidence is a distraction – i.e. it keeps us collecting evidence and appealing to the Government, and waiting, and waiting, and –*

I'll never forget seeing Stephanie Bottrill's suicide note, left for her son, which says, 'Don't blame yourself for me ending my life. The only people to blame are the Government.' Stephanie was 53 when she died. Her family say that prior to her suicide Stephanie had been worried about how she would pay an extra £20 a week due to changes in her Housing Benefit, which came as a direct result of the 'bedroom tax' (the reduction of your Housing Benefit if you have a spare room – introduced as part of the Welfare Reform Act 2012). Stephanie's son told the BBC that he feels 'it's definitely down to them [the government] putting this law in because she would have still been here'.[1] There's something about seeing Stephanie's suicide note – the pain in the letters of her handwriting. The final full stop.

Two years earlier, Paul Wilcoxson, who experienced mental health issues, and died in 2011 while searching for a job, left a suicide note in which he 'expressed concerns about government cuts'.[2] Brian Sycamore, who died by suicide after issues with Universal Credit and running out of money for his electricity meter, left a note which sarcastically says, 'can you thank the people who work at the Department for Work and Pensions (DWP)?'[3] And there's Philippa Day who died by suicide in 2019 after her disability benefits were stopped. Her suicide note, reported in Disability News Service, detailed how having her benefits severely cut had forced her to get payday loans: 'I've been so trapped for so long and then along comes the government who people would assume are there to help. Since January the 11th 2019 my benefits have been severely cut, this has caused me to get payday loans to simply live and that has escalated into a hole I can never get out of.'[4]

Suicide notes are evidence – written by the people at the sharpest edges of welfare state violence, the people we don't get another chance to hear from. But not everyone leaves a note. Some people leave other kinds of evidence about what killed them – their bodies found next to letters from the DWP telling them they were 'fit for work' or that their benefits had been stopped. Roy Curtis (previously known as Ayman Habayeb) was found dead in his home in 2018, six days after being asked to attend a face-to-face Work Capability Assessment (an assessment to determine how a health condition or disability affects your ability to work, introduced in 2008 as part New Labour's welfare reform agenda). The DWP had been repeatedly warned that its efforts to force him into work were making him suicidal. A folder of letters was found in his flat, including the covering page of a capability for work questionnaire, where Roy had written in red letters 'This is when my nightmare began'.[5]

Errol Graham also died in 2018, from starvation after having his benefits cut off. When he died he weighed just 4½ stone. Errol was unable to engage with the DWP's processes due to lack of accommodation for his mental health issues. He left a handwritten note, seemingly for officials at his 'fit for work' assessment but never sent asking:

> Please judge me fairly. I am a good person but overshadowed by depression. All I want in life is to live normally. That would be the answer to my prayers. Thank you to all for taking the time to read this letter, I really appreciate it. I don't know how I'll cope when I see you all. I hope I will be OK.

Writing about his letter, journalist Frances Ryan says, 'it reads as a plea from beyond the grave: a man with severe mental health problems politely asking the state to treat him as a human being.'[6]

Paul Reekie's body was found next to two letters from the DWP notifying him that his Housing Benefit and Incapacity Benefit were being stopped. As a well-known author and poet, Paul's death was one of the first to spark concerns among disabled activists about the harm being caused by the shift to Employment and Support Allowance (ESA), a benefit for people who are unable to work due to disability or ill-health, and the roll-out of the Work Capability Assessment. His death led to the formation, by disabled activists, of the Black Triangle Campaign. Paul Reekie died in 2010, the year that David Cameron became prime minister. In his first speech in this role, David Cameron referred to people on welfare as 'sitting on their sofas waiting for their benefits to arrive'. Despite in the same speech distancing his party from Labour, it doesn't sound that different from the Work and

Pensions secretary of Tony Blair's administration who talked about plans to get tough on 'people who scrounge from the system'.[7] Two years into the Conservative–Liberal Democrat Coalition government of 2010–15, Chancellor of the Exchequer George Osborne stoked up animosity between workers and those on welfare when he asked at a Conservative Party conference: 'Where is the fairness, we ask, for the shift-worker, leaving home in the dark hours of the early morning, who looks up at the closed blinds of their next door neighbour sleeping off a life on benefits?'[8]

Research shows a significant increase over the years in the number of negative stories in national newspapers about disabled people who claim welfare. In a content analysis of media representations of disability in the UK, Emma Briant and colleagues, in research commissioned by Inclusion London (which supports Deaf and Disabled people's organisations in London and campaigns for equality for Deaf and Disabled people), found an increase (post-recession) in use of terms like 'workshy', 'skiver' and 'drain on the economy' to describe claimants of disability benefits, with those claiming benefits due to mental health framed as 'faking it'. Post-2008, it has become common to see headlines such as '75% on sick are skiving'[9] (from 2011) or more recently, 'Britain is becoming a nation of dishonest scroungers who openly steal from supermarkets and defraud the benefits system'[10] (from 2025). The Bad News for Disabled People report compared media stories from the second term of Tony Blair's New Labour government in 2004/5 with the beginning of the Conservative–Liberal Democrat Coalition government in 2010/11. The report found an increase in media stories about benefit fraud – portraying disabled people as 'scroungers', 'workshy', and a 'drain on the economy', with people with mental health conditions more likely to be represented as 'undeserving' and as unworthy.[11] Terms such as 'scrounger', 'cheat' and 'skiver' became more common, reinforcing the idea that disabled claimants were 'undeserving'. Welfare was described more frequently as a lifestyle choice, with those who claim it portrayed as indulgent and wasteful. The Bad News for Disabled People report concludes that much media coverage replicates the government's position on disability and helps lay the groundwork for removal of support structures.

Many have shown how the language of politicians and media portrayals of 'scroungers' is reproduced in the everyday abuse of disabled people, and in increased hate crime against disabled people. In 2011, there were almost 2000 recorded disability hate crimes in England and Wales, double the number in 2008 when records began.[12] This was the same year that David Cameron told us that:

> For years we've had a system that encourages the worst in people – that incites laziness, that excuses bad behaviour, that erodes self-discipline, that discourages hard work ... above all that drains responsibility away from people ... well this is moral hazard in our welfare system – people thinking they can be as irresponsible as they like because the state will always bail them out. I want us to look at toughening up the conditions for those who are out of work and receiving benefits.[13]

The Disability Hate Crime Network carried out a survey finding that benefit scrounger rhetoric can lead to hate crime, with many disabled people describing how they had been verbally or physically assaulted by attackers who called them 'scroungers', told them to get off benefits, or accused them of being too lazy to work. One person explained that 'most of the abuse is from strangers, who now think that everyone who is disabled is lying about being ill. Because this government is spreading so many lies, regarding us.'[14] These lies are not only something that strangers attack people with – we all internalise them. Many disabled people come to see themselves as what the government says they are – 'scroungers', 'burdens', 'undeserving'. This is profoundly damaging for people's sense of self and mental health. In sociologist Kayleigh Garthwaite's research, people describe claiming Incapacity Benefit as 'like a rope around your neck' because of the shame, and as deeply stigmatising, 'if you are on it, you're a scrounger'.[15] The fear of being a 'burden' (explored in Chapter 3) shapes and shows up in people's suicidality – it's part of the way that the welfare system is killing us. Martin Rust died two months after being declared fit for work. Martin's mother explained 'he had attempted suicide before because he feared being "a burden"'.[16]

BURDEN OF PROOF

Could there be much clearer evidence that the welfare system is killing people than Roy Curtis's plea, written in red pen and pain across a capability for work questionnaire. Or Stephanie Bottrill's final words, written in a suicide note that we can now all access online? And yet the burden to prove that governmental and media stigmatisation of benefits claims leads to hate crimes and suicide, and that welfare policy harms and kills people, too often falls on the people most violently impacted. Ellen Clifford, a member of the steering committee for Disabled People Against Cuts (a non-violent direct action group, born from a march against cuts at the Conservative Party conference in Birmingham),[17] and author of *The War on Disabled People*, talked to me about:

> Trying to build awareness of the horrors that have been happening and the devastating impact; we've been fighting against that line you get all the time from the government: 'There is no causal link.' Which is so infuriating. It is always that; there's such a high expectation placed on us [disabled people] to prove the link, and to give evidence.

Ellen is talking about the DWP's stock response when it comes to the deaths of disabled people claiming benefits, or what it refers to, in the murderous language of bureaucracy, as the 'death of a customer'. The DWP says:

> Where it is appropriate, we undertake reviews into individual cases, but we do not accept the argument of those who seek to politicise people's deaths by linking them inaccurately to welfare policy.[18]

This is also true of how the DWP responds when people's deaths are by suicide: that 'suicide is a tragic and complex issue and we take these matters extremely seriously';[19] that it's not appropriate to comment on 'individual cases'; and that 'suicide is always a tragedy and a lot of different reasons are always involved. We look at a number of suicides but on a private basis, as a lot of the information cannot be shared, so that is not a useful approach.'[20] These kinds of statements frame suicide as tragic, complex and individual – as if there are no patterns to spot by looking at people's suicides alongside each other. Of course, feeling suicidal and dying by suicide is complex – our lives are messy, things add up and compound one another, and when we look back it's hard to pick out a single event that started it all (though sometimes this is possible). The DWP weaponises this complexity – using it to deny its role in creating conditions that make people suicidal.

Alongside references to complexity to defer accountability, we also see mental health weaponised in a similar way. This is an old tactic: assuming that suicide is always the result of mental health issues, which are framed as irrational, individual and apolitical, and therefore no one need take responsibility for, or be held accountable for, creating conditions that make life unliveable. I, and many others, have tracked this tactic in our research over years and continents, as a way to obscure structural violence and to deny the role of violent state policies by blaming the victim. Yet recognising the complexity and multiplicity of factors that may contribute to suicide can occur simultaneously alongside invoking government culpability, just as it is entirely possible to recognise mental health as both political and deeply personal. People's accounts of their suicidality, suicide notes left after death, and the stories told by bereaved families and friends paint a picture of how violent policies are lived and felt, how they cultivate an atmosphere of fear, a pervasive anxiety, shame and anger – physically and psychologically wearing people out. No wonder then that a lot of disabled people's activism and campaigning has been around evidencing cause and effect – how the government's 'welfare reform' is killing disabled people.

Evidence and proof come up time and again in disabled people's anti-austerity activism – disabled activists doing the labour of evidencing the harms of the welfare system while living the sharp edges of it themselves. But who decides what counts as evidence of causality? How do we evidence harms committed over and over again by the government, the private companies they outsource to, and the media – whose weapons are a signature on a piece of paper, a memo, a meeting with no minutes, a headline – when the evidence of harms can be found in suicide notes, leaked documents, coroners' reports, hidden in plain sight in banal-sounding reports? There is a violence in constantly being asked to provide evidence of harms. For many disabled people, this mirrors the violence of being made to prove that you're disabled and/or ill and to prove that you're 'deserving' of benefits. Tumu Johnson, co-director of the feminist disabled women's collective, Sisters of Frida, explains:

> There are ways in which the welfare state inflicts violence onto us [disabled people], that is obvious and undeniable ... We are asked to prove over and over if we are disabled enough and are deserving of what we need. Sorted into deserving and undeserving recipients. Disabled people aren't believed. So many people have fought so hard to shine a light on the violence that happens continuously.[21]

Tumu is talking about how disabled people face a welfare system designed not to believe them, where the burden of proof lies with them to prove they are 'genuinely ill', to prove they are 'eligible', to prove they are meeting certain conditions, to prove they are looking for a job, to prove they are 'deserving' of the welfare they need to live. Our current welfare system is one where people are not believed. When I spoke to Ben Baumberg Geiger, who has spent over 15 years researching issues around disability and the benefits system, about the Work Capability Assessment (which we delve into in the next chapter), he told me that 'assessors feel that they are told that to be doing their job, they need to be not-believing what people tell them. And I don't think they're necessarily trying to be malicious; I just think they're set up to be like, "If you just believe everything that people tell you, then what sort of assessor are you?"' And when the system harms and kills them, disabled people have to prove that too – amass the evidence of individual and population-level harm, prove cause and effect – and again, they're not believed. Another person, who wants to remain anonymous, explained to me that the system is 'constantly framed as needed to be this way to protect from people abusing the system or people taking advantage of the system ... This is a system that doesn't start from a position of trust.' This lack of belief is part of what philosopher Miranda Fricker calls epistemic injustice – having one's credibility and capacity to produce knowledge doubted and questioned.[22]

Families speaking after their loved one's death also often talk about governmental welfare policy as causing harm. David Barr died by suicide, in 2013, after learning that the decision to stop his benefits had been upheld. His father says, 'I'm in no doubt this matter was the final straw. I would say they are 90 per cent to blame for him taking his life. He'd just had enough.'[23] By 'they', he's referring to Atos (the private company that at the time held the government contract to carry out Work Capability Assessments) and the DWP that contracted Atos. We'll hear more about Atos and DWP outsourcing in the next chapter. A year later, in 2014, Trevor Drakard died by suicide. Trevor had a brain injury and epilepsy and was 'panic stricken' on being told that his Incapacity Benefit was being replaced with Employment and Support Allowance on condition of him being part of the 'Work Related Activity Group' – meaning he had to prove he was looking for work. He wrote a letter to the DWP explaining that 'I have never been able to work due to my epilepsy. I lost my job because they could no longer cope with my attacks.'[24] Yet his appeal was rejected. His parents, who found his body, said that prior to his death he was 'beside himself' with worry, and that 'there is no doubt whatsoever that is what caused his death'.[25]

Disabled people and allies have and continue to be creative geniuses in using multiple strategies to evidence the harms of the welfare system. This evidence doesn't always look like what the state tells us evidence should be like – it's written in suicide notes and placards, stitched into banners, shouted on the streets. We can learn a lot from disabled people's tactics of evidence-making.

TACTICS OF EVIDENCE-MAKING

Cause and effect: coroners naming the DWP as contributing to suicide

Joy Dove, like many families, fought long battles to have the role of the DWP and/or their outsourced partners to be named as a trigger in their loved one's suicide. This includes urging coroners to write a Prevention of Future Deaths report – made when, in the opinion of the coroner, there are actions that an individual or organisation should take to prevent future deaths. Joy Dove campaigned for eight years for a second inquest to investigate the DWP's role in her daughter Jodey's death. Before the first inquest, Joy wrote to the coroner saying, 'I blame the DWP.' The coroner read the letter out, but she said it wasn't in her remit to involve the DWP, and instead, after a 37-minute inquest, recorded 'suicide'. Joy told Disability News Service that afterwards she felt that 'we need something on that [death] certificate that implies the DWP were at fault'.[26] And Joy's campaigning was successful. In the second inquest, the coroner said that the DWP's decision to stop Jodey's out-of-work benefits after a string of safeguarding failures was the 'trigger' for her to take her own life on 21 February 2017 and that her 'deteriorating' state of mental health had been 'precipitated' by the withdrawal of her benefits.

Two years before Jodey died, in 2015, coroner Mary Hassell concluded that the suicide of Michael O'Sullivan had been a 'direct result of being ruled "fit to work"'.[27] At the time, this verdict was 'thought by campaigners to be the first official link of the Work Capability Assessment to suicide'.[28] Yet that all changed when we found out about Stephen Carré. Stephen Carré died by suicide in 2010, after the DWP confirmed its decision that he was ineligible for its then new out-of-work benefit – Employment and Support Allowance (ESA). For Stephen's father, Peter, the cause of his son's death is crystal clear – the 'DWP and Atos killed my son'.[29] Coroner Tom Osborne came to similar conclusions at Stephen's inquest, where he found that the rejection of his appeal at being found 'fit for work' was a 'trigger' in his suicide. In the Prevention of Future Deaths report, and at Stephen's inquest, a coroner ruled that his death was linked to flaws in the Work Capability Assessment system (including lack of consultation with his GP about his medical history), and that the rejection of his appeal that he was not fit for work was a 'trigger' in Stephen's death. This is clear evidence of the potentially fatal impact of the assessment process, yet the report, buried in the recesses of the Ministry of Justice website, would only come to be publicly known about in 2015, thanks to the constant digging of John Pring.[30] The report was never shown to either of the independent teams reviewing the Work Capability Assessment, despite being thought to be the first of its kind detailing deaths resulting from welfare reform and the assessment. But it's not the last – anyone can search the Prevention of Future Death online database; all you need to know are some names: Faiza Ahmed, Roy Curtis, Philippa Day, Michael O'Sullivan – evidence that future deaths like Stephen's were not prevented.

The coroner for Tim Salter, who died by suicide nine months after his benefits were stopped, is stated as saying that a 'major factor in Tim's death was that his benefits had been greatly reduced leaving him almost destitute'.[31] Also, the coroner for Brian Sycamore (one of many names that MP Debbie Abrahams struggled to read out in Parliament), who died the same year as Jodey, in 2017, named issues with Universal Credit as a trigger in Bryan's suicide.[32] But coroners don't always do as families ask – Gill Thompson (following the death of her brother David Clapson) and Jill Gant (following the death of her son Mark Wood) tried to get coroners to name the DWP's actions as a trigger but the coroners would not.

The everyday complexity and messiness of our lives will always elude a simple idea of cause and effect. For example, DWP policies end up making a lot of people homeless, sleeping rough, in precarious housing, staying in violent relationships which provide a conditional roof over your head. When some of these people die, as many do – the Dying Homeless project recorded 1611 deaths of people who were homeless in the UK in 2024[33] – what caused their deaths? Or to ask the question less passively, what killed them? Welfare, housing, domestic violence? The black mould on the walls of the flat they were forced to move to after cuts to their benefits? The cold seeping up from the concrete streets they were forced to make home after finding themselves facing the 'bedroom tax'? And how does their death get recorded? Into what statistics is it included? And where suicide is recorded as the cause of death, what caused their suicide?

There are patterns to what disabled people, families and coroners name as triggering disabled people's suicides. One of these is around the DWP not seeking further medical evidence before finding people fit for work. Following Stephen Carré's inquest in 2010, the coroner wrote to the DWP with concerns that the system did not automatically seek further medical evidence from a claimant's GP or psychiatrist if they had a mental health condition. Four years later, as investigated by John Pring, another letter was sent to the DWP by a coroner, raising the same concerns and making almost identical recommendations, this time following Michael O'Sullivan's death.[34] Then there's Edward Jacques, who died in 2012, after being found fit for work by a Work Capability Assessment that lasted just 23 minutes. He died by suicide a week after his Employment and Support Allowance was stopped. The coroner at his inquest said:

> I find the assessment process in Edward's case did not fully or properly reflect Edward's physical and mental health at that time. It is conceded by those involved in the [assessment] process that if the information as to Edward's physical and mental health as shared by his GP had been known at the time of the assessment, the outcome would have been very different. It is desperately sad that such evidence was not available either to the nurse or to the decision maker.[35]

The coroner also said the Work Capability Assessment is a 'crude assessment'. For Edward's brother and sister, there was 'no doubt that the decision to stop his allowance was a major trigger which led him on to a severe depression and desperate action. We do not believe that Edward is an isolated case and we think thousands of assessments have been made like this across the country.'[36] And they're right. As Disability News Service has reported, 'the deaths of other claimants have also been closely linked to the failure to ensure that further medical evidence was obtained, including those of Mark Wood, Paul Donnachie, David Barr, and a Scottish woman known only as Ms D E.'[37] Given how life-threatening it is not to ask for, or to overlook, medical evidence, it's no surprise that medical evidence has been a focus of some disabled people's campaigning in relation to welfare state violence. This often takes a harm reduction approach through reform of the existing system (e.g., the First Do No Harm lobby, resulting from disabled people's campaigning).

GPs providing medical evidence can also be an important site for medical allyship with disabled people in a context where the government has crafted suspicion of the reality of illness and disability of those trying to claim benefits, building on and reproducing ideas about 'malingering and illness deception' – influential in DWP policymaking (as we'll explore in Chapter 3). This disbelief is also evident in debates about the 'sick note' (as documented by historian Gareth Millward) – a key tool in gatekeeping, and policing the boundaries of sickness.[38] In 2024, then prime minister Rishi Sunak joined a long line of politicians evoking the idea that benefits have become a 'lifestyle choice' for some, causing a 'spiralling' welfare bill, and blaming this on 'sick note culture' as a way to justify (unrealised) proposals to make it harder to get a sick note, and to remove people's benefits entirely if they are out of work for longer than twelve months.[39] Yet the appeal to medical evidence, and to coroners' verdicts, can make it seem like professionals have superior or more objective knowledge than those with lived experience.

It is a huge win for the families who are able to get 'official' medico-legal recognition that the state can contribute to making people suicidal. This provides vital evidence of how the welfare system kills people, and many families feel validated by it. Coroners and people's families also play an important role in making the DWP aware of 'cases' (and that technical sounding word means people who have died) to investigate through their Internal Process Review process.[40] At the same time, the fact we have to appeal to medical and juridical evidence to confirm something that disabled people and families are telling us is true in effect confirms and replays the systemic disbelief in disabled people built into the welfare system. Dying isn't enough for people to be believed – they need a coroner to back them up. This is the very disbelief (disbelief that you're ill, that you can't work, that you need support) that kills people.

Slow violence, dissociating effects from causes

As John Pring and I were pulling together the masses of evidence that make up the Deaths by Welfare timeline (which as discussed in the Preface was created in collaboration with many other brilliant people named earlier and throughout this book), we noticed something about time, something about violence that is slow.[41] As we waded through documents, our heads full of the stories of the many people we know who navigate welfare state violence – stories of delays, of cumulative effects, of things piling up, of corrosive fear and anxiety – it was like we started to unearth a weapon in this war on welfare, and that weapon is time. We realised that time is key to understanding the everyday, bureaucratic and institutional nature of welfare state violence and how this violence kills people.

Thinking about this with John reminded me of a book I'd read a while back, Rob Nixon's *Slow Violence*, about the slow unfolding of environmental catastrophes: 'violence that occurs gradually and out of sight, a violence of delayed destruction that is dispersed across time and space, an attritional violence that is typically not viewed as violence at all'.[42] The book builds on a literature, including Rachel Carson's *Silent Spring*, documenting the delayed effects of chemical toxicity and petrochemical pollution, where damage is incremental, harm is witnessed slowly because there's a lag between policy and its violent consequences, and this works to weaponise time and dissociate effects from causes.[43] Many people, including John Pring (writing in Disability News Service about the DWP's 30-year 'toxic legacy') name welfare reform as toxic, and so turning to understand how toxicity works, lives inside our bodies, slowly corrodes and kills, is important.[44]

Violence that unfolds at a snail's pace is hard to apprehend and represent. It makes it difficult to trace cause and effect; as time rolls on, people's deaths become disconnected from what killed them. Co-creating the Deaths by Welfare timeline was one way we could think of to make visible the slow violence of the welfare state and to show that there is a pattern to what's killing people. A pattern that many disabled people and bereaved families know only too well. The unfolding of slow violence over time means there is (often, although not always) a lag between the introduction of policies and the harms they inflict. People die miles away from where politicians sign off on policies, and may die months or years after the policies come into being – often after years of the build-up of incremental harms. Creating the timeline together helped John and I to realise that this time lag of delayed destruction and delayed effects is key to how the welfare state kills people, that is, delay isn't just a side effect exploited by the government but is weaponised to avoid accountability and deny justice.

We saw, and felt, delay tactics everywhere – in the freedom of information process, where responses to requests sometimes say the time required to collect data, due to lack of centralised record-keeping, is too costly, and therefore not provided. Delay was especially apparent in the reviews carried out by the DWP into people's deaths (discussed later), including in the framing of reviews into the deaths of people who claim benefits as private, the time taken to redact them as too burdensome, and therefore refusals to share them with the families of those who have died or made public. These tactics are also evident in the limiting of the review to an individual's life, excluding from analysis links to other deaths that occurred earlier or later in time. Delay is there as people wait on hold, and wait for a letter – the fear of the brown envelope. Delay is there in the appeals process – appealing the DWP's decision to stop your benefits because you're fit for work. And it's not only the welfare system that weaponises time. Time (sped up and delayed) is also a well-known tactic in the hostile environment of immigration policies and in how state power shapes everyday practices of bordering, as we'll see in Chapter 3.

Rob Nixon helps us to see 'the temporal distance' between short-lived policies and 'long-lived consequences, as gradual casualties are spread across a protracted aftermath, during which the memory and the body count of slow violence are diffused – and defused – by time', making cause and effect much 'harder to track' and state 'answerability harder to impose'.[45] Many disabled people know that to analyse welfare state violence we need to be attuned to the ways that harms accumulate slowly, over time. Hence, a number of disabled people's campaigning groups have demanded a cumulative impact assessment of welfare reform. The dissociation of cause from effect in conditions crafted not to believe people means that some of disabled people's campaigning involves finding allies in those who haven't been dehumanised, in order to evidence harm.

'Find allies that the oppressors have not put on the blacklist'

Rick Burgess (co-founder of the War on Welfare Petition and Manchester Disabled People Against Cuts) explained to me:

> As a population, we've been targeted. And when you target people, you dehumanise them. So we were treated as something less than human; so they weren't listening to us; they weren't respecting us. So we thought, 'Well, we need some authoritative third-party to say, Actually, guys! There's something really terrible here.' When you're a disregarded cohort – a hated demographic – you need to find allies that the oppressors have not put on the blacklist to try and speak on your behalf a little bit, because they've locked us out; they're ignoring us. And they're killing us.

Rick was involved in one such appeal, when he and other disabled people and allies contacted leading epidemiologists to research, and provide evidence for, what was then already really clear to disabled people, but largely ignored by a lot of other people, which was that the Work Capability Assessment was making people suicidal. This research was published in the *Journal of Epidemiology and Community Health*, and shows that the programme to reassess people on Incapacity Benefit through the Work Capability Assessment was linked to 590 suicides between 2010 and 2013 in England.[46] Despite wide coverage of the research, on reflection, Rick didn't feel the research evidence made much difference:

> One thing that happened is the DWP kept a lot more of their figures secret. I think that there were some attempts to smooth out the rough edges of the WCA. To be honest, I don't feel it was because they were worried about people's well-being; I think they were worried about headlines.

Yet researcher Ben Baumberg Geiger reminds us that impact isn't always immediately clear. Ben, who 'happened to be on secondment at the DWP at the time' when the research came out, says we shouldn't 'understate the significance of it – that report *did* reach into the DWP ... publicly, there wasn't any engagement with it; but it was interesting to see that, on the inside, people were reading it, and paying attention to it'.

This tactic, of appealing to those with more authority, was also used when DPAC co-founders petitioned the United Nations Convention on the Rights of Persons with Disabilities (UNCRPD) to investigate UK welfare reform. In 2016, thanks to pressure and years of research by disabled people, the UNCRPD found that 'grave and systematic violations' of disabled persons' rights had taken place because of austerity measures and welfare reforms since 2010, which had 'disproportionately and adversely' affected the rights of disabled people. In a follow-up report in 2024, the UN found that no significant progress had been made in addressing these concerns, that the government does not consult with disabled people, and that the government uses a 'rhetoric that devalues disabled people and undermines their human dignity'.[47] Ellen Clifford played a key part in petitioning the UN. She says, 'in 2016, 2017, there was so much enthusiasm for the Convention. But then, of course, there were no consequences. The government could just dismiss that finding of grave and systematic violations.'

Trying to hold the government to account by mobilising independent bodies, research, medical evidence, the judicial system, takes a huge amount of energy. It's important in that it can be validating of people's experiences and be a form of collective witnessing but it is also heart-wrenching that it can so easily be dismissed and doesn't necessarily lead to systemic change. We need to better understand the impact of the myriad tactics used by disabled people and bereaved families, and how we feel about that impact within the system – helping the DWP to tinker at the edges of harmful policies in ways that might be life-saving right now, but may ultimately reinforce the system that's killing people. If our evidence is aimed at the government, we have to face the painful reality of whether we might suspect it already knows and doesn't really care. Even if our evidence doesn't change the government, it can impact in other ways, such as by mobilising people to take action and build power; affirming people's dignity; and making connections between different experiences to build cross-movement solidarities. There are many traps and tensions in the practice of evidencing, including the trap of wanting to seem reasonable in order to appeal to the government.

The 'trap of wanting to appear reasonable'

People are not believed, and are devalued, in life or in death, and because of this disbelief, our activism, especially where we appeal to the government, sometimes gets pulled into showing we're reasonable and our evidence is objective. This is the way we're told we should do it, and maybe that's why it often feels like a trap. Ellen Clifford explained that

> It is important on the one hand, that we make sure that the evidence we're using is robust, so it can't be used to discredit us, because they will use every opportunity.
>
> There are people within the disability sector who get held back, I would say, and fall into the trap of wanting to appear reasonable. There are people who think, 'Well, the way that you engage and influence with government is to be reasonable.' But I think we have to understand the limitations of this approach. Policymakers are only going to listen to the evidence that you're giving them if it's already acceptable to their pre-existing agenda. If they don't want to listen, they're not going to listen however you put across your evidence.

This is like the respectability trap that we've probably all found ourselves in, where somehow our testimonies, our pain, become credible only if we're respectable, reasonable, objective, calm. Can you imagine what our actions might be like if we didn't have to appear reasonable to the government? What would our evidence be like, and for whom? Ellen talks about being trapped in a kind of campaigning that assumes that the government doesn't know what's happening, and that if we're 'reasonable' and we calmly present the evidence to them, then they'll change because they're also 'reasonable'. But for Ellen, the government

> aren't reasonable. They're violent. They create injustice. They created a system that's deliberately designed to push people into poverty because our lives are worth less to them than other people's. And so I think it's right that we meet them with a level of anger, which is completely justified.

For a long time, I imagined that evidence of harm is a way to fight for government accountability. But we've seen in doing this that our evidence sometimes risks reinforcing dehumanising ideas of disabled people who claim welfare as damaged victims or lacking agency. There's also plenty of evidence to show that the government already knows that its policies are killing people and that it was told before welfare reform was introduced that the changes would lead to harm. Internal documents show that welfare harm isn't only something that can be seen in retrospect. The DWP's own research reports predicted that some of the policy changes of welfare reform would lead to harm, alongside disabled people forewarning this long before people started to die. In creating the Deaths by Welfare timeline, we found many prophetic early warnings of the harms to come – from the DWP itself, and from disabled people. Hidden in innocuously titled documents, such as the DWP's Research Report 278 – the second report on Incapacity Benefit reforms and Personal Advisers, published in 2005 – are findings of unmanageable workloads affecting advisers' ability to identify risk and resulting in less compassionate support to people in distress.[48] Members of the Mental Health Technical Working Group that was used by the DWP to help design the Work Capability Assessment in 2006 and 2007 also shared with Disability News Service how they thought at the time that the process was 'deeply flawed' and damaging to mental health.[49] In 2006, two years *before* what is usually seen as the beginnings of welfare reform, Professor Alison Ravetz wrote a critique of the government's New Deal for Welfare, warning of incalculable stress for those forced into work and predicting future harms. In a prophetic warning, Ravetz concludes that:

> What might be expected is a slowly accumulating number of bad decisions and blatantly scandalous cases, eventually giving rise to a groundswell of unease ... the cost, in stress, to those people and their families will be incalculable.[50]

We know now that disabled people would come to pay the cost with their lives. And we now know that people were dying as early as 2010. John Pring talks about all the evidence – the coroners' reports, the reviews carried out into deaths by government, 'all building up into a giant pile of evidence. It's continued over three decades ... the evidence is all there. And now they're refusing to carry out research into the impact of their policies: they don't want the proof of what they're doing to people.' If the government knows its policies are harmful, then this suggests that producing evidence to appeal to the government on the basis of its ignorance might be a tempting but flawed theory of change. While we may know that the government knows, is the harm it produces intentional, and how could we ever evidence this?

'THE SMOKING GUN' – DOES PROVING INTENT TO KILL MATTER IF PEOPLE DIE ANYWAY?

One day, talking to John Pring about writing this book, he asked me,

> how will we move from showing/proving that deaths were caused by reckless/negligent actions (which I think we all accept) to proving that there were intentional killings, i.e. state murder? I still think that we have yet to prove any of these killings were intentional, but I know others disagree. Meanwhile, I will keep looking for the smoking gun. I bet it's in the archives somewhere.

John believes that somewhere, hidden in the archives, lies a probably banal looking email or memo that proves beyond doubt that senior politicians knew their welfare policies would kill or were killing disabled people and that they either don't care or more actively want to kill people whose lives they don't value. Something about the idea of this 'smoking gun' draws me in as well and at the same time makes me uncomfortable. I keep wondering why do we keep searching for intent and admission (the memo, the whistleblower, the secret recording) that proves the government knew it was killing disabled people, when we already know the government kills people? And we know the government knows it's doing this because disabled people, bereaved families and allies have worked so hard to make this knowledge public. Is the admission of politicians, or their recrimination in hidden documents, more compelling than the evidence of disabled people dying? Do we need the government to admit it when the policies it cooks up and signs off on kill disabled people anyway? For sure, there could be instances where harm was unforeseen – not part of the original intention. But what about when that harm is then shown to policymakers and they don't change anything or don't listen – is this then intent?

It's largely thanks to John that we have evidence that the DWP knows its policies kill people (whether or not this was their intention). The DWP has been repeatedly warned of this fact and has even confirmed it in its own research, as well as in the reviews it carries out into people's deaths, showing that welfare policy is life-threatening.[51] John submitted over 25 freedom of information requests and several complaints to the Information Commissioner's Office (ICO) to try to find out about the internal investigations that the DWP carry out when it is considered that its activities may have contributed to harm and/or what it sometimes refers to, in the murderous language of bureaucracy, as the death of a 'customer'.[52] What happened on John's journey to get this evidence is a wild story, tracing evidence of the DWP's own (often well-hidden) research into harms.[53]

Between 2014 and 2022, the DWP carried out approximately 220 reviews – previously called Peer Reviews, and since October 2015 called Internal Process Reviews (IPRs) – into the deaths of people who claim benefits. Redacted versions of these reviews contain hundreds of recommendations, including repeated warnings that policies were potentially life-threatening. Yet before 2020, and the introduction of the Serious Case Panel, thanks to pressure from disabled people, these recommendations were not tracked or monitored, meaning the DWP didn't know whether the suggested improvements from the reviews had been implemented. The DWP has been collecting these reviews centrally for more than a decade yet refuses to publish them in full – not even to most of the families of those who have died. Even the design of its review processes, which treats each person's death individually, means that patterns across people's deaths remain invisible, and that policy is seen as outside the scope of these reviews, meaning systemic issues are overlooked.[54]

Chatting to John one day about this he told me: 'It's not by mistake.' The DWP has been told its policies kill people 'by disabled people, by coroners, by their own Internal Process Reviews; they've been told it in parliament, on the streets, by activists, by researchers'. Rick Burgess agrees:

> The first death: that could be a mistake. The tenth death: okay, some unfortunate mistakes; there's a big system! A hundred deaths: okay, they didn't have time to get ahead of it. The 303rd death: that's getting a bit weird. The 407th death: They've had reports back! They're keeping doing this! The one-thousand-two-hundred-and-forty-seventh death: Well. *They know what they're doing.*

Rick thinks of this as 'democide':

> if genocide is mass-murder, then democide is mass-manslaughter; it's not so much killing people, but taking away the necessary elements a human needs to survive in a society, and subjecting them to absolutely inhumane conditions cumulatively; so when you take away their benefits, when you subject them to oppressive assessments, when you have them demonised in the press. And you do that repeatedly for years, and years, and years. We're now fourteen years into this process; that's not an accident, that's not a passing fad – that's a cultural democide against a demographic, that demographic being disabled people benefit claimants.

In *Death by Government*, political scientist R.J. Rummel explains that the intentionality of democide 'is found in the deliberate use of governmental power to cause death, whether through direct killing or through policies that know or are reckless about the inevitable loss of life'. Rummel talks about democide occurring through the 'imposition of lethal living conditions'.[55] These lethal conditions are not accidents, nor are they 'failures'. As we'll keep encountering in this book, they are the way we live historical forces of ableism, colonialism, structural racism and capitalism in our everyday lives. This, then, is 'practical intentionality', meaning that if a government causes deaths through a 'reckless and depraved indifference to human life', crafting lethal conditions through stigma and punishment, then 'the deaths were as though intended. Neglect that leads to death is murder through practical intent'.[56] The evidence of cumulative impact of harm produced by disabled people and bereaved families, of which this chapter only scratches the surface, is full of proof of practical intent, and therefore of democide.

It's significant that Rick mentions genocide alongside democide. At the same time as chatting to John about a 'smoking gun', I was just finishing reading Mohammed El Kurd's (2025) book *Perfect Victims and the Politics of Appeal*, about the ongoing genocide in

Gaza, livestreamed as I write, and the century-long occupation of Palestine. Don't get me wrong, this is a completely different context that is in no way comparable but does share some similar logics and tactics, for example, in using disablement as a weapon. El Kurd asks questions about whether it matters if perpetrators admit to atrocities when we know they are happening – 'why do we give the authority of narration to those who have murdered and displaced us when the scarcity of their guilt means honesty is unlikely. Why do we wait for those carrying the batons to confess when our bruised bodies tell the whole truth.'[57]

Like being trapped into being seen as 'reasonable', I wonder if there's a trap in trying to prove intent, and whether it might function as a distraction. It somehow devalues disabled people's own evidence – treating it like it isn't enough, like it needs to be proved or corroborated through some kind of admission of guilt by those with power. And doesn't that yearning for admission of guilt (however differently we might intend it) repeat one of the very deeply held and horribly dehumanising assumptions of our current welfare system and its outsourced disability assessments – that disabled people shouldn't be believed and should be distrusted, and that the burden of proof is on them to show that they're deserving? Perhaps then we need, as Dean Spade (writer and founder of the Sylvia Rivera Law Project in New York City) urges, to 'look more at impact than intent'.[58]

There's another piece to this and that's a question around what we think evidence of intent would do in terms of accountability and change? If we find proof of intent, what happens next? One way to answer this is to look at other areas where proof of intent exists – where the memos have been found, where the whistleblowers have come forward – and see what this did in terms of change. And while there might be examples where this has led to change, there are lots of examples where it hasn't. Devastating examples. Because I lived not too far away at the time and will never forget waking up to the news, I often think of the 72 people, including many global majority and disabled people, who died in Grenfell Tower in 2017. Grenfell's residents had raised concerns about the building's safety for years before the fire.

The inquiry into Grenfell 'concluded that a failure to act on repeated warnings about the dangers of combustible materials was a key cause of the disaster'.[59] An inquiry and multiple investigations have revealed masses of evidence that those responsible for cladding the building and regulating it knew the risks associated with using combustible cladding materials. There are emails dating from before the fire, available on the BBC, referring to fire-safety risks as 'whoops', and demanding that poor fire test results on the cladding be kept confidential.[60] And despite this and all the damning evidence, where is justice for those who died and those left displaced? A disabled activist who needs to remain anonymous, warned me that 'if we turn to the state to have a conscience – we'll be holding our breath for a long time'. What if we turn in a different direction with our evidence, and stop holding our breath?

CREDIBLE EVIDENCE AND RADICAL ACTION

We need to evidence harm in a way that doesn't dehumanise disabled people and that radicalises those less familiar with welfare state violence, enrages them and moves them to action. Disabled people's tactics of evidence-making teaches us a lot about this. Our evidence doesn't have to be solely focused on harm or only aimed at the government – it can shape more radical action, and it can be a form of bearing witness, a way of validating people's experiences, a tool for disabled people.

Ellen Clifford tells me that we need credible evidence 'not because the government will listen to it', but because it 'validates us and the experiences that we're going through. And I think that's important. I think it's also really important for bearing witness to what's happening. That we're recording it.' This is similar to disabled writer and educator Mia Mingus's call for disabled people to leave evidence: 'We must leave evidence. Evidence that we were here, that we existed, that we survived and loved and ached. Evidence for each other that there are other ways to live – past survival; past isolation.'[61]

This is evidence as a practice against forgetting, against the kind of amnesia that benefits the perpetrators of harm. Judith Herman, who writes about trauma and the connections across domestic abuse and political terror, says that 'in order to escape accountability for his crimes, the perpetrator does everything in his power to promote forgetting' through secrecy, attacking the credibility of the victims, ensuring no one listens, and denial. And the 'more powerful the perpetrator, the greater is his prerogative to name and define reality, and the more completely his arguments prevail'.[62] The powerful craft welfare's story: they want us to forget those they have killed, and to forget that there are other ways of doing welfare, more dignified and caring. But people remember – and those memories are part of our resistance.

Disabled activists are creative and strategic in evidencing harms, in making evidence legible to different people. Here radical action can be informed by evidence, and is partly about getting the evidence out there – not to government but to the public. Ellen explains:

> we create political change by using the evidence we've got, but recognising it's only one part. We have to have credible evidence in order to convince those people, but we also have to be prepared to take quite radical action in order for us to get noticed, because the media don't tend to want to cover our issues. Then we have to use forms of resistance that are unlikely to get funded, that are more political, that are trying to raise awareness among the public, but also educate them.

In a different way, Dolly Sen asks, 'How do we share evidence and make it irresistible?'

And beyond documentation of the 'problem', how do we start to not only document and provide evidence but also demonstrate, prototype and build different ways of doing welfare – welfare without deservingness, welfare without borders, welfare that affirms dignity, safety, belonging, that values all of our lives. What evidence would we need to be able to do this?

It's also not just about what the evidence is but also *how* we provide evidence. This means we could understand *evidencing* as a practice – a practice through which we sometimes reproduce state logic; a practice that can be rooted in critique or opposition; or a practice committed to dignity. What might shift if we understood evidencing as a practice rooted in dignity, as a life-affirming practice, as a practice defined by those most impacted, that bears witness, is grounded in resistance, and is in service to building different futures? As Ellen Clifford shared: 'I'm hopeful that there might be a different time in the future when we're able to use what's happened now to create a different kind of society.'

2

Work Does Not Define Our Worth

The Work Capability Assessment (WCA) was introduced in October 2008 to assess entitlement to Employment and Support Allowance (ESA), a benefit for people who are unable to work due to disability or ill health, which has since become synonymous with death. The assessment was the key element of the New Labour government's welfare reform agenda, which was introduced with the intention of cutting spending on out-of-work benefits through a stricter conditionality regime. With the assessment came three new categories for those who have been assessed: those who are fit for work, those seen as having limited capability for work, and those who have limited capability for work and work-related activity (the so-called support group). Rick Burgess (co-founder of Manchester DPAC) knows the WCA well because it nearly killed him:

> Progressively, over time, not only have they kept this not-good assessment – [laughs] being very diplomatic – *shit* assessment, monstrously cruel assessment, but they've also tightened other things around it, so that cumulatively (I think it's important, here, to talk about the cumulative impact of this, because that's one of the things we asked for originally, back in the debate- and petition-years), the cumulative impact on people is extremely nasty, and that is why there are suicides – *because it's just unbearable.* I mean, the last time I went through one was the end-of-2011, and 2012: I barely survived that year. That was probably the closest I came, recently, to suicide. And I've probably been through four or five work capability assessments.

A year after Rick barely survived the WCA, Michael O'Sullivan went through something similar and didn't survive. He took his own life in 2013, after being found fit for work and ineligible for ESA. He had been claiming Incapacity Benefit since 2000, due to depression, social anxiety, agoraphobia, and general anxiety disorder that had gradually worsened since he first moved to London from rural Ireland at the age of 19. He had been told in March 2012 he would be reassessed for ESA. He was assessed in August 2012 by a physiotherapist, an assessment that lasted just twelve minutes and left him 'humiliated, mortified, and feeling like a criminal'.[1] He was declared fit for work, and although he asked the DWP to reconsider, the appeal was turned down. He was told to attend a two-week training course but was constantly mocked, harassed and teased by the other, much younger students. At the end of the first week, he tried to end his own life. He survived and was deemed 'unfit for work' by his GP for six months but was called for another WCA just four months later. His assessor, a former orthopaedic surgeon who had been working for Atos for 15 years, took just 31 minutes to assess him, and only a further eleven minutes to complete the paperwork. He had made it clear on the pre-assessment ESA50 form that he had suicidal thoughts. He took his own life on 24 September, just hours before he was due to start a four-week job placement.

I can't do justice here to the extent to which disabled people have resisted the WCA regime. This has included evidencing the harms caused by the assessments, showing the assessment doesn't do what the government claims it does, lending equipment to disabled people to record their assessment, documenting how many people it has killed, and imagining alternatives. In 2012, the Spartacus Network (a group of disabled and chronically ill people across the country who research issues relating to disability and social security), produced the *People's Review of the Work Capability Assessment*, documenting its fatal impact on benefit claimants, and the links between being found fit for work and people's deaths.[2] The report includes people's harrowing experiences with the assessment process:

> Everyday I panic when the post arrives, waiting for the brown envelope from DWP. I've got to a point now that I have nightmares over the work capability assessment, I'm so frightened, I, like many other disabled people are worried to the point of suicide.

This person is far from alone. As we saw in Chapter 1, the WCA was linked to 590 suicides between 2010 and 2013 in England.[3] And a 2016 survey by Mind (a mental health charity working in England and Wales) asking over a thousand people about their experience of WCAs found that 87 per cent of people said that the system caused distress and 51 per cent said that they had suicidal thoughts as a result of it.[4] In a later report by Mind, in 2020, Sarah talks about her experience of the assessment, where 'The worst bit is being asked to tell the assessor "why haven't you killed yourself yet?"'[5]

Rick is a survivor of the WCA, who with Jane Bence and Wayne Blackburn (all disabled people who were formerly part of the War on Welfare petition campaign) and lawyer and benefits expert Nick Dilworth created the campaigning organisation New Approach, dedicated to abolishing the WCA and developing a replacement. Together with others, the group led a survey of 884 people who have been through the WCA. Rick explains that they wanted to 'give the survivors of the WCA a chance to assess the people and system that assessed them, thus 'Assessing the Assessors' was born. Launching in Edinburgh with a mass party outside the Atos assessment centre in Edinburgh, 'we had cake, we had tea and coffee, we had a conjurer! And we had the questionnaire presented in accessible format.'[6] The report concludes that the assessment is 'abusive', 'disrespectful', 'callous and inhumane', discriminates against disabled people and appears to promote unprofessional activity on the part of assessors and to cause hardship and poverty. At a House of Commons Work and Pensions Committee, a manager of the Welfare Benefits Advice Service at Mind in Croydon says something similar: 'without exception clients are terrified, anxious and panicked by the process of ESA, particularly the WCA'.[7]

Ben Baumberg Geiger (who researches disability and the benefits system) talked to me about how in 2015–16, while on secondment at the DWP, he tried unsuccessfully to get the assessment changed:

> There's three things that the WCA is, at least on the face of it, trying to do, and does very badly: one of them, we could call assessing the genuineness of people's conditions; one of them is about linking those impairments to work-capacity; and then the third one is about conditionality and sanctions.

For him, a big piece is lack of transparency and evidence in the creation of the WCA, and how it relates to actual working conditions. It focuses on finding people's most significant impairments, despite the fact 'that most people claiming benefits (or at least about half the people claiming benefits) have got multiple conditions that affect them in multiple different ways'. Assessors are told they 'should be doing these informal assessments of noticing: if somebody reaches into their bag for a tissue, which hand is it with? … The sort of thing people hate.' Neither is there clarity on 'the extent to which you give somebody the opportunity to explain why, even though they said they've had depression for a certain period of time, they've not gone to their GP. Which is, again, one of the things people say: "Well, it probably isn't that serious, then," without talking to somebody about the many, many reasons that people have of being very distrustful of GP services.' Basically, he sees it as 'set up to be trying to judge on the genuineness of you going and trying to explain your life to them. But it does it in an incredibly bad way. I just think it's a terrible combination.' And we know it's a lethal combination, where people's accounts of the impact of their impairments are undermined and disregarded by assessors (e.g., documented by the Welfare Conditionality: Sanctions, Support and Behaviour Change research project).[8]

Unlike many people, Ben argues that A Better Work Capability Assessment Is Possible (the title of a report he wrote with Demos).[9]

He suggests reforms such as audio recording assessments, giving claimants the chance to explain any evidence which seems to contradict their impairments, changing the assessment descriptors to better reflect the actual labour market (including allowing for the impact of multiple impairments), and reducing conditionality to ensure people aren't unfairly sanctioned. These changes would likely help ease the harm of the assessment, for sure, and that is huge. Might they also, though, ultimately strengthen the hold of the assessment process and of the DWP?

While Rick wants to abolish the WCA, he still thinks some kind of assessment would be needed – he wants a replacement that doesn't harm people. Something that allows for the fact that work isn't for everyone, while also making work far better for those who can and want to do it. In the foreword to the Spartacus Network's *People's Review of the Work Capability Assessment*, Peter Beresford, who researches user involvement in mental health, says the assessment should be judged in the wider context of what the government is doing to create an accessible meaningful labour market (i.e., not much, arguably because this isn't the real point of WCAs, right?). He also warns us that it's a 'mistake to see the WCA in isolation' because the involvement of the private insurance industry and the outsourced assessment process create a 'perfect storm of irresponsibility and unaccountability'.[10]

MALINGERING, POINTS-BASED ASSESSMENTS, AND THE INSURANCE INDUSTRY

> When I got through it in 2003–04, I said, 'This is a horrible system, and if this is rolled out, there's going to be a lot of deaths.' And unfortunately, that is what happened.

In 2003, Rick Burgess, unbeknown to him, was subject to a trial of what would become the WCA. He remembers the context, tracking 'the various Labour Secretaries of State for the DWP as they worked with the media to create an opinion against benefits-claimants', cultivating a 'toxic atmosphere' that enabled them to pass punitive policies. For Rick, one of the early indications of this was the Malingering and Illness Deception in Welfare Benefits Conference, which took place in Woodstock, near Oxford (in 2001), and saw 'malingering' as a lifestyle choice for many claimants of long-term sickness benefits.

Malingering means pretending to be ill or exaggerating symptoms in order to claim welfare (or for another incentive). In a twist of irony, malingering came to be medicalised in the early nineteenth century in association with people feigning illness in opposition to joining the military. It has since come to be applied to people claiming disability benefits via a long stigmatising battle and sustained resistance, and to be used to label people with medically unexplained symptoms and chronic illness, especially chronic fatigue (evident in the work of Catherine Hale and the Chronic Illness Inclusion project).[11] Though, as we'll see throughout this book, the idea of using poor relief and welfare to distinguish between those who are 'genuinely' ill and cannot work, and are therefore deserving, and those who are not, has a long history going back to before the 1800s. According to disabled activist and writer Ellen Clifford, the 'fear that giving money to disabled people, and disability benefits, would encourage malingering' is built into the foundations of the welfare state, making it 'deliberately exclusionary' of disabled people.

'Malingering' is part of the ideological warfare that comes under the name of 'benefit fraud', which even when consistently low is used over time to justify stigmatisation and punishment of people claiming welfare, and throughout the 1990s/2000s, mobilised to enable deeper involvement of the private insurance industry in UK welfare. In 1992, Peter Lilley (then secretary of state at the Department of Social Security, in John Major's Conservative government) gave a speech about 'closing down the something for nothing society' and tightening up on 'scroungers' and 'bogus asylum seekers'. Cultural studies scholar Jonathan Rutherford tracks how two years later, in

1994, John Major's Conservative government hired John LoCascio, a senior executive of US insurance company UnumProvident Insurance, to offer guidance on welfare claims management to limit the UK welfare budget and advise the UK government on how to reduce the number of claimants of long-term sickness benefits.[12] This revealed the influence of US corporations in shaping the development of the UK's approach to 'welfare reform'. In 1995, John LoCascio co-wrote a journal article with the principal medical officer for the Department of Social Security, Mansel Aylward, suggesting that the increase in the number of recipients of Invalidity Benefit in the UK and long-term disability benefits in the USA were due to doctors accepting patient's subjective health assessments (i.e., how they describe how they feel about their health) as the basis for diagnosis and capacity for work. Here we see the idea that most claimants of Incapacity Benefit were living with 'psychosomatic' conditions, and that GPs should not determine people's capacity to work.[13]

The 'malingering' conference is significant because it aimed to transform welfare and how we understand illness as a means to push growing numbers of people into work. Mo Stewart, a disabled researcher who has long been investigating the influence of corporate America in the planned destruction of the UK's welfare state, explains that the people who attended and the ideologies they represented would be key in justifying the 'future demolition of the welfare state'.[14] The conference took place in the same year that the Department for Work and Pensions was formed – through merging together the Department of Social Security and the Employment Service. In one of our many chats, Rick would point out the significance of the name of this new department – clearly signifying a shift from social security to work.

The conference took place amidst the Labour government's welfare reforms of 1999, which were steeped in this same rhetoric – cutting invalidity benefit for thousands of disabled people as a way to 'think the unthinkable' and reform a welfare state said to create cultures of dependency.[15] The anti-welfare rhetoric underlying these reforms sought to frame disabled people's unemployment as the result of individual 'dependency' rather than an exclusionary labour market.[16] At the time, one newspaper reported that '[s]ick and disabled people who refuse to look for work will face the withdrawal of their state benefits under a tough new government drive to slash "welfare dependency"'.[17] And, at the same time, over the Atlantic Ocean, the new president, George W. Bush, was reading from the same script, saying 'too many Americans with disabilities remain trapped in bureaucracies of dependence'.[18]

Back to Oxford – many of the presentations at the malingering conference, including John LoCascio's chapter on 'Malingering, insurance medicine, and the medicalization of fraud', were published in 2003, by Oxford University Press, in the book *Malingering and Illness Deception*, edited by Peter Halligan, Christopher Bass and David Oakley.[19] Testament to how the most chilling details can be found in the most banal places, in the book's acknowledgments section, we find out that the conference 'would not have been possible had it not been for the enthusiastic support of Professor Mansel Aylward and funding from the Department for Work and Pensions'.

Mansel Aylward, Philip Sawney (a GP) and John LoCascio were among the first to advocate a functional capacity assessment approach (which focuses on capacity to work regardless of diagnosis) that would come to define disability assessment medicine as a way to generate profits.[20] They would play a key role in suggesting that so-called 'malingering' is a lifestyle choice for many claimants of long-term sickness benefits. This approach would get a real-world application in the Social Security (Incapacity for Work) Act 1994, which replaced Invalidity Benefit with Incapacity Benefit, and introduced the points-based All Work Test – whose scoring system treats impairments in isolation with no reference to the environment or how what we can do one day might be different from what we can do the next. That means asking people questions about whether they can move about unaided, reach things or make themselves understood, and assigning them points depending on their answers. The then Department of Social Security (DSS) would make decisions on eligibility for benefits through non-medical adjudication officers – a process that, according to Jonathan Rutherford, was advised by John LoCascio.[21]

Interestingly, according to law scholar Nick Wikeley, just a few years before, in 1991, the government had rejected using a points-based system for assessing entitlement to Disability Living Allowance because it was seen as 'humiliating' and 'intrusive'.[22] But new regulations did introduce regulation 27, decided by a doctor, which provided a 'safety net' for those who faced a 'substantial risk' of harm if they were found capable of work because they did not score enough points on the test (suggesting some government awareness that determining capacity to work is linked to potential and significant harm).

Actual benefit fraud – which amounted at the time to less than 0.4 per cent of Incapacity Benefit claims – was not the issue.[23] The people at the conference were proponents of welfare to work – linking conditionality of benefits to work-related activities – used in the USA since the 1990s. This created a huge cultural shift from more of a collective to an individualised responsibility for health and welfare. In 1996, Bill Clinton's government created massive welfare reform in the USA – replacing Aid to Families with Dependent Children (AFDC) with Temporary Assistance for Needy Families (TANF) – mandating that low-income parents had to work in order to receive welfare benefits, and removing the safety net. The Personal Responsibility and Work Opportunity Reconciliation Act, of which TANF was a part, also played a key part in what political scientist Sanford Schram calls the medicalisation of welfare through framing welfare 'dependency' as an illness.[24]

Something else linked these welfare-to-work ideologies, and that was their association with the giant US insurance company UnumProvident, which has a long history of lawsuits against it for denial of, and deceptive practices in, disability insurance claims. Throughout the 1980s and 1990s, welfare state privatisation went global, largely promoted by international trade bodies such as the World Bank and International Monetary Fund through coercive and punitive Structural Adjustment Programmes. In order for many countries, impoverished through colonialism, to be eligible for loans for development, they had to meet certain conditions – including opening up welfare and health as markets for the private insurance industry. For many Latin American countries, this began in the 1980s – with the World Bank insisting on reforms that privatised social security and disability pensions. This means that welfare reform has always been a key point of struggle in violent structural adjustment policies, meaning that what is often treated as national reform of welfare systems is globally connected.

A few years after the Malingering Conference, after a career as chief medical adviser, medical director and chief scientist of the DWP, Mansel Aylward retired from the civil service to become the first director of the UnumProvident Centre for Psychosocial and Disability Research at Cardiff University. One of his first tasks was to design a 'non-medical' assessment model for the DWP, using research sponsored by UnumProvident Insurance.[25] Unum executives and people representing Atos were both part of the Labour government's mental health and physical function 'technical working groups', set up in 2006 to review and develop the new, stricter 'work compatibility assessments'.[26] In the same year, David Freud, a senior banker at UBS AG, was commissioned to conduct a review of New Labour's welfare-to-work policies – published in 2007 as 'Reducing Dependency, Increasing Opportunity: Options for the Future of Welfare to Work'.[27] Freud recommended involving the private sector on long-term, outcome-based contracts to help the government reach its targets in cutting welfare, and (citing Aylward) to enable a business model for workfare.

The biopsychosocial (BPS) model of assessment, put forward by Aylward, was adopted by the DWP in October 2008 in the form of the WCA – which kills so many disabled people. This approach was hugely influential to the 'benefits crackdown' of the then incoming Coalition government in 2010, which, as Debbie Jolly, co-founder of DPAC put it, meant people 'getting rich on disability denial'.[28]

OUTSOURCING ACCOUNTABILITY

Within a few years of being introduced, disability assessments were being outsourced to private companies. In 2000, the All Work Test was reformed and renamed the Personal Capability Assessment, and outsourced to the company SEMA, which would be bought out by Schlumberger in 2001. SchlumbergerSema would then be taken over by the French corporation Atos Origin in 2004. This process would make Atos the sole provider of the government's assessment contracts. In 2005, Atos would win a £500 million contract to carry out the assessments for the next five years (it would win a further three-year extension in 2010 and then another extension that would take it to 2015).

In August 2012, while still holding the contract for the WCA, which was increasingly being linked to disabled people's suicides, Atos became the official sponsor for the Paralympics. (No, I'm not joking.) During the Paralympics, disabled activists from Disabled People Against Cuts (DPAC) arrived at the Atos head office to deliver a coffin filled with messages drawing attention to the over one thousand (at the time) people who had died after being found 'fit to work'.[29] Paula Peters from DPAC told researcher and campaigner Debbie Humphry that she remembers:

> We raised awareness of how toxic the work capability programme was, how toxic this government was, how toxic these companies were ... We had 400 people there and the press were all over us ... Before that people weren't making the connection that Atos were the contractor. The only way the companies understand is when you hit them in the profit margin. So you trash their reputation.[30]

For a long time, it was common to see disabled protestors holding placards with 'Atos Kills' scrawled in red pen – made to look like blood. In March 2014, after extensive reputational damage and declining share prices, Atos bought themselves out of their £400 million state contract.[31] And it was Maximus, in 2015, who replaced them. Maximus got the job thanks to their extensive experience in the USA, where, according to journalist Tracie Mcmillan, they secured the USA's first privatised welfare contract in 1987, making huge profits capitalising on the idea of 'welfare fraud', and using technology to restrict access to benefits through old tropes of deservingness.[32] In the USA, they also have a hand in prisons and in child enforcement; they oversee workforce programmes in Israel and Australia; they ran contracts in Africa and Latin America and for the World Bank and the US Agency for International Development;[33] and in the UK, they have contracts with the Home Office and Ministry of Justice, as well as the DWP.[34] They also, according to their website, make profits from war – providing defence services based on their 'vast experience in mission-centered cybersecurity, AI and machine learning, data analytics'.[35]

As with Atos, DPAC resisted Maximus, making public the role it played in Medicaid fraud in the USA. Multiple lawsuits over false claims have been filed over Maximus's incompetence, discrimination and alleged fraud and corruption in the USA – all in the public domain at the time that Maximus was given the contract by the DWP.[36] Despite (or maybe because of) this history of deception, the UK government continues to outsource to Maximus as part of government plans to reduce eligibility for certain benefits (specifically Personal Independence Payment (PIP) and the health component of Universal Credit). In 2023, the DWP awarded Maximus the contract to carry out disability assessments in the north of England and Scotland, worth an estimated £800 million over five years, according to investigations by the *Guardian* newspaper.[37] It will also work as a 'delivery partner' to the company Capita in Wales and the Midlands, worth another £150 million.

A year after this contract was awarded, Bruce Caswell, the chief executive of Maximus, was paid a base salary of $886,904, with stock awards, incentive plans and other compensation taking his total package to $10.2 million, and in 2025 the company reported a 23 per cent rise in profits.[38]

According to then minister of state for disabled people, health and work, the DWP awarded Capita two five-year contracts to carry out assessments of disabled people, one across Wales and the Midlands (£450 million), and the other in Northern Ireland (£110 million).[39] This is despite the fact that the actions of Capita were found by a coroner to be 'the predominant factor and the only acute factor' that led Philippa Day to take her own life in 2019. Disability News Service reported that the safeguarding review into her death in October 2019 found the actions of Capita had had a 'profound impact' on the 27-year-old and caused her 'debilitating anxiety', thanks to systemic problems in the PIP assessment system.[40]

Undercover filming for Channel 4's *Dispatches* about PIP assessments showed Capita's chief medical officer telling a trainee assessor that the company needs its assessors 'to be doing as many assessments a day as you can possibly manage' and to 'forget your mental health background and park it to one side' when carrying out assessments.[41] Undercover footage also shows one experienced assessor admitting that he sometimes completes his assessment reports before even meeting the claimants, which he says is standard practice.

Alongside Capita and Maximus, Serco was one of the five companies given UK government contracts to carry out assessments for disability-related benefits – worth over £2 billion – from 2024 to 2029. According to Serco, as well as carrying out assessments for disability-related benefits, their 'services span justice, migration, defence, space, customer services, health, and transport'.[42] That means they make their profits from assessing if disabled people should get benefits, border control, and from occupation and war, including providing services for Israeli naval projects.[43] Serco also profits from immigration, by running some of the UK's immigration removal centres and has a government contract to run hotels that house asylum seekers. It's because of the horrendous conditions that people are housed in, and the huge profits made on the back of their dehumanisation, that Refugee and Asylum Participatory Action Research (RAPAR), a human rights organisation founded in Salford in 2001, has a campaign called Serco Must Go!

Ellen Clifford said that outsourcing has the effect of massively reducing transparency, allowing the government to avoid accountability for wrongful assessment decisions and punitive processes. Outsourcing disability assessment is a key tactic to extract profit, and for the government to avoid accountability by distancing itself from the deaths its policies cause – and it's also the part of the grinding bureaucracy that is most synonymous with people's deaths. Former assessors told the *Big Issue* about pressure to 'ramp up numbers' with little empathy for vulnerable claimants, leading to people being refused support or facing a distressing appeals process, and that disability assessment is 'run as a business. It is not run to help people. As long as it's run like that, nothing will change. It will remain target-driven. It will remain profit-based. It is not putting the best interest of the people using the system at its heart.'[44]

Greg Wood, a GP who worked at Atos as a senior adviser on mental health issues, told the *Guardian* that assessment was not 'even-handed', that assessors were trained to award points 'begrudgingly' and encouraged to find 'reasons not to award points', and that medical staff were told to change reports if they were too favourable to claimants. He says: 'I think the Department for Work and Pensions is the real culprit here. It's the government training that makes Atos assessors do this.'[45] Outsourcing makes for a complex bureaucracy that seems to me intentionally hard to follow, especially because it makes it even harder to trace cause and effect, and accountability for people's deaths. My struggle to explain this in a way that doesn't give you a headache is an example of how the bureaucracy of welfare infrastructure is violent. But in that complexity is a pattern – politicians tell us the immigration and welfare bills are unwieldy, expenditure is seen as unproductive, while they simultaneously open up these areas to the market, creating sites of huge profits.

ABANDONMENT – ORGANISED AND EXTRACTIVE

Summarising the testimony collected from people who have experienced the WCA, collected for the Assessing the Assessors report, Rick Burgess writes:

> Page after page contains what can only be described as horror stories from a Kafkaesque nightmare, in a country that seems to have engaged upon a regime of removing disabled and ill people from society by the most opaque and brutal bureaucratic means possible. There is no doubt the WCA causes deaths. There is no doubt it is not fit for the purpose, there is no doubt it must be abolished as a simple matter of morality, human decency and basic human rights.[46]

Companies like Maximus make money from devising complex eligibility rules and from running complex systems related to welfare-to-work programmes. This is the kind of complexity that former benefits advisers told the *Big Issue* make assessments 'soul destroying' because they're designed 'to catch people out'.[47] This means that the brutal bureaucracy that harms and kills so many disabled people is by design and for profit.

Maybe then the assessment is fit for a different purpose than the one we're told – the purpose of getting people off welfare by any means. We can see this in impact (and often explicitly in intent) in the USA, where, according to journalist Tracie Mcmillan, 'before Clinton's reforms, more than 60 percent of the families in poverty in Indiana got cash assistance. By 2016, only 7 percent did.' A decade after welfare reform was first rolled out in the USA, Maximus had annual revenue of $701 million.[48] Violent bureaucracy is their business.

When Rick Burgess says that outsourcing is a 'horrific example of a highly-privatised government system, where it's just impossible to actually get a handle on the bureaucracy that's oppressing you' – this is what he's talking about.

Thinking about how systems can be designed to weaponise complexity and deny accountability makes me think about how abandonment is organised. Geographer and prison abolitionist Ruth Wilson-Gilmore asks us to imagine an unregulated or deregulated rental unit, where the landlord doesn't keep the lightbulbs working and someone, an elderly lady in her example, falls down the stairs. This is 'organized abandonment and vulnerability to premature death' because, while premature death can happen to anyone, in this example, it's the 'decisions that make that vulnerability so pervasive and frightening' because they are the result of choices.[49] Ruth Wilson-Gilmore's writing describes the deliberate manipulation, disinvestment and dispossession of resources from poor communities (who are often made up of Black people and people of colour, Indigenous people in the US context from which she writes, and disabled people), in ways that render them vulnerable to adverse health and premature death – as 'organized abandonment'. This abandonment is racialised – where she defines racism as 'state-sanctioned or extralegal production and exploitation of group-differentiated vulnerability to premature death'.[50]

Although many disabled people in the UK understandably detest the word 'vulnerability' as the state has weaponised it against them, the framing of being made 'vulnerable' – the structural forces that render certain populations more vulnerable to harm and premature death is very relevant to understanding and resisting welfare state violence. We see over and over how the idea that some people are framed as a social 'cost' to the state, a 'burden' or a 'drain' on the economy is central to creating the state-sanctioned devaluation of life (something we explore further in Chapter 3). Building on Ruth Wilson-Gilmore's work, Beatrice Adler-Bolton and Artie Vierkant (in their book *Health Communism*) show how

> the surplus population has become an essential component of capitalist society, with many industries built on the maintenance, supervision, surveillance, policing, data extraction, confinement, study, cure, measurement, treatment, extermination, housing, transportation, and care of the surplus. In this way, those discarded as non-valuable life are maintained as a source of extraction and profit for capital.[51]

When talking about the system creating a 'burden of proof' for disabled people and people who claim welfare, a disabled activist who wants to remain anonymous explained to me that the idea of benefit fraud, so foundational to welfare as we know it, 'makes it seem as though people are extracting from the state ... when the reality is the state is extracting from people'.

It is through abandonment that the state extracts profit from the very people it deems to be burdensome.

This is 'extractive abandonment' – making certain populations profitable to capital. Whole industries are built on extractive abandonment and huge profits made, and welfare is no exception. We have seen this in the outsourcing of assessments determining people's eligibility for disability benefits. We also encounter it in how the global insurance industry not only profits from 'welfare reform' but is also complicit in the occupation and genocide of the Palestinian people – investing in and underwriting companies that have supplied – or whose equipment has been deployed for – Israel's military operations in Gaza.[52] Here we see that disablement, or what Jasbir Puar (who writes about how disablement is used by Israel to maintain occupation of Palestine) calls 'maiming' is a 'source of value extraction from populations that would otherwise be disposable'.[53]

Disability is key to understanding extractive abandonment and capitalism more generally – especially as disability as we now know it was created by capitalism. Marta Russell and Ravi Malhotra's 'money model of disability' brilliantly explains how disability is a 'product of the exploitative economic structure of capitalist society: one which creates (and then oppresses) the so-called "disabled" body as one of the conditions that allow the capitalist class to accumulate wealth'.[54] The 'money model' explains how industrial capitalism created disability for those who didn't embody being a standard worker, erasing their labour power because only paid work was seen to count. Here disabled people came to be seen as a problem, whose solution lay in exclusion in asylums, prisons, workhouses, and also through eugenics (including sterilisation). Yet disabled people shore up capitalism in two key ways: through disability-related impoverishment and lack of a real safety net creating a fear among workers of becoming disabled and destitute, and through making disablement into big business – from privatised social care and outsourced disability benefits assessments, to some of the same companies profiting from disablement through conflict.

The idea that resources are scarce and that people should meet certain criteria to be able to access support, what is often called 'eligibility', is foundational to what we now call welfare. Written into 'eligibility' is the idea that some people deserve support more than others, and assessing who they are (sorting, categorising, surveilling) occupies centuries of attempts to classify poor people and determine who should receive relief and welfare, and what forms it will take.[55] Much of this classification is about determining who can and can't do waged labour, and who therefore deserves support. The Vagabond Act of 1530 categorised poor people as either 'impotent', unable to work, and therefore 'deserving' of relief, or as 'vagabonds', people who beg for relief in a context where begging had been outlawed and therefore who deserve only to be whipped (perhaps some current day politicians would still agree). In England, and much of Europe, poor relief tended to be organised by local parishes. Then came the Poor Relief Act (known as the Elizabethan Poor Law) in 1601 – a nationwide system of relief, which put the responsibility on each parish to collect taxes to fund poor relief, assigning some people as 'overseers of the poor' – responsible for punishing 'vagrants' (i.e., the 'undeserving') and forcing the 'able-bodied' poor to work. Around this same time came the Enclosures Acts – the carving up and privatising of common lands which sustained people outside of paid work.

Frances Fox-Piven and Richard Cloward, in their book *Regulating the Poor*, see poor relief systems, from the sixteenth century onwards, as developing a way to control mass disturbances and poor people's resistance against the long and violent transition to capitalism:

> Some of the aged, the disabled, the insane, and others who are of no use as workers are left on the relief rolls, and their treatment is so degrading and punitive as to instil in the labouring masses a fear of the fate that awaits them should they relax into beggary and pauperism. To demean and punish those who do not work is to exalt by contrast even the meanest labour at the meanest wages.[56]

The Elizabethan Poor Law solidified ideas of, and connections between, deservingness, able-bodiedness, work, productivity and worth, still evident over 200 years later in the Royal Commission into the Poor Laws, in 1832, and the subsequent passing of the New Poor Laws in 1834 – often cited in contemporary disability activism as comparable to what's happening now. The 1832 Commission recommended that the able-bodied poor could be given relief in the workhouse under conditions less eligible than the working poor. They explained the idea of 'less eligibility' as 'the first and most essential of all conditions' – that the situation of the recipient of relief 'shall not be made really or apparently so eligible as the situation of the independent labourer of the lowest class'.[57] This means that relief must always provide for less and support a lifestyle less than the lowest paid forms of work. This was referred to as the Workhouse Test – a regime designed to be so awful that it would deter people from seeking relief in the first place. Here the system is designed to reduce the need for time-consuming tests of merit or means to determine who is truly needy.[58] Describing workhouses, the Poor Law Commissioners' Report (1834) states that 'into such a house none will enter voluntarily; work, confinement, and discipline will deter the indolent', providing 'an unerring test of the necessity of applicants'. Fear was written into the infrastructure of workhouses, which, according to historical geographer Felix Driver, in his book *Power and Pauperism: The Workhouse System 1834–1884*, were designed to be a 'terror to the able-bodied population'.[59]

Beatrice Adler-Bolton and Artie Vierkant document how poor people were sorted into the 'impotent poor' who were seen as deserving because they were seen as legitimately unable to work; 'able-bodied poor' – willing to work but unable to find jobs; and the 'idle poor' who 'refused to be productive citizens'.[60] These ways of classifying appear banal and administrative, and yet they create divides between poor people, by separating poor people based on who is and isn't a worker, and who is seen as a legitimate non-worker (deserving of welfare). Even the 'impotent poor', framed as deserving of support, were treated as suspect – the relief they received kept meager as a way to stop people abusing the system. This idea of abusing the system (as if the system isn't also abusive) seems to have been around for as long as poor relief and welfare – making it hard to imagine welfare without it. No wonder then that the history of paid work, as criminologist Jon Burnett documents in the book *Work and the Carceral State* is one of coercion, force, punishment and policing.[61] Yet there was massive resistance to the Poor Laws and an anti-Poor Law movement which saw them as inhumane, calling workhouses 'prisons of the poor'. Much of this resistance came from poor people.

Part of the divisive power of 'work' is how it is mobilised in different ways for different groups, and this is used to pit us against one another. For example, the UK government currently doesn't allow people seeking asylum the right to work – something opposed by a coalition of 300 organisations advocating to 'Lift the Ban'. Yet while we campaign for asylum seekers to be able to work (if they want to, if they are able), we must also recognise that the 'right to work' has been weaponised by the state against disabled people and others who claim welfare.[62] From the perspective of those in power, another very important alliance to prevent is between workers and people who claim welfare, while also underplaying that many people claiming welfare do also work. Rick Burgess pointed out to me the significance of the beginning of the Covid pandemic when there was a massive increase in the working population who suddenly had to claim Universal Credit. At this time, the amount paid to people in receipt of Universal Credit was increased (an uplift) but other more long-standing benefits, including Employment and Support Allowance (claimed by many disabled people) were not increased. Rick understands this as a tactic by the government to ensure that working people not usually on welfare, who have been targeted through anti-welfare propaganda to hate people who claim welfare, don't come to realise the awful reality of welfare, preventing solidarity from growing. Those on the older benefits took the decision to court and lost because, as Rick explains, the High Court judge making the decision reproduced ideas about people on benefits as 'sub human, who should get treated worse than other people' – showing how cultural ideas about deservingness shape the law. This is part, as my dear colleague at Healing Justice Ldn, Sarah Joynt-Bowe explains, of the state's endless 'contortions to prevent migrants, disabled people, and workers from resisting together. It's a strategy to divide and deprive for the sake of maintaining capitalism and often reinforcing nationalism.'

WORK DOESN'T EQUAL WORTH

Martin Hadfield, who was unemployed and desperately looking for work, died by suicide 24 hours after his last meeting with Jobcentre staff. His stepfather told the *Mirror* that 'despite being unemployed for months, proud Martin refused to accept state handouts ... He got nothing off the government and was proud not to.'[63] But he was driven to despair after being rejected for 40 jobs, leaving him feeling 'put down with no self worth'. At protests, when I see people holding placards saying 'work doesn't equal worth', I often think of Martin. The history of the centrality of work to welfare, traced above, shows us why we need to keep telling ourselves, militantly, that our worth is inherent and not tied to productivity.

If the history above sounds all too familiar, that's because the New Poor Laws laid the foundations for ideas about poverty and undeservingness that continue to shape policy today. These laws instituted the idea of paid work as the measure of human worth, where those who can't or won't work and therefore need state support are called 'burdensome'. This is evident in the 'work first' approach to welfare that saw early iterations in 1996 in the USA under Clinton – where welfare reform meant mandating that low-income parents had to work in order to receive welfare benefits. It's evident in the widespread global use of workfare – making welfare conditional on work and compliance with work-related activities. It's evident in the Labour government's 'Pathways to Work: Reforming Benefits and Support to Get Britain Working' Green Paper, launched in March 2025, which proposed tying welfare to mandatory engagement with work coaches – designed to push disabled people into work through sanctions. But work has always come first, and welfare was designed to be a deterrent by a state intent on forcing as many people into paid labour as possible.

When we hold our placards saying work does not equal worth, this is what we're up against – centuries of this. And it's this history, and historical continuities, that some disabled people's organising mobilises as resistance. Against a backdrop of people on welfare being described as 'work shy', disabled activists came together to form the Black Triangle Campaign, in 2010 (a year when multiple disabled people's campaigning groups were formed in response to the violence of welfare reform and austerity). The black triangle was a badge used in Nazi concentration camps to mark people as 'asocial' or '*arbeitsscheu*' (work shy), which was later adopted in feminist lesbian organising. Coming across the Black Triangle Campaign, which maintained a list on its website of some of the people killed by welfare reform, played a big part for me in creating the Deaths by Welfare project. That some people can be portrayed as 'work shy' makes sense in a welfare system always organised around, and also increasingly more explicitly focusing on, work, and where being assessed for and found 'fit for work' has led to so many people's deaths, including many by suicide.

Maximus, Serco, Capita – we know the names of those who are harming and killing us, and so we should say them out loud, chant them in public, write them into public consciousness. We know the companies, we can find out the CEOs – there is something powerful in naming them all as perpetrators. At the same time, we need to name the system enabling the perpetrators to kill people. This is important because we've seen how DPAC successfully campaigned to stop outsourcing to Atos, and yet the contract was immediately given to another company, Maximus. We need to campaign against the companies whose names we know, while also campaigning against outsourcing as a practice – not necessarily because we think the DWP would do it better in house but because outsourcing is a tactic to deny accountability.

This feels especially important now, as those of us who want to ultimately get rid of the WCA find ourselves encountering a government that says it wants to abolish it by 2028. Isn't that what many of us have been demanding for a long time? The consultation process, which disabled people have called out as a sham, would suggest not. Disability News Service report on concerns about the financial impact, especially as the Institute for Fiscal Studies (IFS) estimated that while scrapping the WCA could see an increase of £390 a month in benefits for 320,000 disabled people, it would also see a fall of £390 a month for 520,000 disabled claimants.[64] The changes will mean that disabled people will likely instead be assessed through a PIP assessment, which shares many harmful similarities with the WCA, and will enable DWP work coaches, who, as John Pring points out, 'usually have no health-related qualifications – to decide if a disabled person should carry out work-related activity'.[65] This is deeply worrying because work coaches will likely still work in a system that offers targets and financial incentives for getting people into work, meaning likely imposition of inappropriate work-related conditionality, and sanctions if people do not meet it. And it gets worse. The Child Poverty Action Group (CPAG) shows that the proposed changes will mean the end of appeals against WCA decisions – meaning that discretionary decisions, potentially shaped by targets to push people into work, will lose judicial oversight.[66]

This is part of a continued attack that many of us know well, some of us are newer to, and that binds all of our lives. It is also an invitation for us to be clear on the kind of welfare we want, and whether assessment would be part of this, or not. We've met people, like Ben Baumberg Geiger, who call for better assessments, and do this by giving concrete examples of how other countries do assessments. In 2015, Ben, Jon Warren, Kayleigh Garthwaite, and Clare Bambra looked at how seven other countries assess capacity, finding that 'real world' assessment is not 'utopian and unworkable' and 'instead, it is the WCA that appears strange when viewed in an international perspective'.[67] 'Real-world assessment looks at whether someone's functional impairments interfere with their ability to get or keep a job', taking into account non-medical factors (such as employability) that make it easier or harder for different people to work. They recommend the UK adopt this approach, involving disabled people in it from the beginning, and always making sure that unemployment benefits are a 'safe place' for disabled people.

If part of our collective vision is welfare (and a world) without extractive abandonment, what are the smaller moves that might get us there? Designing more humane assessments is important, as is delinking assessment from profit, and removing outsourcing and private insurance industry influence. There's a bigger piece too – something we'll keep coming back to – about growing our collective capacity to reimagine welfare. Whether that's better assessments, or welfare without assessment, eligibility requirements and conditionality – that's for us to decide.

What feels especially important as we imagine beyond current systems is how we unlearn centuries of our inherent worth being tied to our ability and desire to work. This takes us back to Marta Russell and Ravi Malhotra's 'money model of disability', which teaches us the importance of fostering solidarity across those of us harmed by productionism. They remind us that

> buying into the largely capitalist-induced belief that work equates with self-esteem or is a condition for membership of the human race – that people are labourers first and human beings second – only serves to oppress us all.[68]

When we feel, or are made to feel, worthless because we're unemployed or can't work, we can find the reason why in centuries of being told some people are deserving because they can work or somehow meet criteria for being 'genuinely ill', and some people aren't. It's important to understand how hierarchies of worth and deservingness are not 'human nature' but centuries old – imposed and reproduced, with constant repetition and resistance. We need to know so we can resist them and take away their hold on us – how they shape the way we talk to ourselves and each other, untethering the power they hold over how we understand human worth.

3

No 'Burdens' and No Perfect Victims

Martin Rust died two months after the DWP found him fit for work. The coroner said the DWP's decision 'caused distress and may well have had an adverse effect'. Martin's mother explained 'he had attempted suicide before because he feared being "a burden"'.[1] Coming to feel we're a 'burden' because we're told we are by government and the media shows up in people's accounts of feeling suicidal, in suicide notes, and in family accounts of those who have died by suicide. To counter the way their loved ones were made to feel undeserving, and to try to appeal to the government to recognise the value of their life, some families tap into the script of undeservingness and burden. Remember Trevor Drakard, who died by suicide after being found fit for work despite never working due to his epilepsy? His brother Michael explained, 'the system is not appropriate for someone like Trevor, who really needs help. It was never about the money. He did not drink, smoke, he had the most frugal existence – he probably had about ten shandies a year.'[2] And then there's David Clapson, who died with just £3.44 left in his bank account, after his Jobseeker's Allowance was cut because he missed an appointment. He couldn't afford food or electricity and died from diabetic ketoacidosis – caused by not taking his insulin. His sister, Gill Thompson, believes he was in a desperate situation, telling the *Daily Mirror* that 'my brother was not a scrounger. He was getting £71.70 a week. He was not living on champagne and caviar.'[3]

Families say these things to justify why someone deserved support and was failed by the state. People say this because they want their loved one to be grieved and grievable. And to be grievable their life has to be seen as having value. And, as we explored in the previous chapter, by far the dominant way we have of seeing lives as valuable is their proximity to paid work. As one disabled activist told me, 'we've been conditioned to think that some people are "undeserving of support" and that what's happening to them is their fault – people have been blamed and demonised, even in death, in ways that position them as responsible'.

Joy Dove, Jodey Whiting's (who died by suicide in 2017) mother knows this well. She told me: 'Would you believe? When Jodey died, there was a lot of discrimination because she had nine children. When the story come out, you wouldn't believe how much the trolls were saying things – "Where's all the fathers?"' 'Where's all the fathers' taps into another script we all know well – of women supposedly choosing to have children in order to live some kind of imagined life of luxury on welfare. And when these scripts are used against our loved ones, we want to redeem them. Like Joy does for Jodey – explaining that she had two sets of twins and there weren't loads of different dads. But also, so what if there were loads of dads and loads of kids – Jodey would still have deserved to live.

Jodey would likely have known the stigmatisation of welfare well, as she lived on the Tilery estate in Teesside (in the North-East of England), where *Benefits Street* would later be filmed – just one of many UK TV programmes portraying, in often dehumanising ways, the lives of people who claim benefits. Alongside systemic dehumanisation of people who claim benefits by the government, these TV programmes portray welfare as a lifestyle choice in need of strict eligibility and punishment. It's no wonder we reproduce this when desperately affirming our loved one's deservingness so that we can publicly grieve. Yet in appealing to the public and the government to grieve for our loved ones, to see them as victims, we are repeating the same ideas that have killed and continue to kill people. It's painful to recognise how trapped we are by these ideas – how hemmed in. This framing of some people as a cost to the state, as a burden, is one way that certain groups are devalued and made vulnerable to premature death. It shapes our grief – who can be mourned, whose lives we see as worth living, whose death is grievable, who we see as a victim and of what.

Talking about disabled people as 'victims' of welfare state violence is fraught. Disabled people have fiercely resisted the dominant story of disability as tragedy. 'Piss on Pity' is a famous slogan of disability activism, rooted in the Disabled People's Direct Action Network (DAN) – a grassroots network of disabled people who use non-violent civil disobedience as a means to fight for equality and disability rights. Yet even this problematic framing of 'tragedy' is conditional and differentially distributed. We need to hold the truth that while many disabled people rightly resist having their lives understood as a tragedy, some disabled people are never seen as victims, never pitied. And what about those of us disabled by systems – disabled on purpose by settler colonial militaries, incarcerated in prisons and immigration detention centres designed to be maddening, losing all sense of our inherent worth in a welfare/health/mental health/social care/education/criminal punishment system that tells us we're nothing. There's another trap here too – that in trying to show how the welfare system, as part of the wider state, disables and kills people, I inadvertently, unintentionally use disability to exemplify injustice, as something to be prevented (see the work of Sami Schalk and Eli Clare as they warn against this).[4] This means taking seriously that the welfare system, as part of the capitalist state, is built on both disablement (i.e., impairing people, driving people mad) and on the exclusion and deaths of already disabled people.

Since 2017, I've been writing about how framing people as 'burdens' creates conditions that make people feel, and contribute to people feeling, suicidal. I felt driven to write it because I was, and still am, incensed by the way some dominant psychological theories of suicide talk about how suicide is linked to people perceiving themselves as a burden.[5] This is often framed as though people's perceptions are individual and irrational, when often people perceive themselves this way because they are told they are a burden – day in, day out, by the system that's supposed to support them, and in the headlines that hate them. This is just one example of how the state weaponises mental health to deny accountability in killing people – to make it seem like some people's deaths are inevitable.

Disabled people's anti-austerity activism grapples with using tactics to try and shock the public into seeing how the welfare system is killing people against a backstory of ableism that assigns value to particular types of (hyper-productive) embodiments, while writing disabled people's lives as not worth living and disabled people's deaths as inevitable (though it's not only disabled people who are harmed by ableism). Anthropologist João Costa Vargas and political scientist Joy A. James write about similar tactics in relation to the killings of Black people in the USA. They ask: 'What happens when instead of becoming enraged and shocked every time a Black person is killed in the United States, we recognize Black death as a predictable and constitutive aspect of this democracy?'[6] Predictable not because of something inherent to Blackness, just as tragedy is not inherent to disability, but because the status quo depends on Black and disabled people's exclusion, neglect, premature death, disappearance and mass incarceration. Therefore, to become redeemable and grievable, Black people must become angelic, prove their innocence, in order to be seen as worthy to fight back. We saw this play out with Treyvon Martin, a Black teenager, who was killed by George Zimmerman, a neighbourhood watch volunteer, in Miami in 2012. Competing media narratives took pains to portray Trayvon as child-like and innocent (in his football kit), or as a troubled youth (tattooed, gold-toothed) – as if his death can only be grieved if he is innocent (of what?) Trayvon's supporters, just like many families bereaved by the welfare state, portray him as an 'innocent victim' and at the same time reproduce the anti-Blackness that is the soundtrack to his and so many Black people's deaths.

Infantilisation (making people seem child-like), respectability and innocence as strategies for redemption – we know this well, from Trayvon, to the conditional partial public mourning of Palestinian children but never Palestinian adult men, to the lack of public grief for people killed by welfare state violence – unless they can prove they were hardworking or were 'genuinely' ill. Certain people's deaths are foretold, and we're made to feel that public grief is scarce, conditional, one of many cuts under austerity. And of course, it's much easier to kill people who have already been framed as disposable. In fact, the state does so with almost complete impunity – making welfare state violence the perfect crime as it makes life for certain groups unliveable.

This reminds me of something El Kurd writes about Palestine and the ways that believability and grievability are reliant on playing or framing our loved one as a 'perfect victim'. He says, 'to practice a politics of appeal is to utilize all the tools made available by the institution … sometimes with moderate success. And always in line with the institution's logic.'[7] Using the tools of those who oppress us to try to dismantle oppression is fraught. This is what feminist, lesbian, warrior, poet Audre Lorde warns against when she says:

> the master's tools will never dismantle the master's house. They may allow us temporarily to beat him at his own game, but they will never enable us to bring about genuine change.[8]

What are the 'master's tools' here? Are they the official channels we have to appeal through freedom of information requests, complaints procedures, appeals, tribunals, statutory inquiries? Will those tools ever allow us to dismantle the Department for Work and Pensions? The idea of 'deservingness' is one of the 'master's tools' – we use it to appeal to the humanity of the government (do we really believe it has any?); to beg the public to recognise our loss and our loved one's pain; or when we need to appeal a benefits decision. We also talk to ourselves through these tools – they shape our inner voice, they are in our bodies, in the way we clench and relax, how our heart beats race, in our breath. And at the same time, as we speak about our loved one as 'deserving' of welfare, care, life, we create and solidify the idea that some people don't deserve these things and we abandon those who don't have the resources to escape being dehumanised or the family to redeem them from being labelled as a 'burden'.

Who would be a perfect victim of welfare state violence? Does one exist? When I think about the lists of people who have died that many disabled activists have created, I wonder about all the names we don't know. About those who make it into one newspaper story but then we never hear anything about them again, and those who never make it into any press – what about their families and friends? I often wonder – what about the people who weren't anyone's 'loved ones'? The people who will never be seen as 'perfect victims'. The people abandoned by or who abandoned their family, people from abusive homes, and people who were abusive, the people who pissed everyone off or were really unpleasant to be around. People no one cares about because they were no fun, because they were ill all the time, had no money, got tired, were in pain and cranky, bailed at the last minute, then rescheduled, then cancelled again, forgot birthdays, cried all the time, got too drunk, took too many drugs, were too complicated. People who never worked, hated working, did everything they could not to work. How do we grieve these people, and how do we honour them? Do they not deserve to live? Aren't we all messy and complicated?

Why do we know some names and not even recognise so many others? Perhaps because some people actually had families and friends, or had the resources, time and money for a lawyer, for belief they had a 'case', for feelings of shock and outrage rather than being resigned to a system whose brutality cleaves people's everydays. That dull violence – there in the aching joints of the morning, stitched into the duvet kept on all afternoon in lieu of central heating, in the drip of the switched off fridge, collecting like dust in the rim of an unbranded tin of beans, like concrete in the night's clenched jaws. And what about families who did love these people but didn't see them often, and then get judged if their loved one's body is found months later in a flat they never visited? And then there's the families who dare not make a legal case because they themselves claim benefits and live in fear of DWP surveillance. There are people I've spoken with as part of Deaths by Welfare, people who have profoundly shaped my thinking, and whose names I don't know and may never know – people whose cameras are always off while on Zoom, people who write in the chat so as not to reveal their voice – people living in fear of having their benefits removed after seeing what the system has done to their families and friends, people desperately trying to stay alive when the system wants them dead.

We've probably all encountered, maybe even been part of, and signed the petitions for, the campaigns that ask for some people to be recognised as deserving – for example, for some people, often those who are terminally ill, to not have to go through assessments for benefits. Of course, people who are terminally ill shouldn't have to spend what time and energy they have left fighting with the government over disability benefits assessments (the very fact this needs saying makes my heart ache). And neither should anyone else. How can we resist the trap to fight each other for scraps? How can welfare be for all – not just for those who can somehow prove they are 'really' ill, not only for those who are easily redeemed, or more appealing. We need to grow the available frames for grievability and victimhood – not apply eligibility and conditionality (foundational to the welfare system) to determine who will be publicly mourned or only conditionally grieved. We need to find a way to describe the messy complexity of people's realities – their agency and resistance – not, as prison abolitionist Mariame Kaba warns, flatten their lives to make them into perfect victims.[9] If our movements are fuelled by grief, then let it not only be for the 'perfect victims'.

'BURDENS' ON THE STATE AND WELFARE AS EXTRACTION

Histories of state violence are also histories of the ways different groups have, over time, been framed as costing the state too much, and therefore cast as deserving or undeserving. These ideas, past and present, are foundational to how the state differentially distributes life chances and premature death – whose lives we're told are worth living, and whose deaths grievable. This mirrors the way that welfare itself is often framed as an economic cost and burden that needs to be reduced, instead of, for example, being seen as a social investment or redistribution of wealth. In their book *Health Communism*, Beatrice Adler-Bolton and Artie Vierkant show how the categorisation and certification of people as worker, property or surplus is central to capitalism – where those deemed to be surplus are seen as a threat to the national population (often imagined as coded into their faulty genes) and/or a drain on society's resources.[10]

One way to understand the framing of people who claim welfare as economic 'burdens' is as a distraction and disavowal of the history of the welfare state itself as dependent on the violence and extraction of colonialism. Sociologist Gurminder Bhambra traces how after the Second World War, Britain had huge debt while also committing to building a welfare state. To navigate this, Britain depended on its Empire – by running down the debt it owed to India and Pakistan after independence, and subordinating the economies of its remaining colonies. This meant that British colonies were made to use funds that otherwise could have been used for their own development to give Britain cheap credit to develop the welfare state.[11] As an example, historian David Fieldhouse shows that between 1946 and 1951, colonised countries 'were lent or given some £40 million' through the Colonial Development and Welfare Acts and, at the same time, were required 'to lend or tie up in London about £250 million'.[12] In India, and beyond, Britain's colonial extraction created recurrent famines – the money extracted created a British welfare state, while those being extracted from were left to suffer and to die. This means that the welfare of the national population (and not all of it) depended on colonial extraction and violence.

When we hear 'welfare reform' many of us think of 2008 (austerity, cuts, assessments) onwards but welfare reform has been central to nation-building. The great Liberal reform programme of 1906–14, including the 1908 Old Age Pensions Act and the 1911 National Insurance Act, aimed at breeding an imperial race, through getting rid of people of 'poor stock' or 'unfit', i.e. eugenics.[13] Post-Second World War, an expanding welfare state provided increased provision of social services alongside increased regulation of receiving state support. The report of William Beveridge, which became the basis of the Labour Party's welfare programmes, advocated for the 'defeat' of 'want, disease, ignorance, squalor and idleness' in a context where welfare was part of Britain's 'reconstruction' following the Second World War.[14] The drive for the welfare state then, far from a benevolent concern for the population, was about increasing national efficiency, and as Debra Hayes, who has written extensively about the connections between welfare and immigration controls, puts it, through getting white men 'fit for work or war' in order to win back imperial power – building nationalism into the foundations of the welfare state.[15] It was also at exactly this time when there was significant immigration of Black people to the UK – people who were technically citizens not aliens, but who were constructed as migrant workers and denied full rights of access to the emerging welfare state and National Health Service (NHS), as well as being largely excluded from housing reforms by the post-war Labour government, leaving people in the hands of the private market. Legal scholar Nadine El-Enany shows how while colonised people were forced to fund the development of the welfare state, when they tried to come to the UK they were deemed to be 'aliens', written out of the welfare state, and constructed as a burden and a drain on public funds.[16]

Anti-Black welfare

In their 1985 book *Heart of the Race: Black Women's Lives in Britain*, Beverly Bryan, Stella Dadzie and Suzanne Scafe show how Black women's relationship with the welfare state was (and is) presented as 'parasitic' – described by the media as 'scroungers' and depicted as 'having a child-like dependence on a benevolent caring (white) society'.[17] *Heart of the Race* shows how the framing of people as a burden on the state is a cover-up of the way 'Black women's labour has propped up this country' for centuries of European colonialism and capitalism, and how Black women have been 'the producers of its wealth'.[18] The framing of being a burden on the state continued throughout the 1960–1970s, where a moral panic was crafted about the cost of the immigration of Black British citizens from the Commonwealth to the nation, crime and disease, and was used to justify a whole host of anti-Black legislation (1962 and 1968 Commonwealth Immigrants Act, 1971 Immigration Act and the 1981 British Nationality Act). In the UK, the government introduced the Child Benefit Act of 1975, payable only to mothers whose children lived in Britain. Brixton Black Women's group, and others, campaigned against this as racist legislation that targeted and tore apart Black families.[19]

Something similar was at play at the same time across the Atlantic, in the construction of 'welfare mothers' and 'welfare queens', who, we are told, have children to increase the size of their welfare payments, while using their benefits to live extravagantly. According to writer, lawyer and abolitionist Andrea J. Ritchie, the 'welfare queen' was used as a device to frame all Black mothers as 'a deviant and fraudulent burden on the state who must be punished through heightened surveillance, sterilization, regulation, and punishment'.[20] In the USA, the 'welfare queen' emerged when civil rights victories meant access to welfare was expanding to other groups beyond the white people they had been designed for, and when welfare mothers organised together through the grassroots National Welfare Rights Organization to fight for huge changes to the welfare system. In the 1980s, Ronald Reagan used the 'welfare queen' to symbolise so-called welfare dependency, and to justify his neoliberal agenda to reduce federal spending – cutting funding for means-tested programmes and food stamps. In the early 1990s, as UK politicians were making speeches about benefits cheats, and representatives from the insurance industry were co-writing articles on illness malingering with people high up in the DWP, the Clinton administration was reigniting the 'welfare queen' as a way 'to end welfare as we know it' by introducing punitive welfare reforms.[21] This ended the New Deal promise of welfare for children living in poverty (although let's be real, welfare before Clinton was not ideal and was never intended to end poverty. But things can be crappy and still get a lot worse).

While the figure of the 'welfare queen' shows how the idea of welfare dependency has been racialised, Black people have in fact been excluded from welfare in the USA for most of its history. Sociologist Dorothy Roberts, who has written extensively about the USA's racist child welfare system, traces how 'mothers' pensions', which lay the foundations for modern welfare's approach to single motherhood, enabled 'deserving' (often white) mothers to do unwaged labour at home, while providing the availability of less 'deserving' women to do low wage work.[22] As elite white people shaped the US welfare movement, Black women (who were also excluded from the white feminist welfare activist network) and low-income immigrants were framed as in need of control and surveillance. The New Deal assigned mother's aid into a different programme of aid – Aid to Dependent Children (ADC) separate from the social insurance (social security) administered to white men in paid work and their wives. ADC would be designed to humiliate – full of surveillance, eligibility criteria and work requirements. This would then morph into Aid to Dependent Families and Children (AFDC), which would become associated with Black mothers – the so-called 'welfare queens'. This is what Clinton wanted to end – by using welfare as a tool of social control to change people's behaviour – casting children even deeper into poverty if their mothers would not or could not conform.

The idea of the 'welfare queen' was crafted in 1970s–1980s USA, cutting and pasting old but ever-present white supremacist ideas of Black women used by the powerful to justify slavery. Disabled and chronically ill storyteller, healer and revolutionary, Aurora Levins

Morales talks about how people who kidnapped and enslaved people during the Atlantic slave trade justified it to themselves and others – how, through projection, they talked about enslaved people as lazy, as needing to be enslaved and punished to make them useful.[23] She asks us to consider how the idea that Black teenage mothers on welfare who are reliant on a tiny fraction of the welfare budget are somehow bankrupting the economy functions in a similar way. This is part of what scholar Jina B. Kim calls 'a persistent history of state-sanctioned assaults on racialized maternity, which range from the breaking of kinship ties along the Black Atlantic to the punitive surveillance of state foster care practices' (something Dorothy Roberts also writes about).[24] For abolitionists Mariama Kaba and Andrea J. Ritchie, this means that 'strictly policing "undeserving" Black women has ramifications for all people accessing a social good that has become gendered and raced as Black'.[25] This makes me think about what threads tie together the groups who are framed as burdens on the economy, and what these ideas are in service of, as public wealth is redistributed upwards – making the wealthy even wealthier.

Throughout history, as Robbie Shilliam traces in *Race and the Undeserving Poor*, there has been a racialised distinction between those deemed deserving and undeserving of social security and welfare – spanning from the abolition of slavery and the introduction of the Poor Laws, through eugenics and national insurance, welfare and colonial development, into so-called universal welfare and workfare.[26] As early as 1596, in a context of repeated failed harvests, leading to a sharp rise in poverty, Queen Elizabeth I issued an order to deport Africans and those descended from Africans from England on the grounds that they were consuming 'the Relief' that rightfully belonged to her subjects.[27] This echoes today, where hostile immigration policies have been used to target long-term, legal Commonwealth Black citizens (the Windrush generation) – making it impossible for them to prove their status, and resulting in denial of services, including healthcare and welfare, and in some cases deportation. This means that the welfare system's exclusion of, and violence towards, Black people, has shaped how migrants and disabled people (who, of course, may also be Black) have been treated, and how Black people's resistance to welfare state violence contains lessons for everyone.

Anti-migrant welfare

As with the demonisation of Black women on welfare, there is an oft-repeated story of migrants, including refugees and asylum seekers, as a 'burden on the taxpayer', as fraudulently trying to claim welfare, and thus as undeserving, as documented by Hannah Jones and colleagues in the book *Go Home: The Politics of Immigration Controversies.*[28] An early example of this is the Aliens Act 1905, often seen as the first UK legislation to formally introduce immigration controls, and initially directed against Jewish refugees fleeing anti-Semitism, but largely only applied to poor people. Those rejected fell into four main categories of undesirability: the diseased, the insane, the criminal and those thought likely to be a burden on the public purse, that is, showing that those who are likely to claim poor relief are deemed too economically costly to be allowed to stay in the UK. The Aliens Act of 1905 created deep connections between immigration status and welfare entitlement, showing the centrality of the nation state to our current welfare system. It also laid the foundations for the current denial of entry to anyone who may have 'recourse to public funds'.

In the same year as *Heart of the Race* was published (1985), the Child Poverty Action Group (CPAG) and Runnymede Trust published a small book called *Passport to Benefits*, documenting the by then widespread, yet still largely officially denied, practice of checking passports to determine eligibility for benefits, targeted at Black and Asian people.[29] The closure of factories and mines, and the heavy suppression of constant resistance and strikes, synonymous with Prime Minister Margarat Thatcher, hit hard – leading to massive rises in unemployment. More people, including many more people of colour, now found themselves having to navigate the welfare state. It is in this context that it started to emerge that some local Benefits Offices (part of the then Department for Health and Social Security (DHSS)) had started asking to see people's passports as a condition of receiving benefits. This would later come to be enacted, and, despite huge resistance, largely normalised within the NHS.

In the run-up to this, in 1982, the Indian Workers Association in Bedford supported a number of cases of Indian workers being 'subjected to humiliating checks by local welfare officials', while the following year, Sheffield's Asian Welfare Association raised issues of 'racist motives behind demands made by social security officials to examine the passports of black claimants'.[30] (It's worth noting that in this period 'black' was often used by people who may now be more likely to identify as people of colour, as well as by Black people.) The Legal Action Group alleged that the DHSS 'guidelines encourage checks on all "blacks"'.[31] While Oldham Council for Racial Equality received complaints from the Unemployed Workers Centre in Oldham that Asian people were under greater suspicion when claiming sickness benefits, and their sick notes were more heavily scrutinised by the DHSS than those from white claimants.[32] Articles appeared in the local press about 'Black claimants getting a raw deal',[33] and Black families being forced to live at starvation levels.[34] The DHSS then commissioned a report on staff racism within the department but part of it wasn't published, and apparently includes quotes from staff 'who regard claimants as grasping, devious, and undeserving', and refer to them in overtly racist language.[35]

The *Caribbean Times* featured an interview with Don Christopher, a Black man working in the DHSS, who talked about being 'appointed to snoop on black people', and showed a leaflet used in DHSS training that described West Indians as promiscuous. Unsurprisingly, this racist and humiliating treatment meant that many Black people and people of colour did not access welfare despite being entitled. It was in this context that people came together to create the Committee for

Non-Racist Benefits, in 1986, whose members said that the practice of checking passports in relation to welfare targets Black people and has given 'the green light for DHSS staff to harass black claimants', as it legitimises 'the racist assumption that black people are a burden to the welfare state'.[36]

A few years later, in 1992, Peter Lilley (then secretary of state at the Department of Social Security, in John Major's Conservative government) connected the ideas of tightening up on benefits 'scroungers' and 'bogus asylum seekers'. This shows how the story of benefit fraud is used to justify cuts to disability benefits and punitive immigration policy, of which restricted or complete denial of access to welfare for migrants is a key part. The 1993 Asylum and Immigration Appeals Act and the 1996 Asylum and Immigration Act portrayed asylum seekers as 'socially costly' in order to justify their exclusion from welfare provision – restricting and removing access to social security benefits, social housing and child benefit for asylum seekers. This continued and intensified under New Labour from 1997, and the introduction of the Immigration and Asylum Act 1999, where there would be 'no recourse to public funds' for people 'subject to immigration control', effectively excluded people seeking asylum from welfare benefits.[37] The harms of no recourse to public funds, which was expanded in 2012 by Theresa May (then home secretary) to include those who moved here to live with their British families, are well documented, including preventing survivors of domestic violence from accessing emergency accommodation because they don't qualify for Housing Benefit – leaving people with the choice, as Southall Black Sisters put it, to 'leave and face destitution, or stay and risk their lives'.[38]

The Immigration and Asylum Act 1999 also replaced cash benefits with vouchers – justified as an anti-fraud measure and used globally to stigmatise people – to mark them out and control what they spend money on. Fast forward to the departing Conservative government, in 2024, when Rishi Sunak, under the guise of changing 'sick-note culture' (echoes of malingering ringing strongly here), proposed reforming Personal Independence Payments (PIP) (a cash benefit designed to help people with a disability, long-term illness or a mental health condition with extra living costs) by introducing vouchers to replace cash payments. Little wonder then that the Immigration and Asylum Act 1999 was framed by those campaigning against it as 'the New Poor Law' – direct and collective action forming the sharpest form of opposition to immigration-linked welfare provision.[39] Chatting to Rick Burgess one day, he reflected on the Immigration and Asylum Act 1999:

> There was definitely something about that Act, about basically saying we can be incredibly horrible to a part of the population and we can justify that enough with our friends in the media that enough people will go along with it that we can do it. And when they saw they could do that to refugees and asylum seekers, they also thought, could we start cutting other groups off from the support that they got used to in this little post-war settlement?

Rick is saying that 'no recourse to public funds', a policy which explicitly weaponised welfare for asylum seekers, was a test case for punitive welfare reform later expanded to disabled people. This played out again in the hostile environment policies – announced in 2012 to describe a set of policies crafted to make life as difficult as possible for migrants, including refugees, in the UK. These policies turned many people (employers, landlords, healthcare workers, teachers) into border guards, and cut people off from services – saying they have no recourse to public funds – through the logic that migrants are not deserving of dignity and humanity. As I trawled through evidence of disabled people killed by the welfare system, I can remember coming upon the story of Mercy Baguma. She was from Uganda, and seeking asylum in the UK's hostile environment. She had lost her job after her limited leave to remain immigration status expired, had no recourse to public funds, and was living in extreme poverty with not enough food. In 2020, she was found dead next to her malnourished young baby – an 'unspeakable, avoidable tragedy' that is 'indicative of the inhumanity that is embedded in our immigration system'.[40] I have never been able to get Mercy's face out of my mind.

As with welfare reform, parallels are often drawn with the hostile environment and England's New Poor Law of 1834, and many disabled people, including journalist Frances Ryan, have pointed out that the UK is a hostile environment for disabled people too (including disabled migrants).[41] All these acts and policies (the 1905 Aliens Act, the weaponisation of welfare for Black people and for migrants) are part of a process that has been taking place for over a century – the systematic removal of access to welfare from people without British citizenship. And citizenship itself is tenuous – it can be removed, especially for racialised people. Migrants Rights Network has tracked the expansion of deprivation of citizenship powers since 2003 – powers that primarily target British Muslims and make more and more people deportable.[42]

Burdens unite! Solidarities of the 'undeserving' and transformative coalitions

While it is only recently that politicians name these policies as the 'hostile environment', the policies have been hostile for a long time. Yet the interconnectedness of welfare control and immigration control has been a rich site of resistance – going back at least to those opposing the Aliens Act, including the establishment, in 1902, of the Aliens Defense League, based in Brick Lane. Given this long history, it's little wonder then that anti-deportation campaigner and barrister Steve Cohen wrote about the long lineage of Black people's 'militant, collective and grassroots' resistance to the state-imposed tying together of immigration and welfare.[43] Tracing the connections and continuities in the way welfare is weaponised against disabled people, Black people and migrants, including refugees and asylum seekers, has helped me see patterns. Patterns in how both welfare itself and those who are entitled to it are framed as too costly, as an economic 'burden'. At different times, in different places, this narrative has been used to cut support, and deny entry, citizenship and access. This is also about recognising the centrality of ableism and racism to anti-welfare. Doing this, for Jina B. Kim (who we met earlier) holds 'radical potential for "progressive transformative coalition work" among the groups most antagonized by antiwelfare policy: racialized, low-income, and disabled populations'.[44] We need this kind of coalition building because, as Beatrice Adler-Bolton and Artie Vierkant remind us – 'it is immeasurably threatening to capital to see a group of those it has deemed to be waste come together in solidarity'. Burdens unite! And we don't have to only imagine it – we can trace these coalitions historically and in real time.

Parveen, Manjeet and Osime: the radical solidarities of anti-deportation campaigns

I first came across Parveen Khan in the archives. Parveen came to the UK in 1980, not realising her husband had entered the country 'illegally' – he was 13 when he arrived. Parveen applied to the Home Office for a pardon and they deemed her to be 'illegal' too. Her husband was forced to go into hiding, leaving her with two children. The then Department for Health and Social Security (DHSS) also refused her supplementary benefit and child benefit, which in the early 1980s was for anyone living in Britain for six months or more. Parveen was not alone. In 1982, the Workers Against Racism group picketed outside Oldham's social security offices over their refusal of supplementary benefits to 680 Asian and Black workers.[45] This didn't end without a fight. A tiny snippet from a 1982 copy of Spare Rib, a feminist publication from the UK, describes how

> 30 women and children occupied the DHSS office in Longsight Manchester in support of Parveen Khan and Manjit Kaur [another woman who was refused benefits] ... Despite the arrival of the police,

> who threatened to remove us forcibly if we did not leave, we remained in the building until a manager agreed to a meeting.[46]

Most of the women involved were also single mothers who experienced daily 'humiliation and despair', saying 'we are not going to stand by and watch the continued harassment of Black women by the DHSS'.[47] The piece then advertises a national day of action on 31 January 1983 with picketing outside DHSS offices – protesting the link between welfare entitlement and immigration status – with pickets in Manchester, Leeds and Birmingham. Without this, as part of a wider campaign for Parveen, the authors of *Passport to Benefits* think 'it is likely that the Khans would have been starved out of the country'.[48] The campaign showed the role that welfare (the then DHSS) played in the enforcement of immigration control – illustrating 'how far the DHSS is prepared to go in using the immigration laws to deny benefit and thereby to act, itself, as an arm of immigration control'.[49] For some Black people, the DHSS was an arm of the Home Office, meaning people avoided claiming benefits for fear of their immigration status being questioned. This is because information is passed between the Home Office and the welfare system, who, according to the Joint Council for the Welfare of Immigrants (JCWI) at the time (1982), 'cooperate to starve people out of the country'.[50] They also noted that 'given the treatment which Asian women appear to receive in DHSS offices, it is not surprising if many do not even claim in order to avoid subjecting themselves to what they know will be a degrading experience' (leading to the Sandwell Welfare Rights Take Up Campaign with respect to Asian Minorities, at Sandwell Citizens Advice Bureau).[51]

In 2011, there was another anti-deportation campaign in support of a South Asian woman in Manchester – Manjeet Kaur. Manjeet, who died in 2020, was a disabled activist and chair of RAPAR (Refugee and Asylum Participatory Action Research, a human rights organisation in Manchester). She connected, through her own experience and in her movement organising, activism led by disabled people, and activism led by migrants, including refugees and asylum seekers. In a tribute to her life, Dennis Queen (another Manchester-based disabled organiser) remembers in 2011 when Manjeet's right to remain was refused and her landlord was going to evict her onto the streets, from housing that was practically inaccessible to her as a wheelchair user, but still, it was a roof over her head (barely). Women Asylum Seekers Together (WAST, a grassroots network campaigning to improve the rights of women seeking asylum in the UK) contacted Manchester Disabled People Against Cuts, and together they gathered as many people as they could within their grassroots networks, so that on eviction day 'a collaboration of disabled and nondisabled activists gathered together at the property ... and we barricaded ourselves in with Manjeet, daring the landlord to get the police to drag us out'.[52]

Two years before Manjeet died, Osime Brown, a young Black autistic man, was convicted of (despite denying) stealing a mobile phone, given a five-year prison sentence, and threatened with deportation to Jamaica where he hadn't lived since he was five years old. Osime and his family describe being 'terrorised by the state for years'.[53] Osime was convicted under joint enterprise laws – where guilt may be deemed by an individual's presence within a criminal group. There is huge resistance to joint enterprise, evident in the work of Manchester-based organisation Kids of Colour, as a 'racist doctrine', which disproportionately punishes Black communities – with many calling for it to be abolished.[54] Mothers of people incarcerated through these laws have come together collectively to lead the resistance, including the group Mothers Against Joint Enterprise (JENGbA), set up just down the road from me in Manchester. Osime's mother, Joan Martin, said his deportation would be a 'death sentence'. She led Osime's anti-deportation campaign – building alliances with disabled and autistic people's groups, Black Lives Matter and migrants rights' activists. And they won – Osime was not deported. But many others have been.

Grassroots campaigns against deportations, and especially those co-led by or organised with Black and disabled people, are an important site of resistance, especially as they deny the state should determine controls, and emphasise abolition of all controls. Steve Cohen was involved in many of these campaigns from the 1980s onwards, combining legal battles with community campaigns, and establishing and running the Greater Manchester Immigration Aid Unit for many years. Steve was an abolitionist when it came to immigration – there could never be 'fair' immigration reforms – and his booklet *No One Is Illegal* informed the manifesto of the No One is Illegal Group and the No Borders Network. For Steve, anti-deportation campaigns, often rooted in Black communities, didn't rely on courts or Parliament to succeed, and 'during the Thatcher years they probably represented the most consistent form of extra-parliamentary opposition to government generally and the Home Office in particular'.[55] For Steve, 'the demand for no [immigration] controls means rolling back the entire welfare system to its inception and reformulating it ... It means fighting to break the link between welfare and nationalism.'[56]

Similarly, a disabled activist I spoke with as part of the Deaths by Welfare project talked about how

> welfare operates under a nation state. The nation is racialised, ableist, transphobic, and homophobic – it generates ideas of the deserving recipient of welfare ... reimagining welfare is about recognising that we have to think of welfare differently than the way the nation state does, and that's really dependent on developing communities on a local and national scale that are in relationship to each other.

This is also an invitation to imagine welfare beyond nation states, welfare without borders. And we don't only have to imagine – anti-deportation campaigns are one example of these coalitions in practice. Anti-deportation campaigns are often reactive and oppositional (they are against something, they are a critique) but these campaigns are important to welfare activism for many reasons. They are nearly always led by people who are most impacted, and as we've seen have deep roots in Black communities, often impacting and led by disabled Black people and people of colour. They tend to ask not for pity or compassion but instead, according to Steve Cohen, demand solidarity with those under threat, arguing that 'emphasising the "compassionate" circumstances of a case simply reinforces the assumption that the right to stay here depends on proof of "exceptional" circumstances'.[57] Disabled activists call this pissing on pity. This is important given how much we're pulled into telling the story of a 'perfect victim' – how our loved one is different, how they are deserving, how they're not a burden – all the time repeating the logic of deservingness that made them disposable, kill-able, in the first place. Anti-deportation campaigns also don't tend to appeal the deportation of one person yet condone deportation overall. Deportation, and often immigration controls as a whole, are understood as inherently racist and ableist – there's no reforming them to make them somehow less so. This isn't nostalgic reformism – to tweak the system, to tinker at its edges – this is abolition. For example, there was a lot of campaigning about the Windrush generation being wrongly targeted by hostile immigration policy, implying that the Windrush generation are deserving but others are not. A different approach is to campaign against the entirety of the violent immigration system.

Anti-deportation campaigns cultivate cross-movement solidarity in the spaces of nationalism, borders and the welfare state. Disabled asylum seekers are one group doing this work – resisting the immigration system as a form of disablement (e.g., the Disability Murals project, and the Disability and Migration Network).[58] Rebecca Yeo, a scholar and activist who works closely with DPAC, shows how the social model of disability can be applied to understand the disabling impact of immigration policy, acting as a way to build solidarity and collective resistance between disabled people's movements and people subject to immigration controls.[59]

The histories we've traced so far show us that disproportionately distributed harm and premature death, targeting racialised, low-income and disabled populations, seems to be a feature of the (welfare) state, not a bug. Yet I have rarely come across lineages of Black women's or migrant's resistance to welfare state violence, and what we can learn from it in our current organising, being publicly acknowledged in welfare activism and movement work, or in welfare research and scholarship. Partly, this is because of the whiteness of some disability rights organising and racism in disabled people's movements, and also because some women of colour don't identify as disabled, even when they experience disablement. There's lots of complex reasons for this, and one, as Mia Mingus points out, is that 'it can be very dangerous to identify as disabled when your survival depends on you denying it'.[60]

Yet as we learned from Rick Burgess earlier, policies which explicitly weaponise welfare for asylum seekers were a test case for punitive welfare reform later expanded to disabled people. These histories are deliberately excluded because they lend themselves to solidarity infrastructures that are a fundamental threat to the current system. We need solidarity not simply because the impact of welfare state violence is similar across different groups but because anti-welfare ideas and practices are anti-Black and ableist (and anti-Blackness is also ableist). Jina B. Kim, in an article called 'Cripping the welfare queen', writes about how 'the phantom of the welfare queen, alongside other bogeymen of reform (e.g., the undocumented immigrant), provides the narrative support for an ideology and praxis of resource austerity, in which the looming threat of parasitic others enables divestment in public services'.[61] This gets at the connections between ableism, scarcity, state violence and the dismantling of public infrastructure. This means that only by 'recognizing the links between the marginalization of welfare queens and their disabled kin can we develop critical analytics that can [confront] the linked yet varied sites of power in this country'.[62] And one way to do this is to actively seek out longer lineages of resistance to welfare state violence – the kind that help us sense that this violence is by design, not by mistake.

4

Policing Welfare

WELFARE AND THE POLICE

'The Department for Work and Pensions is a shadow penal system, punishing people for the crime of living in poverty … If you live under the DWP, you live in a parallel system, there's not the Britain that other people live in. It's a police state'. This is what Rick Burgess from Manchester Disabled People Against Cuts (DPAC) told me one day. Michael O'Sullivan, who died by suicide after a long battle over his 'fitness to work', knew this well. His daughter, Anne-Marie, told Disability News Service that assessments 'left him "humiliated, mortified, and feeling like a criminal"'.[1] The criminalisation of poverty sits alongside decades of simultaneous cuts to social welfare while increasing spending on surveillance, policing and prisons (in the UK, the USA and beyond). Sociologist Loïc Wacquant calls this the 'double regulation of the poor' – neoliberalism's dual strategy of replacing social welfare with punitive control, combining restrictive 'workfare' with expansive 'prisonfare' – as a way of surveilling and punishing economic insecurity.[2] Following the trend of mass incarceration set by the USA, the UK's (and especially England and Wales) prison population has almost doubled in the last 30 years – attributed by social work scholar Ian Cummins as a 'punitive turn' occurring alongside a decimation of the welfare state.[3]

In 2017, disabled activists from the Disabled People's Direct Action Network (DAN) and DPAC criticised 'heavy-handed' police tactics at a direct action protest in Manchester that blocked tram lines outside the Conservative Party Conference. Terry Hutt, an 82-year-old DAN activist, showed Disability News Service the purple bruises he said he received on his arm from being grabbed by a police officer during the protest. He sat on his walking stick on one of the tram lines during the protest, and said: 'If they can push me around, they can push anybody around.'[4] In 2019, Greater Manchester Police admitted (after previously denying) that it has an agreement 'to share information about disabled people and other activists who take part in protests with the DWP'.[5] Greater Manchester Coalition of Disabled People (GMCDP) said they were 'extremely concerned' about the police 'spying on disabled protesters and passing on their details onto the DWP'. Brian Hilton, from Greater Manchester Coalition of Disabled People, asked 'Are we now saying if you can protest you should not be in receipt of benefits? What's next? Are the police going to run undercover operations at festivals to see if disabled people are brazen enough to sway in time to the music or, god forbid, dance?' For Brian, this is 'yet another example of the punitive and unwarranted targeting of disabled people'.[6] Disabled activist and DPAC member Andy Greene explained to researcher and campaigner Debbie Humphry that

> Greater Manchester police have a written agreement with the Department for Work and Pensions to report disabled people if they are protesting, on the basis that if they are fit enough to protest, they must be fit enough to get around and to work, and shouldn't be getting disability benefits ... So for me the state is always violent in different forms.[7]

Ellen Clifford, also part of DPAC, told Debbie that 'it's part of police protocol. Just for participating, because the implication is that ... if you're able enough to get to the protest then you're committing benefit fraud'.[8] While data-sharing agreements between the DWP and the police have been clouded in secrecy, data sharing between the Home Office and the DWP are available for all to see. Under the auspices of 'preventing fraud and illegal immigration', the Home Office 'conducts large-scale data matching with DWP' in order to 'identify individuals living in the UK illegally and to "make it harder for people to live and remain in the UK illegally"'.[9] Information from the Home Office is then used by the DWP to criminalise people for so-called benefit fraud. We saw in Chapter 3, the longer history of the then DHSS, the police and the Home Office sharing information, in order, according to the Joint Council for the Welfare of Immigrants, to 'starve people out of the country'.[10] Talking to Rick Burgess one day about who might be missing from activism and movement work, he explained that 'some people can't risk being reported to the DWP', which casts a 'huge shadow' stopping people from being part of movements. Rick mentioned that one group of people who are especially 'oppressed and suppressed are disabled asylum seekers' – often forcibly dispersed around the country with no money, and subject to conditions which mean they 'can't risk any trouble with the authorities'.

But the welfare system doesn't only work *with* the police, it actively *polices* people, and it always has done. Tracing the linkages between the police and the DWP is important because it shows us that the DWP is deeply connected to the police and implicated in policing. The DWP is not just 'like' the police, nor does it only work with the police, but it polices people. This goes deeper than policing; this is a carceral way of thinking about and organising welfare – through suspicion, surveillance, criminalisation and punishment. Long before we had a DWP, welfare was about policing eligibility for 'relief' from poverty through ideas of deservingness. Welfare policing also manifests in the 'detective work' that frontline workers told researcher Jamie Redman and colleagues is done to 'smoke out' those unwilling to work and/or suspected of committing benefit fraud. Staff at Jobcentres and delivering work programmes talk about being under pressure to use tactics such as evaluating people's appearance and checking their social media accounts.[11] While staff themselves have their daily work digitally monitored and audited for compliance with reducing claimant numbers.[12]

The logic of 'benefit fraud' and 'welfare fraud' (going way back before those words had even been put together) means that welfare has long ties to the criminalisation of poverty and to the policing of work under capitalism. Prison abolitionists Mariame Kaba and Andrea J. Ritchie see the push to get people off welfare into paid work as part of a wider police project – 'humiliating, degrading, and denying social welfare recipients is one way that social policy acts as social policing'.[13] And this policing can lead people towards more explicit police violence. This is evident in the findings of a large independent study of benefit sanctions in the UK, where the destitution caused by sanctions lead many into survival crime.[14] This is welfare under what scholar Jackie Wang calls carceral capitalism – a parasitic form of governance that extracts and incarcerates,[15] while framing those it extracts from as parasitic. This carcerality lives inside us, it polices our imaginations – just think how difficult it is to imagine welfare without some form of conditionality, some form of policing of eligibility.

In 2011, in a context of uprisings following the police murder of Mark Duggan, then Prime Minister David Cameron talked about the need for a more punitive criminal 'justice' system because of an overly lenient welfare system.[16] Cameron frames poverty as the result of individual bad behaviour and poor choices, and welfare as inciting laziness, excusing bad behaviour and eroding self-discipline. The centrality of punishment to welfare is part of the carceral state, which exercises power not only through criminal punishment but also through surveillance and policing deeply embedded in the welfare system, social care, social work, the mental health system, education and more. Here many of us are managed and controlled through the fear and punishment designed into our welfare system – from the forbidding architecture of the workhouse, to how the fear of destitution and stigmatisation become weapons to deter and punish people who claim benefits.[17]

In 'A heavy nonpresence', a piece of research by Derica Shields, where they interview Black Londoners navigating the welfare system and reckoning with the 'gaslighting, surveillance, and dehumanization that accompany the "care" of the state', we see 'how welfare services extend the carceral and disciplinary mechanisms of the state into the homes and lives of Black people'.[18] Sociologist and legal scholar Dorothy Roberts shows that the USA's 'child welfare system's surveillance, control and destruction of Black families is part of the same carceral regime as prisons and police',[19] and of the settler colonial logic that disproportionately polices and tears apart Indigenous and First Nations' families (and has done for centuries). Just as many people refer to the 'criminal justice system' as the more aptly named 'criminal punishment system', Dorothy Roberts refers to the child welfare system as the 'family policing system'.

Talila A. Lewis, a Black queer disabled abolitionist and community lawyer in the USA, reminds us that disabled people too 'have always been a target of the carceral machine'.[20] In the UK and the USA, disabled people are disproportionately brutalised and killed by police and over-represented in the prison system, as reported by journalist Mary O'Hara.[21] This, as someone I spoke to who wants to remain anonymous explained, means the 'police, policing, prisons, the whole prison-industrial complex is a disabling event itself'. Many disabled people, including those who have had any contact with the mental health system, know the control, surveillance and punishment hidden under the guise of 'care' – what Liat Ben-Moshe calls 'carceral sanism'.[22] These historical continuities matter. For example, historian Gareth Millward shows how medical evidence such as the 'sick note', as well as disability assessments (such as the Work Capability Assessment) perform the role of 'sickness policing'.[23]

The police have always been about policing poverty and work under capitalism. The history of the development of policing in England, especially in the eighteenth and nineteenth centuries (as the Poor Laws are being consolidated) is the history of capitalism and industrialisation. Police power, according to political economist

Mark Neocleous, has never simply been about responding to crime, instead it produces capitalist social order by regulating labour.[24] In the late 1700s, small specialised forces, such as the Thames River Police and the Bow Street Runners, were created to protect property, profits and plantation owners, and to manage workforces. The ruling class back then told the same story, almost word for word, as the one told now – that poor people are lazy and should be forced into work. In 1839, a few years after the New Poor Laws and the introduction of the workhouse, a Royal Commission on Constabulary Forces recommended that a national police force be created, to project industrial capitalism. Edwin Chadwick – a central figure in Poor Law reform, was one of the committee members.

WELFARE SURVEILLANCE

> Because I realise now: I've become institutionalised. I live inside an invisible cage built by the DWP (and Social Scare, of course. Let's not forget them. Bastards). By institutionalised, I mean, for eg – I anticipate and strategise against DWP sanctions automatically whenever I think, open my mouth, and especially if I leave the house. Any time I think about doing anything out of the house that might improve my life, (eg an art class, or an event that a photographer is at) I freak out over whether it will trigger sanctions. The DWP is absolutely a panopticon. I'm living in a fucking panopticon. Except it's invisible. And specifically designed to marginalise already vulnerable people … Most people don't even know it exists. And often don't believe you when you tell them. And it fucks you up so sometimes, you forget that you're living in a panopticon and just blame/hate yourself.[25]

This is Nila Gupta, who co-founded the Onyx Collective, a group of seven artists who shared the lived experience of disability and racism. Jeremy Bentham, a philosopher and social reformer in the

1700–1800s, whose preserved skeleton, dressed in his own clothes, and topped with a wax head sits in a cabinet in a hallway of University College London (yes, really) is famous for designing the panopticon – a circular prison with a central tower that in theory allows one person to see into all prison cells at once, potentially observing all those incarcerated at the same time, and creating the conditions for people to police themselves (as we'll explore later). While Bentham is most famous for the design of the panopticon, he also, in the late 1700s, proposed privatising 'poor relief' by creating a National Charity company that would build industry houses for 'pauper management', from which he planned to profit.[26] This privatised system of poor relief was Bentham's utopia, his dreams of a microcosm of a new world.[27] While Bentham's design never became a reality (or at least not in the way he envisioned it), we saw earlier that through the New Poor Laws of 1834, workhouses were designed to create fear and to deter people from entering. Anyone with any experience of the current DWP is likely reading this and wondering if Bentham truly died and isn't still running the show from his cupboard.

In a newspaper article titled 'No wonder people on benefits live in fear. Supermarkets spy on them now', disabled activist and consultant clinical psychologist Jay Watts writes that as well as information from the police, the DWP uses CCTV surveillance and monitoring data provided by businesses, airports, public buildings, gym memberships and social media, to build cases against disabled claimants.[28] As I write this book, the Public Authorities (Fraud, Error and Recovery) Act 2025 (note yet another banal sounding title hiding something nasty) is currently moving through the House of Lords.[29] If realised, it would, according to Disability Rights UK, give the DWP 'unprecedented powers' to monitor the financial activity of people who receive benefits, forcing banks to carry out mass surveillance of millions of people's bank accounts looking for potential breaches of benefit eligibility rules, to pass onto the DWP.[30] As part of this, the DWP promised to hire 3400 people to create a 'benefits police force' to check people's bank accounts using artificial intelligence.[31]

Disabled people, civil liberties groups and independent MPs have been vocal critics. Independent MP Zarah Sultana says this algorithm-driven 'mass surveillance' treats disabled people, carers, jobseekers, pensioners and parents 'as suspects by default, simply because they receive state support'.[32] Yet, as sociologist and legal scholar Dorothy Roberts documents, there is a long history (in the USA where she writes from but also in the UK) of public welfare being structured around 'bureaucratic supervision' based on means and morals testing that assumes that welfare benefits are an 'undeserved subsidy', placing people under surveillance, and waiving people's right to privacy.[33] This is very different for the middle classes, whose publicly subsidised benefits come in the form of entitlements and tax breaks, which entail no loss of privacy, no surveillance, no degrading treatment.

Labour MP John McDonnell points out that the Fraud Bill targets people who are already in desperate need rather than the group of people who do actually have a history of fraud – MPs.[34] The 'climate of fear' that John McDonnell says is exacerbated by the Bill is summed up perfectly by Liz Kendall, one of its proponents (and previously secretary of state for work and pensions between 5 July 2024 and 5 September 2025), when she directs the Bill 'to every single individual knowingly cheating the system, our message today is clear: we will find you, we will stop you and we will get our money back'.[35]

We've heard this before. As John Pring points out – Liz Kendall's threat sounds very similar to something we heard from Tom Pursglove, previous minister for disabled people, as he stood in a stab-proof vest in front of a police van in a video the DWP released in late April 2023, saying 'We will track you down, we will find you, and we will bring you to justice.'[36] The video supposedly shows a raid carried out by the DWP with the Metropolitan Police cracking down on 'fraudsters who are cheating our benefits system'. Pursglove tries to reassure us that 'we of course want a safety net that protects the most vulnerable ... but we just cannot have people cheating the system'. When I first saw the video, I thought it was an eerily well-made spoof of the DWP. In fact, it is a spoof but made by the DWP of the film *Taken* starring Liam Neeson. What makes this even more surreal (yes, even more surreal than the minister for disabled people parodying a line from a Liam Neeson film) is that he could just as easily have said the original line from the film and it would also be true of the DWP: 'I will look for you, I will find you, and I will kill you.' Also parodying Liam, Tom Pursglove explains that the DWP has 'a very particular set of skills that we use in conjunction with the police to tackle fraud'.

As well as prying into the bank accounts of people on benefits, the Public Authorities (Fraud, Error and Recovery) Bill proposed to give some DWP staff the same powers of search, entry and seizure as the police, and powers to use 'reasonable force' against benefit claimants.[37] A number of MPs have criticised this – some claiming that only the police should be able to use force. Indeed, as we've seen, the police do use force against disabled people (and many others). But rather than feeling trapped into arguing that only the police should use force, it feels important to critique both DWP *and* police use of force.

Welfare state surveillance and policing also extend into the ways the DWP operates to get us to police each other and ourselves. This happens in both insidious ways and can also be very in your face – perhaps no more so than the DWP's campaigns about so-called 'benefit fraud'. From 2006 to 2014, the DWP ran a range of campaigns. One, 'No Ifs, No Buts' (2006–08) emphasised criminalising benefit fraud and surveillance. The campaign cost £9.3 million. One black and white poster with a photo of a street of houses that could be almost anywhere in the UK reads: 'Benefit thieves, our technology is tracking you.' Another says: 'Benefit thieves; do you know who's following you?'

In 2009 came the 'They thought they'd never be caught' campaign, including TV adverts and posters with a photo of two people holding cardboard cut-outs of their criminal convictions, overlaid by an image of a target. This campaign cost £2.4 million. Going down the rabbit hole of DWP 'advertising' (read: propaganda of mass dehumanisation), I was sucked into a 136-page report about the objectives of these campaigns: 'increase the perception of risk and fear of getting caught'; 'increase awareness of the consequences of getting caught'; and 'maintain public acceptance that benefit fraud is wrong'.[38] The report concludes that considerable investment was needed to 'build awareness and start to reframe attitudes' and that it's important to 'drip feed ... messages'. In a way, this is heartening because it means that in order to be convinced that 'benefit fraud' is 'wrong', the government has to pay companies to drip-feed constant negative messaging. Heartening because it implies without that 'drip-feeding' or with different messaging, we already understand that claiming welfare doesn't have to be negative, and could potentially see claiming welfare differently. Just imagine for a minute if that money – more than £16 million (between 2006 and 2014) on campaigns about benefit fraud – had been spent on actually supporting people.

The objectives and findings are important because they explicitly focus on cultivating fear, and do so through emphasising surveillance of people who claim benefits (surveillance by the government, by our neighbours and by ourselves). Many of these advertising campaigns feature the number for the National Benefit Fraud Hotline that we're all encouraged to phone if we want to report someone we think is claiming benefits who shouldn't be, and no I'm not putting the number here because nobody should be calling it! This is part, as racial justice researcher Tarek Younis pointed out to me, of a broader culture of 'crowd-sourced snitching' on each other – known well to anyone in the UK who gets any form of public transport and is inundated with 'See It, Say It, Sorted' (a British Transport Police campaign), or who remembers the Home Office-branded vans driving round in 2013 telling people: 'In the UK illegally? Go home or face arrest', with a picture of a person wearing a Home Office badge holding out a pair of handcuffs.

Critiques of these kinds of campaigns talk about the negative impact of this governmental crafting of fear. People, like me, do research into how these kinds of campaigns make people feel fearful.

We then try to get these findings onto the desks of policymakers – as a way to get them to change. But there's another way to read these findings – and that is as evidence of the campaign's success in achieving its objectives to create fear in the first place. If the fear is by design, then to the DWP, evidence of fear confirms money well spent.

SANCTIONS AS POLICING

Investigating people's deaths linked to and caused by the welfare system would be impossible without looking at the DWP's sanctions regime. Sanctions are a key part of the conditionality of the welfare system – the whole premise that if you don't do the things that you've been told to do (such as search for a certain number of jobs, attend interviews, etc.), then you can be sanctioned, which often means having some or all of your benefits stopped for a specific amount of time. This is destitution as punishment. Disabled activists and bereaved families have repeatedly shown the links between sanctions and people's deaths.

People like David Clapson and Faiza Ahmed. David died in July 2013, three weeks after being sanctioned. When he had his Jobseeker's Allowance taken away from him, David, who had diabetes, couldn't afford to pay for electricity to power the fridge where he kept his insulin. He died from an acute lack of insulin and despite his death having clear links with the sanction system, no inquest was ever held, although this decision was challenged by David's sister through judicial review.[39] A year later, in 2014, Faiza Ahmed died by suicide hours after telling a Jobcentre work coach that she was suicidal. She'd previously been sanctioned by the Jobcentre for turning up late and missing appointments. Her brother later spoke about how DWP's sanctions regime is based on threats and intimidation. He is certain that racism lay at the heart of the way his sister was treated by the DWP.[40]

David's and Faiza's deaths are two of too many, and when you hear stories like theirs, it's hard to understand how and why sanctions operate. Sanctions, like much of the welfare system, are intentionally complex and bureaucratic. I needed to talk to many people to help me navigate this complexity and understand how this system harms and kills people. Two of these people were Caroline Selman and Sara Lomri (then both based at the Public Law Project – a national charity in England and Wales, set up to ensure that those who have been marginalised through poverty, discrimination or disadvantage have access to justice and can hold the state to account) – who at the time I met them in 2022 were researching benefit sanctions and supporting those who experienced them. I immediately liked Caroline and Sara – their passion and slightly dark sense of humour. Sara's deep laugh, the way she slanted her laptop camera so she couldn't see herself on the Zoom Self View because she finds it distracting and says it makes her think she needs botox. I scribbled notes furiously despite knowing the audio recorder was rolling.

Caroline and Sara explained that sanctions have been around for a long time in the welfare system but during the introduction of the Welfare Reform Act in 2012,'we saw a real increase in the severity of sanctions' and a 'change in culture' leading to the following years seeing 'really very high levels of sanctions and people being sanctioned'. The impact of sanctions is 'potentially very severe ... losing up to 100% of your standard allowance. For some people, that's all of their income, and that has a huge impact on people'.

There is a lot of evidence that sanctions and conditionality are associated with significant mental distress. Two longitudinal studies (Welfare Conditionality, 2014–17 and Lived Experience, 2011–16) found sanctions consistently lead to 'acute suffering', feelings of worthlessness and suicidal thoughts.[41] Inclusion London found that the impact of sanctions and of being required to undertake 'work-related activity' leads some people to 'constant anxiety' and 'chronic fear', and has been described as 'life-threatening' for claimants with existing mental health issues.[42] Ben (not his real name) is one of these people. I first contacted Ben through Twitter, where, through his account

@BenClaimant, he provides signposting and support to so many people navigating the welfare system. Ben also campaigns with Unite Community and with DPAC, and has spoken in Parliament about the benefits system. When Ben tells his story, it's like he's trying to make sense of a system that doesn't make sense. If you really want to understand how a system can break someone, how it can threaten someone's life, then you need to talk to Ben. And so I did – and have done many times since. Chatting over Zoom, Ben told me about how being sanctioned just before Christmas left him with no money or food, and made him suicidal:

> Christmas comes along … I've got nothing. I've got absolutely nothing to eat. I've got water, that's it. And as soon as it gets dark, I'm trying to go to sleep. But, you know, you can't really sleep. Not in that situation. You try. It's … The nights become really, really long. And something just broke within me at that point.

Ben got an appointment with his work coach in the new year, who told him 'the sanction indicated to her that I didn't have a work ethic, and therefore, she wanted to put me on this workfare'. This meant working for four weeks, for a company, for free. And Ben remembers,

> at that point, I stopped listening to her. It was just too much, I couldn't cope. We did go through the rest of the meeting, but I just don't know what she said after that. And I just made a beeline, I went home and tried to take my own life.

Ben explains to me that 'you can't think properly when you've got a sanction. You know, even if you've got those support networks around you, it's just all consuming.' It's tempting to listen to Ben and imagine that maybe he just got unlucky and had a particularly nasty work coach. But then I spoke to researcher Jamie Redman about his research with those working in frontline roles at Jobcentres, and it became clear why we need a structural analysis of this brutal system.

Jamie talked about why the government has made sanctions a more prominent part of the welfare system, despite evidence that they are harmful. He talks about how over the past few decades, 'a sort of common sense thinking around poverty and unemployment' – that they are 'not a structural problem, a problem of society, but a problem of individual behaviour' has 'travelled across successive administrations and political leaderships'. This is the idea that we need 'to change claimants behaviour, to make sure that they conform to pro-work behavioural norms and values'. Jamie's research shows how sanctions are a weapon used against unemployed people, which inflict shame, punishment and abandonment, while policing the boundaries of the labour market, preserving accumulation in times when waged work pays low and is insecure.[43] Sanctions are yet another tool in making people out to be, and making people feel like they are, undeserving.

In his research, Jamie spoke with eleven frontline workers – including coaches in Jobcentre Plus, 'welfare-to-work' advisers on the work programme, and managers – all working when the Coalition government came into power (the same time as David Cameron was talking about 'toughening up the conditions for those who are out of work and receiving benefits'). These frontline staff told Jamie that they were subjected to pressures to achieve off-benefit flow targets – that is, to get people off welfare – case closed. This was done through a 'range of stringent managerial pressures, some of which are numerical, some of which are articulated through authority, through the chain of command, in performance reviews, to essentially find ways of either shifting claimants off the books … or finding ways to sanction people'.

Jamie also told me something else about sanctions, how frontline workers talked about targeting non-native speakers, and specifically Roma people, for sanctions. One work coach talked about working in an area where a lot of Roma families had recently moved and how they 'were subject to incredibly harsh, strict benefit regime based on their ethnicity'. The fact that many people didn't speak English was weaponised, with work coaches demanding people sign claim closure forms that they couldn't read. This systemic racism came from management, and is not confined to welfare benefits. As documented by the *Travellers Times*, Gypsy, Roma and Travellers have long resisted the disproportionate forcible state removal of their children by social services.[44] There is mounting evidence of the institutionalised racism and xenophobia of the sanctions regime. In 2017, using data published by the DWP, researchers found that across almost all ages and genders, claimants of Black and mixed ethnicity were the most likely to be referred for sanction.[45]

RESISTING SANCTIONS

Speaking to people like Ben who have tried to end their lives because of sanctions (not to mention all the people we can't talk to because they have died by suicide because of sanctions) and to people who have been under pressure to deliver sanctions makes it extremely difficult to believe politicians as they try to justify sanctions. Sanctions are such a visibly violent part of a wider system where conditionality, complexity and bureaucracy are used as weapons to punish and shame people. And yet, people fight this system in different ways and with different tools. Some say sanctions are needed but shouldn't be applied to vulnerable groups, others argue about whether sanctions are effective at deterring benefits claims and getting people into work. People resist through sharing their experience of sanctions and providing support to others, through litigation, through exposing how the system damages both benefits claimants and frontline workers, and through practising forms of support that prefigure what we might dream a welfare system could be, a system with no conditionality and punishment.

Resistance to sanctions can be tricky when we use evidence to show that some groups shouldn't be sanctioned – an argument that Disability Rights UK and others have made about people with 'limited capability for work', including disabled and chronically ill people.[46] This can, often despite intentions, very easily sound as though we think some people shouldn't be sanctioned but others are fair game. It reminds me of debates around some groups as being 'over-policed' – as if there is a right amount of policing, as if some people deserve to be policed more than others. Research by Del Roy Fletcher and Jamie Redman, with 480 out-of-work claimants in eleven locations in England and Scotland, found that unemployed people claiming welfare were largely supportive of welfare reforms that increase poverty and destitution and exacerbated ill health, because of the idea we've been told for centuries that it's 'necessary to punish/deter migrant, fraudulent and feckless populations from making claims on public resources'.[47] Here people reproduce deservingness to claim it for themselves in a context where they are made to feel worthless, or as one research participant put it: 'sanctions are good for some people but not for someone like me who actually genuinely does their job search'.[48] Later Jamie Redman told me that what struck him about this at the time was 'just how powerful these ideas weigh on the psyche. People would talk in detail about the problems they've personally faced through the benefits system yet remained staunchly in favour of it for "others"'.

Tensions also come up in campaigning, when we argue against sanctions by saying they're not effective at getting people back into work, which is the government's justification for using them. And it's true. Even the DWP's own research, for which there was a battle to have the findings made publicly available, found that sanctions were not successful in getting people into long-term work.[49] How we measure employment rates is also an issue – often employment is simply assumed if someone's case is closed but forcing them off welfare doesn't mean people have found jobs. Of course, saying sanctions don't 'work' is a tactic in using the government's own claims against them. But when I listen to people talking about their experience of sanctions, it makes me wonder if actually sanctions are effective – not at getting people into work, but at getting them off welfare, and as weapons of state violence, as tools of dehumanisation that contribute to making life for many unliveable. If sanctions are designed to instil fear, punish people, make people suffer and get people off welfare whatever the costs, then what does us evidencing them doing all these things achieve?

The DWP's report into sanctions, which it seems they'd hoped to keep secret, shows that welfare conditionality and sanctions have a wider role than only getting people into work – this is about incentivising compliance with conditionality and punishing those who don't comply.[50] Since capitalism was forced upon us, as we traced in Chapter 2, people have had to be coerced and violently pushed into working – it's just we've mostly forgotten this because we're constantly told that capitalism is natural and common sense. This means the histories of work and welfare are histories of each other, just as much as they are histories of capitalism and punishment. Welfare has always had elements of conditionality and punishment aimed at changing poor people's behaviour – as if their behaviour is responsible for structural inequality. Sanctions reproduce old scripts of the Poor Laws 'less eligibility', while their rising use and severity is inspired by behavioural economics (another banal name for something which makes me nauseous).

Behavioural economics, which uses the word 'nudge' for something I would call coercion, aims to motivate people to behave in certain ways. It is hugely popular – bestselling books, influential lobbying of the government, and all that jazz. Conservative anti-welfare people within the DWP started exploring its potential for use with people who claim welfare around 2008 (just as we saw massive attacks on welfare through welfare reform). As reported in the *Guardian*, the DWP claimed that those receiving welfare were 'more likely to look for work because of the threat of sanctions'.[51] But sanctions were being 'nudged' before this too. In 2005, Waddell and Aylward (the same Mansel Aylward we met in Chapter 2, DWP chief medical adviser and medical director who retired to be the director of a research centre funded by insurance company UnumProvident and a supporter of research into 'malingering') wrote a book explaining the number of people on Incapacity Benefit as being due to people assuming a 'right' to Incapacity Benefit (how dare they?) for which the solution is to use 'sanctions as a "motivational tool" to prise people out of their sick role'.[52] Sanctions are based on the theory of 'loss aversion' – that people prefer avoiding losses to receiving gains, meaning sanctions aim to 'nudge' compliance to welfare conditionality. But, as disabled political activist Kitty S. Jones points out, sanctioning welfare recipients by removing their lifeline benefit – originally calculated to meet the cost of only the basic survival needs of food, fuel and shelter – isn't *nudging* ... it's 'dystopic, psychopolitical behaviourism'.[53]

'SOFT POLICING'

'Have you ever been policed by an official who wasn't a cop?' asks Project NIA, a grassroots organisation that works in the USA to end the arrest, detention and incarceration of children and young adults by promoting restorative and transformative justice practices.[54] We've explored so far how welfare is not only connected to policing but also does its own policing – determining eligibility, doling out sanctions, refusing access to benefits, separating people from their kids. Some people call this 'soft policing' – not because it's gentler or more cushioned but to show how the police are not the only people with the power to police us. For example, prison abolitionists Mariame Kaba and Andrea J. Ritchie show how the 'policing of Black women, queer, and trans people through the administration of welfare benefits is just one of many ways that soft policing operates'.[55] Just as the police are not the only ones who surveil and punish us, prisons are not defined only by bars. In their book *Prison by Any Other Name*, writers and activists Maya Schenwar and Victoria Law painstakingly trace how many marginalised people are surveilled from birth – whether the eye that's upon is that of the police, child protective services, a parent's parole officer or state welfare agencies, and how punitive logic shapes even so-called 'alternatives' to prison.[56]

Many people who access welfare are also entwined with other systems of state violence and surveillance, for example, with the mental health system, child welfare, healthcare, social care, education, immigration, criminal justice, and counter-terrorism policies such as Prevent. Partnerships between business and government in administering mental health and social care, outsourcing disability assessments, running immigration centres (as just a few examples) are part of what prison abolitionists, including Angela Y. Davis, call the 'prison-industrial complex' – a system that profits from punishment, incarceration and carceral logics within and beyond prison walls, and which impoverishes communities by devouring the social wealth needed to address some of the root causes of poverty.[57] Prison-industrial complex abolitionists, like Mariame Kaba and Andrea J. Ritchie – the people who want to create worlds which meet all of our needs and make prisons and policing obsolete – talk about 'soft policing' as a way to teach us that if our organising focuses only on explicit police violence, 'it can keep us from identifying and addressing the subtle ways the logics of policing are embedded in social policy and hidden in the day-to-day functions of the state', that is, how 'the state's police power is also located in the social welfare and medical systems offered as "alternatives" to policing'.[58] This is important to abolitionists because without reckoning with policing as a whole, we run the risk of replacing more explicit state violence (the police) with violence that is less obvious, more insidious – violence cloaked in the language of welfare and care.

Many disabled people experience welfare as a disability policing system. Remember Tumu Johnson (from feminist disabled women's collective Sisters of Frida) telling us that 'control of disabled people is present in all areas of the welfare state' – in the conditions people have to meet, the appointments they can't miss, the care schedules that dictate when people sleep and wake, and the fear about being reported if seen out having fun. While a future without police might mean ending ties between welfare and the police (and yes, we should absolutely do this as a start), a future without policing would require radically transforming our welfare system – imagining welfare without conditionality and punishment, and stopping the policing of our imaginations.

THE WELFARE STATE IN OUR HEAD – POLICING OURSELVES, POLICING OUR IMAGINATIONS, POLICING EACH OTHER

Remember it was Nila Gupta who told us about the panopticon of the DWP and how 'it fucks you up so sometimes, you forget that you're living in a panopticon and just blame/hate yourself'.[59] Nila is showing us how the DWP gets in our heads – telling us that paid work equals worth and that being on benefits is a failing. This psychological effect is part of the panopticon's design, where prisoners are aware they can be observed at any time, meaning, according to philosopher Michel Foucault, that they internalise this surveillance and discipline themselves whether or not they are being watched.[60] Jay Watts, a disabled activist and consultant clinical psychologist, when asked to comment in Disability News Service on the messaging in the DWP's anti-fraud spoof of the film *Taken* (the one with the minister for disabled people telling people that the DWP will track them down), said:

> The DWP video not only plays on fears of persecution and being accused of wrongdoing, which claimants tell us in clinic provokes terror, despair, and anxiety – quite understandably, unfortunately, given the cruelty of our current welfare system – but also ramps up the messaging with highly evocative and persecutory language almost perfectly designed to trigger fear responses in the body. For any member of the public deluded enough to believe the DWP's likely response that the messaging will only affect people considering fraud, let me tell you this: mental health clinicians such as myself spend a considerable amount of time convincing people in desperate need that they deserve benefits because the pervasive fear we nearly all hold is that we've done something wrong. When I say that this

> policy will get inside people's heads in terms of intrusive thoughts and persecutory auditory hallucinations, I mean it quite literally.[61]

The crafting and triggering of fear also has massive implications for resistance – for pro-welfare activism and movements. Nila Gupta explains that one impact of the panopticon of the DWP is that 'many of us are scared to leave the house, post any pictures of us looking happy on social media, be photographed at events/protests. We're cut off from participating in civil society.' So many disabled people experience this fear. This fear is why some people cited in this book need to remain anonymous. This fear is why we don't know the names of so many of the people who have been killed. Threaded through the ways the DWP crafts fear of criminalisation is a deep fear of destitution that has been designed into welfare for centuries.

One way to think about this is the internalisation of oppression or, given the way this is designed to make us police ourselves and each other, as a 'cop in the head'. 'Cop in the head' is a concept developed by Brazilian theatre director Augusto Boal, famous for the *Theatre of the Oppressed*, to refer to how oppression comes to live inside us, takes on our voice and stops us practising our beliefs and limits our longings. Augusto Boal explains that when oppression has been internalised, there is a 'cop in the head' doing the work of repression that would otherwise require a 'cop in the street'.[62] Yes, 'the cops are in their heads, but the headquarters of these cops are in the external reality. It is necessary to locate both the cops and their headquarters'.[63] This is important because it focuses attention on both actual material ways we are policed, and the ways we internalise this, meaning it looks to transform root causes and not only change the way we *think* about oppression while leaving root causes intact. This is really different, for example, from the way some popular theories about suicide talk about the need to change individual people's perceptions that they are a burden, while doing absolutely nothing to change the way the state, media, corporations tell us that certain people are burdens, and treat them as such.[64]

Paula Peters (from DPAC) told me: 'For the first few years of the coalition government, I had Iain Duncan Smith's voice in my head every single day' (Iain Duncan Smith was Secretary of State for Work and Pensions from 2010 to 2016). The DWP is in our heads but it is *not only* in our heads. This is vitally important to name, given we've seen how welfare is designed on disbelief, and has a long history of gas-lighting people trying to claim benefits, to make people doubt themselves. The welfare state weaponises this disbelief and doubt – uses it as a way to get people to stop claiming welfare. People's deaths by suicide are one way to achieve this, written off as a sad but inevitable symptom of poor mental health – the age-old use of 'craziness' as individual pathology to deny any accountability in driving people mad. Or as an individual tragedy, where the complexity of suicide is weaponised to deny accountability. If I sound angry, that's because I am. It is objectively horrible and I am rightly enraged.

Some people talk about killing the 'cop in our head' or in this case the DWP in our head, that is, getting rid of the oppressive messaging that has come to live inside us and police our imaginations of how things could be different. For me this is a massive YES, and (rather than but) while we still live within our current system, some people's survival depends on the DWP being in their heads. How can we resist internalising this dehumanising 'burden', deservingness and surveillance crap, while also knowing the sticky truth that, like Nila, many people need to 'anticipate and strategise against DWP sanctions' in order to get and keep their benefits. Maybe for now we have to help each other to endure welfare as disbelief, dehumanising, punishment – but by refusing to reproduce this when we talk to ourselves and each other, we start collectively building the foundations for a different kind of welfare (something we turn to in the final chapter). Another way to put this is that we may need, for now, to hold the voice of the DWP lightly. Many navigate these tensions by supporting people going through sanctions in the here and now, while building power against welfare state violence in the long term.

5

Deadly by Design: Building Power Against Welfare State Violence

What happens if I take the deepest breath I've taken all day, and really name what I think we're facing, without appeasing you, without trying to persuade you, recognising your dignity and mine, and doing it because however different we are, and whether we like each other or not, our liberation is deeply connected – we will only get free from this bin fire that we are currently smouldering in, together. Disproportionately distributed harm and premature death, targeting racialised, low-income and disabled populations, is a feature of the welfare state, not a bug. The welfare system is violent by design – it generates profits by extracting, excluding and abandoning certain people – those it tells us are a burden, too costly. There, I said it. But I haven't always known this. I had planned to write this book differently – maybe something softer, more persuasive. Maybe you would have preferred the other version. But there isn't time. I haven't got the energy. And anyway, this isn't a 'choose your own adventure'. Other people have already made the choices, they've written the story, and we live and struggle inside it every day.

ENTRY POINTS BEYOND AUSTERITY AND CUTS

Can you remember when you first realised that the welfare state is violent?[1] Was it in 2008 when we were hit with 'welfare reform' and austerity? Or in 2014 when Stephanie Bottrill's suicide note was published by the BBC, telling her son 'Don't blame yourself for me ending my life. The only people to blame are the Government.' Or was it very recently (in 2025) when Leeds Disabled People Against Cuts (DPAC) organised a die-in to remember 'the thousands of people who have lost their lives as a result of the cruel UK welfare system'.[2]

Or does your knowledge come from further back? Maybe from the 1990s when immigration status was explicitly connected to welfare, creating whole populations who had no recourse to public funds? Maybe you've always known the welfare state is violent – the bureaucratic terror of assessments and paperwork, the waiting, the delays, being looked down on and told you're worthless – knowledge passed down through generations.

When you first realised, or how long you've known – these are our entry points into how we understand welfare state violence and this shapes our resistance. If you think the problems began from 2008 but things were good before that, then you're probably going to campaign against cuts and maybe for tweaks to the system and reforms, nurtured by nostalgia for how things used to be. If you have always encountered the welfare state as violent, then 'cuts' aren't going to cut it for you.

A lot of campaigning about the very real and deeply harmful story of 'cuts' takes the entry point of welfare state violence, or at least it's intensifying, as happening in the government response to the 2008 financial crisis. It's true that for some disabled people, this may have been the entry point to welfare state violence. It's important to meet people where they're at – at the point they realised something, their entry point into an issue. And some of us know welfare state violence only too well and feel like we've been saying it for a long time and not been listened to. There's something about entry points to understanding and activism that keeps coming up for me as a sticking point, a block that often seems to lead us to feel angry with each other and to polarise, even though our enemy is shared and our liberation is connected. The longer lineages of welfare state violence and how people have resisted it show us that if our focus remains on anti-austerity/anti-cuts, we risk overlooking and devaluing the knowledge and analysis of people who have long lived at welfare's sharp edges, and who are very familiar with its extraction, exclusion and its weaponisation.

Well over a decade after the welfare reforms of 2008, cuts are still killing people and we face more cuts ahead. Our placards from 2010 still apply, however much we might want to compost them. But cuts were killing people before 2008 – Brixton Black Women's group were mobilising around 'cuts will kill' in relation to the health service in 1980.[3] A common way we fight the decimiation of the welfare state is to mobilise against cuts. We saw this in 2010, two years into austerity-driven 'welfare reform', when many activist groups led/co-led by disabled people started to form and solidify – groups such as Disabled People Against Cuts, Black Activists Rising Against Cuts, and more recently with Crips Against Cuts. These groups literally have 'cuts' in their names, and 'cuts' are an important, though not the only, part of the stories they tell and the actions they lead.

Austerity is part of the origin story of many groups and campaigns, yet sociologists Akwugo Emejulu and Leah Bassel show far from austerity being new, 'well before the 2008 crisis, women of colour on the whole were already living in an almost permanent state of austerity'.[4] This means if we mobilise only around post-2008 austerity 'cuts', we risk focusing mainly on their impact on (some) white people, while normalising the way poor racialised people, and especially women of colour, have long been impoverished. This means we treat cuts that impact white people as a 'crisis' demanding action, while we treat more long-standing state violence targeting racialised people and others who are framed as economic 'burdens', as business as usual.

The structural devaluation of certain people's lives not only pre-exists austerity but makes it possible in the first place. We explored in Chapter 3 how many different groups over time have been framed as 'burdens' on the state. In her book *Crisis, Austerity, and Everyday*

Life, Gargi Bhattacharyya shows how centuries-old ideas of who is deserving or not of social rights shift and reshape – expanding to include those previously seen as deserving.[5] There can be real tension when those who have previously been privileged as 'deserving' (possibly without even realising it) come to realise they are now being categorised as 'undeserving', and that the state isn't protecting them. As these people wake up to state violence and neglect, they are rightly outraged. And this outrage, and the activism it sometimes informs, can feel hard for people who have long known and named the state as violent, and it can mean the long-standing analysis and activism of those long deemed 'undeserving' is overlooked. There's loads of examples of this – sometimes hard to name. Tensions between people newly disabled through the pandemic (impaired by Covid and disabled by the state's responses or lack of) and those who have been disabled a long time (as documented by health justice researcher Stephanie Davis).[6] Or, as disability justice activist, Leah Lakshmi Piepzna-Samarasinha remembers, when many non-disabled people 'discovered' mutual aid during the early days of the ongoing pandemic, yet never realised or referenced that 'sick and disabled people had been practising it for years', or 'that the term "collective care" was invented by radical disabled women and nonbinary people of color who were and are part of the disability justice movement'.[7] Then there's the tensions between people newly impacted by welfare reform and people who have always known the violence of welfare. People have different entry points and we need to meet them where they're at to build a movement against state violence and to build the systems we need. And we sometimes have to do this while feeling really pissed off that people new to state violence haven't been listening and seem only to care when something impacts them.

A disabled activist who wants to remain anonymous remembers starting to make lists, in 2012, of the names of disabled people who had died because of 'welfare reform' and sharing them on social media. She remembers people responding in shock – saying that 'the DWP would not have done that', a 'government department couldn't behave in that way'. That incredulity can come from deep shock and hurt for those of us who haven't yet realised that the institutions we think of as, and are frequently told are, benevolent and good also surveil, regulate, criminalise, abandon and kill us. Anna Susianta came up against this when her 17-year-old son, Komang Jack Susianta (who adored his older brother, and could run faster than anybody else in their family), was killed by police in 2015 while suffering a mental health crisis. Jack drowned in the River Lea in east London after jumping into the water as police officers chased him. She told me:

> Our campaigns need to be spread beyond just the-death-of-our-children or the-deaths-of-individuals because people who aren't affected by the tragedies that we've been through – When they hear about it, they go, 'Oh no! That – *That* wouldn't happen in a hospital!' 'Oh no! *That* doesn't happen! The police don't *do* that! That doesn't happen.' They have no idea! It's just so important to reach out to people who've never experienced what we've experienced; what our loved-ones experienced. The key thing is about caring for each other at every chance we get because you just don't know that – that person passing you in the street might be going through some terrible time.

For many people though, the fact the (welfare) state kills people would not be a shock. Artist and editor Derica Shields explains that 'prior to the 2008 crisis, the accelerated rollback of benefits was enabled by the media's depiction of Black people as the most frequent recipients of welfare, and as a drain on resources that are meant for all'.[8] Black people, people of colour, displaced and disabled people were also no strangers to being framed as a burden prior to the austerity policies of 2008 onwards. In 2021, Derica Shields carried out a multi-generational oral history project that gathered seven Black Londoners' accounts of their interactions with the UK welfare state – a reckoning with the 'gaslighting, surveillance, and dehumanization that accompany the "care" of the state, while sharing strategies for survival'. Derica writes:

> For Black people, there is no idyll of the welfare state to which we might return. So I have a hard time dealing with the nostalgia (which is especially pronounced ahead of elections) for a postwar contract between citizen-subjects and the state, the conjuring of a just government that apportions funds without discrimination, to provide public services for all. Even when this origin story is being invoked to push back against cuts, the promise of restoration is sustained through the elision of Blackness – specifically, the correlation between Blackness and the undeserving poor in the British imagination.[9]

The exclusion of Black people from, and their abandonment by, the welfare state from its very beginnings shows why many Black people, and especially women, know welfare state violence better than most. Yet I rarely encounter Black women's lineages of resistance to welfare state violence being explicitly acknowledged in welfare activism. The book *Heart of the Race* shows that Black women have long questioned the power of the welfare state because:

> there is no single area of our lives which better exposes our experience of institutionalised racism than our relationship with the various welfare services. Here we deal regularly with people who are vested with the power to control, disrupt and intervene in our lives on behalf of the State.[10]

This is why the women who wrote *Heart of the Race* – Beverley Bryan, Stella Dadzie and Suzanne Scafe – tell us that 'welfare is deliberately designed to make us believe in the myth that we live in a society that is fundamentally humane', meaning that Black feminist activism 'cannot be confined to campaigns against cuts'.[11] We have a lot to learn from Black feminists about campaigning against welfare state violence beyond a focus on cuts, nostalgia and reforms. Dorothy Roberts (who writes about abolishing the family policing system) says something similar in the USA, that 'the fight to salvage pieces of the existing welfare system tended to overlook its serious flaws', including that it has been 'designed to subordinate' Black people, devalue work often done by women, and dampen demands for economic justice.[12] If we only mobilise around 'cuts' to welfare services, we might overlook how harmful welfare itself can be, and the ways in which the welfare state is weaponised by design.

BY DESIGN AND DEADLY: LINEAGES OF RESISTANCE TO WELFARE STATE VIOLENCE

Underneath public campaigning *against* cuts and *for* reforms, I hear something else from many disabled activists – that the welfare system is deadly by design. If you've made it this far in this book, you'll have noticed this too – Rick Burgess (from Manchester DPAC) points out the sheer numbers of deaths, and how the government knows what they're doing, and how we should name it as democide. John Pring (editor of Disability News Service) tells us that people's deaths aren't by mistake because the government has had so many warnings, seen so much evidence, and yet continues. Ellen Clifford, a member of the steering committee of DPAC, and author of *The War on Disabled People*, explains that the government has 'created a system that's deliberately designed to push people into poverty because our people's lives are worth less to them than other people's'. The idea that disabled people's lives are 'worth less' to the government underlies much welfare policy. Paula Peters (DPAC activist and trade unionist) teaches us that welfare (or at least the DWP's version of it) is 'deliberately, intentionally, cruel to wear us down, to stop us claiming. And their attitude is, "The more of us who die, the better."' Tumu Johnson, co-director at the feminist disabled women's collective, Sisters of Frida, shares something eerily similar:

> there are ways in which the welfare state inflicts violence onto us, that is obvious and undeniable. We see a spectrum of control exerted by the welfare state: appointments at the job centre with no leniency,

> dictating where you have to be and when ... Care schedules that dictate what time you'll go to bed and what time we can get up in the morning. Fear that if we are seen attending events or having fun, that will be reported and held against us. Control of disabled people is present in all areas of the welfare state. Sites of health care continue to be used as a tool to inflict violence. The connections between the different sites of violence are compounding in nature: there is a repetition, a pattern, a relentlessness present, which is designed to wear people down.

According to Tumu, this wearing people down is a form of 'violence that is by design and deadly'. The deadliness of its design is there in the constant, cumulative, relentless repetition of violence. People are worn out – it's hard not to be as the world burns around us. Ellen Clifford says she's noticed a shift as the years of austerity and welfare reform roll on, where people are exhausted with fighting the government just to survive. If spoons (as a unit of energy) are limited, then it matters where we put our energy, whether that's into reforming a 'broken' system or uprooting one that's harmful by design. In documenting Black Londoners' experiences with the welfare state, Derica Shields wanted to

> expand what can be named as state violence ... challenge the renaming of daily violence against Black life as 'welfare,' 'benefits,' 'allowances,' and 'relief,' which wraps the causes of our rightful anger in the honeyed language of care. And, before I became immobilized by despair, I wanted to channel my rage at the state, which wastes our time, erodes our health, exhausts and slowly kills us.[13]

For me personally, naming the ways the welfare state harms people as 'welfare state violence' has helped to shift my understanding, and locate these harms not as something only perpetrated by one government department but as part of a much more interconnected web of state harm. I wanted to share this with you not because it is 'interesting' or because it fills some kind of 'gap' in the theoretical literature but because it *does* something – it opens up different kinds of actions and practices. It shows connections between the welfare state and wider forms of state violence, revealing that much of this violence is covered up by framing those impacted as 'burdens' and 'scroungers', and that these frames are connecting threads in violence against differently oppressed groups, especially racialised, disabled and poor people. Naming the violence of the welfare state as state violence can be a connecting thread for cross-movement solidarity, a tapestry that grows and solidifies our ecosystems of resistance (just as Vickie Cooper and David Whyte bring together those writing about *The Violence of Austerity*).[14]

A disabled activist and healthcare worker who wants to remain anonymous explained to me that

> there is such a long history of people working against welfare state violence ... All these movements are built on organizing that's happened before us and organizing that will come after us. And so, once we situate ourselves in the grand scheme of history, it helps us move away from the constant sense of pressure, the weight that feels unbearable, and the isolation.

As a counter to this pressure, this isolation, in October 2023, at Healing Justice Ldn's Rehearsing Freedoms festival, we brought together some of the people cited in this book – Stella Dadzie (who co-wrote *Heart of the Race*), Derica Shields and Tumu Johnson to talk about resistance to welfare state violence. Tumu shared that

> resistance to me looks like the demos and the banners and the lock-ons and the wheelchair blockades, and the campaigns, the endless emails, the meetings held, the conversations, the sharing of knowledge from one disabled comrade to another. What I have learned I've been taught with patience and generosity. It looks like the relationships that we build with each other where we hold space for our own and

> each other's needs, where we relate in a different way and reject the idea that we are burdensome. It's deep listening to what others are experiencing and connecting with them in joint struggle; it's disabled folk bringing me food when I'm sick; and it's meeting lying down. Survival is also resistance. Sadly not all folks have survived the violence of the welfare state and holding them in spirit is so important. As many have said before, one death is too many.[15]

WELFARE SOLIDARITIES

'Reimagining welfare', as a disabled activist explained to me, is 'contingent on developing communal relationships more tightly on a local scale'. We 'can get siloed in struggles, experience frustration when we don't taste progress' so we need to 'deepen our connections across struggles and sectors'. Those in power have tried hard to stop us from seeing the connections in our struggles but there are long lineages of resistance to welfare state violence from the many groups who the state tells us are a burden – opening up space to rethink or refine our demands through threads of cross-movement solidarity. Chatting to Paula Peters (from DPAC), she explained that

> DPAC work on a cross-solidarity campaigning and movement network. Because it's really important to stress that every cut that the government have implemented, and every attack on our rights, impacts on disabled people. From attacks on libraries, denial of … the cuts to social care which have a devastating impact on disabled people. But also, I think the joint solidarity that we show in other campaigns … you know, Fuel Poverty Action being one. Because disabled people are in fuel poverty, especially with rising energy prices. During the pandemic, when many of us were shielding, we had high energy costs, high fuel costs and food costs and everything. It's important to show solidarity to one another's campaigns to build our movement. That's massively, massively important.

As usual Rick Burgess tells it how it is, extending

> solidarity to other groups targeted by the British state – migrants, asylum seekers, people in criminal justice, sleeping rough, people subject to police oppression – the British state is an international criminal. Applying colonial violence to the domestic population. We shouldn't separate our struggle to just welfare – this is the wide attitude of the ruling class to the people it chooses not to favour to live … small tweaks around a fundamental system that is horrible. The change is going to come from all of us. For the victims and survivors to feel justice, the ideal would be that the DWP is abolished. That level of harm and trauma has been reached.[16]

Solidarity rooted in racial, migrant and disability justice is especially important given racism within disabled people's organising. Both Inclusion London and DPAC know this well. In September 2025, Inclusion London (who support Deaf and Disabled people's organisations in London and campaign for equality) launched a series of adverts for its Justice for Disabled Victims of Hate Crime campaign, including adverts featuring disabled people of colour. The adverts were met with a raft of disablist and racist comments. At a similar time, DPAC were forced to delete racist responses to a post they made about the involvement of two disabled activists at an anti-racist demonstration outside a hotel that houses asylum seekers and had been subjected to far-right protests. Some of these racist responses were written by disabled people. Louise Holden, senior policy officer on disabled people and crime for Inclusion London, told Disability News Service that 'The racist and disablist online comments about disabled people of colour, written by disabled white people, make clear that their ongoing hostile environment tactics are working' – 'we are turning on each other'.[17] Paula Peters from DPAC pointed out that recent polling had found that 29 per cent of disabled people intended to vote for far-right party Reform.[18] In this context, it is more important than ever that we cultivate capacities for solidarity.

One way to move towards these solidarities is to recognise that dependency has always been central to welfare – in the creation of economic dependency of colonised states on the colonisers, the disavowal of the dependency of the colonisers on the colonised, and the stigmatisation of dependency on the state of those in receipt of disability or unemployment benefits. Where so many different people over time have been named as a burden, scholar Jina B. Kim invites us to wonder if 'dependency might function as an unexpected axis of affinity between groups framed as drains on the state', and for all who want to liberate pathologised bodies and minds.[19] We can learn a lot about interdependency from Disability Justice. For Mia Mingus, who is a disabled writer and educator based in California, 'interdependency is both "you and I" and "we." It is solidarity, in the best sense of the word … Because the truth is: we need each other.'[20] And one of the ways we need each other is to learn about longer lineages of resistance to welfare state violence – the kind that helps us sense that this violence is by design, not mistake.

Cultural theorist Fred Moten puts it yet another way:

> The coalition emerges out of your recognition that it's fucked up for you, in the same way that we've already recognized that it's fucked up for us. I don't need your help. I just need you to recognize that this shit is killing you, too, however much more softly, you stupid motherfucker, you know?

This isn't solidarity built on the 'it could happen to you anytime' kind that we hear a lot around disability – though of course, non-disabled people are often more accurately referred to as 'the not yet disabled'. This is solidarity built through 'this is happening to all of us in different ways' – it's disabling us all, it's killing us all – some of us just have more of a buffer zone, more time. We need these solidarities, between those deemed 'burdens', 'dependent', 'scroungers', 'bogus', to understand how our oppressions are all connected, the ones we are complicit in as well as the ones that wear us down and kill us.

WELFARE NOT WARFARE

These solidarities aren't only in the future, they are now. In the UK, many of us have been part of increased cross-movement mobilising around 'welfare not warfare'. In March 2024, I joined disabled people and allies coming together to demand No More Benefit Deaths, as part of a national day of action called by DPAC. We gathered outside the DWP's Caxton House, my two-month-old baby strapped to my chest, freeing up my arms to carry a sign that read 'Fund welfare not genocide'. Rallying cries for 'welfare not warfare' have got even louder since Labour announced plans to cut £5 billion from disability benefits – the biggest cuts on record (though largely since scrapped due to opposition). At the same time, the government unveiled plans to increase core military spending to £62.2 billion for the 2025–26 financial year, an increase of £2.2 billion from what was already one of the highest global figures. Fast forward to a rainy 7 June 2025, when the People's Assembly organised a demo demanding 'welfare not warfare' in Whitehall. The 'Welfare not Warfare' campaign comes from a coalition of groups, including Stop the War and DPAC.[21] The campaign opposes 'all cuts to welfare, especially those affecting disability benefits and PIP, to justify huge increases in defence spending'. It argues that instead of spending money on weapons, the government should be 'protecting the most vulnerable in our society, funding the NHS and schools properly, building council homes and saving our broken social care system'. Then in September, the relatively newly formed Merseyside DPAC organised a protest outside the Labour Party Conference in Liverpool – connecting genocide abroad and democide at home. Almost every speech highlighted complexity and cross-movement struggle – especially solidarities with people in Gaza, with asylum seekers, and with trans people. Rick Burgess, who started us off and introduced the speakers, talked about Gaza as a lens through which we need to see everything – if the government sees genocide as a viable option anywhere, then they'll use it on disabled people here. Some people were there because they found

DPAC through organising for Palestinian solidarity. In between speeches and taking turns holding banners, I chatted to people about the shifts we've seen in campaigning recently – it's like the capacity for cross-movement struggle has grown. Some people reflected that it used to be common that disabled people felt they had to position themselves as getting the worst of everything but now something has shifted – something that allows us to feel the connections in all of our oppression. The framing of genocide abroad and democide at home also shows us that our fight for welfare justice has to be global – because the companies profiting from our welfare systems are global and also because the ideas shaping punitive welfare systems are used to manufacture scarcity, justify austerity, and kill people all over the world. And our collective grief over these killings can be the foundations of our solidarities.

REBELLIOUS GRIEF, WITNESSING, COMMUNITY

When I speak about justice to disabled people and bereaved families, many of whom are themselves disabled, patterns emerge; there are certain repetitions, particular words and practices echo – grief, witnessing, solidarity, care. Across disabled movement organisers, activists who describe themselves as abolitionist, and family members who find themselves sometimes unwittingly thrust into campaigning, there's a resonance in how people are practising and dreaming justice, even if spoken in different words, in whispers, even if the tactics sometimes seem in friction, incommensurable. The roots of every space I've been part of along this journey of campaigning against welfare state violence are wet with grief. Everyone knows someone, more than one person, who has died. Paula Peters, from DPAC, says, 'Every human being we've lost is etched on our hearts. Is etched on our minds. Every single day, we carry them with us. Every single day.' Disabled and chronically ill storyteller, healer and revolutionary,

Aurora Levins Morales asks, 'how do you mourn endless numbers of people in endless numbers of places? Is there a form for it, a requisite time and place for mourning? Is there ever an end to it?'[22] And what are the costs for building new worlds if we don't mourn those killed by our current one?

Grief is often the fuel for the fire of our campaigning. Maybe there is justice in not sanitising our grief – keeping it raw and its texture rough. Talking about solidarity with other families bereaved because of the welfare system, Imogen Day shared that 'we're aware that we need each other in this community; we share our grief publicly in-the-hopes that we can bring about positive change to the welfare-system; and that relies upon us leaning on each other for strength. Whilst our loved-ones die alone, *we* are not alone in this journey; and I take comfort in that.' I have come across so much solidarity enabled by grief. DPAC has campaigned alongside many families, and families have campaigned in solidarity with disabled people. And yet there have also been times when the grief feels too heavy, too repetitive, when someone's longing to name the death of a loved one, in detail, is too much for others, too triggering. I've spent lots of time on calls after meetings, checking in on people, reconnecting people who have hurt one another (often with only love intended). This, too, is our work.

The refusal to mourn only in private, and instead to grieve together, publicly, for the people we're told don't matter, would have died anyway, deserved it, had no value, is our rebellion and our healing, our movement towards justice (whatever we think it means). The activism of many mothers, often Black, Indigenous and women of colour/femmes across the world, of disabled people, of trans people, show us the importance of making space for, and collectively practising, grief in our organising. This can be many things – reading out loud and in public the names of some of those who have died, organising vigils, disrupting the workings of the powers that cause mass death. In a context that wants us 'to deaden and dull our capacity for grief', prison abolitionists Kelly Hayes and Mariame Kaba see grief as rebellious – a 'rejection of mass death and an insistence on the humanity' of those who have died and been killed.[23] This is a lever for change because the state is 'wholly unprepared to confront a multiracial, intergenerational movement of people who share a loving practice of grief and who are prepared to care for one another and act in one another's defense'.[24] This shows us that to build new worlds, we must hold love and grief alongside each other.[25] We can resource ourselves, as Camille Barton shows us, to collectively tend to our grief – to reduce our isolation, and clarify what we care about and how we can move towards this together.[26]

The solidarity, love and joy that comes from connecting with others who share similar experiences was by far the thing that the bereaved families with whom I've spoken talked about the most in relation to justice. Listening to many families bereaved by the state describe the love they cultivate in their journeys towards justice reminds me of something I learned from Prentis Hemphill (who works on healing, embodiment and justice) in a room on Bethnal Green Rd in 2025 – that 'the kind of change we are after is cellular as well as institutional, is personal and intimate, is collective as well as cultural. We are making love synonymous with justice.'[27] When I heard Prentis say this, I thought of Imogen Day, and how my chest tightened when Imogen tried to put into words her family's grief after her sister Philippa's death – that 'our love wasn't enough to counteract the state violence'. Could our love build practices and systems outside of the state, not just to survive state violence, but to tear it out by its roots?

There's something incredibly painful and powerful for people in realising they are not the only ones. This is especially because the 'weight' of welfare state violence feels 'unbearable' – it creates isolation and makes 'people feel like they have no one in the world they can turn to' (anonymous). Imogen Day was there in October 2021, at the opening of the Museum of Austerity (an exhibition which features the stories of people killed by austerity), when several of the families of disabled people killed by welfare state violence met for the first time – making connections and starting conversations that continue today. Imogen talks about how

> while none of our loved-ones knew each other, our stories and our experiences are so similar and interconnected … we've really leant on each other, and taken strength from each other as well; and the continued need to-keep-going. And I know that, if any of us were ever struggling with the circumstances that happened, that we could just pick up the phone, and call each other, and we would be there.

Disability News Service has also played a huge role in people coming to understand that they're not alone.

While families impacted by welfare state violence don't have a formalised network, families impacted by deaths in police, prison and psychiatric custody do come together in formalised coalition. The United Families and Friends Campaign (UFFC) was formed in 1996 by Brenda Weinberg, the sister of Brian Douglas who was killed by police in May 1995, and Myrna Simpson, the mother of Joy Gardner, who was killed by police restraint in 1993. Filmmaker and activist Ken Fero from Migrant Media, and community activist Minkah Adofo from the African People's Liberation Front, supported this mother and sister – whose 'simple, but militant idea was to unite the families to strengthen each other and fight the state'.[28] This act of Black resistance to state violence, drawing on a long history, some of which we've traced in this book, created a unity which has drawn in so many families who share similar experiences. Black families and especially Black women, like Brenda, Myrna, and Aji (below), are integral to resistance against racist state violence – they know this violence, and the tactics needed to fight it, very well. An important part of this resistance, according to Adam Elliot-Cooper, in a context where Black families are demonised, is resisting the 'normative nuclear family structure' by extending who counts as family into a 'wider set of Black and activist community networks'.[29] Mothers, and often Black mothers, are at the centre of organising for justice in the face of state violence – whether it's the welfare state, policing, prisons, the family policing system, social care, mental health, or all of them tied together in a knot. This reminds me of the activism of (mainly) Black mothers closer to home, with Mothers Against Joint Enterprise (JENGbA) (in Manchester), and of multiple other campaigns led by mothers – such as Single Mothers' Self-Defence and Disabled Mothers' Rights Campaign.

Aji is one of those mothers who joined UFFC:

> Every October, we have what we call the UFFC March (it's Trafalgar Square-to-Downing Street); and the families talk, and – It's just growing. Everybody is involved. And the other thing, I would say, is now UFFC – Before, it used to – It started as a co-operative for Black families; those, with Black families, that were killed in-custody. And we're finding now that a lot of State-deaths, suicides, are white families – it's across-the-board; it's across the-board.

The informal networks and relationships between disabled people and families bereaved by the welfare state have, according to Alison Burton (Errol Graham's daughter-in-law, who we met earlier and we'll meet again in the next chapter), led to some change:

> I think our fight, our journeys, our solidarity has really, really driven-and-pushed the DWP to do things it was reluctant to do (or rather, it didn't *want* to do) ... When you come together as a group, and you really fight these people, that's when they *do* notice, and that is when the DWP starts to really fall over its own feet, as we've seen; I don't think they expected the solidarity that has come over recent years, and it's been powerful because things have come out that the public had a right to know.

When I hear Alison say this, I hear the power that lies in solidarity, in collective grief and witnessing, and how the powerful (the rich, the state) are afraid of this. A disabled activist who wants to remain anonymous talked to me about how

> people are organizing to have their pain witnessed and when it is witnessed by the state it's all performative. It's all for the sake of giving the presentation that people are being listened to. When you think about justice, it means to be witnessed – to have your pain held intimately and not just treated as something that can be weaponized and used against you and actually used to maintain the violences being done to people.

Through collective sharing and witnessing people can come to realise that what we've been told is our fault is really the result of systemic injustice, meaning the pain and anger people feel makes complete sense, and enabling us to heal together in community. This kind of community witnessing is often impromptu, without formal organisation, but it can also be by design. One of the ways people are currently organising to witness pain is through creating spaces that listen and pay attention away from the state – through people's tribunals and movement assemblies.

PEOPLE'S TRIBUNAL ON POLICE KILLINGS

A university building in Regents Park seemed somehow a strange place for the People's Tribunal on Police Killings, but I bumped into lots of people I knew, including many who like me had come down from Manchester to attend.[30] It wasn't quite as hard to get a seat as I'd imagined but the space at the front for families was packed. The Tribunal (which started officially in 2025) mobilises on the basis that: 'The disproportionate number of Black people killed represents the depth of racism that is ingrained in the police forces of the UK. Policing structures are corrupt and must be abolished.' The People's Tribunal formed out of failures to prosecute police who murder people – 'following more than 3000 deaths at the hands of the police over the past 50 years there have only been 4 successful prosecutions leading to police officers being convicted and imprisoned. This figure is one of the lowest in the world.'[31] The People's Tribunal is supported by the UFFC, Migrant Media, Black Lives Matter and 4WardEver. As a method of bringing people together and connecting specific experiences to wider global struggles, international people's tribunals started in the 1960s and 1970s, examining US war crimes in Vietnam, and the crimes of military dictatorships in Latin America.

Families shared things at the tribunal that sounded so familiar to the families I've spoken with who are bereaved because of welfare state violence – the dehumanising stories that the state and media craft to justify violence and murder by the police, and the bone-deep racism that even without thought makes the police restrain a Black person a bit harder, a bit longer, grab a bit tighter. This is a connected story to the one the state tells about people who claim welfare, including racialised and disabled people, as scroungers and fraudsters – the bone-deep anti-poor ableism that makes us feel entitled to question people on welfare, interrogate their decisions and behaviours, decide if they're deserving, punish them if they don't meet the conditions we impose.

Families at the tribunal talked about torturously long waits to get an inquest, constant delays – the slow bureaucratic violence that families bereaved to welfare state violence know in their bodies as a deep ache. I can't describe hearing Ajibola Lewis, whose son Seni was killed by police while he was a voluntary patient in a psychiatric hospital, speak about Seni – the way her grief commands a room, the hush as she describes how as a mother she thought the hospital would care for him but he was murdered and she will never forgive herself. Aji talked about how she sat and listened to over 29 days of evidence at Seni's inquest, hearing how her son was restrained in two sets of restraints by eleven police officers, on the floor, saying 'I can't breathe.' When the pathologists gave their evidence at the inquest, Aji screamed. The police walked away with impunity. Years later, we have all heard those words 'I can't breathe', while we watch as police kill Black people, how racism steals breath. And the DWP also disproportionately produces premature death – when it sent Jodey Whiting a letter telling her she was fit for work and her benefits would be stopped (despite the fact that she'd just come out of hospital after finding she had a cyst on her brain). Her mother, Joy, says she 'panicked ... she said to me, "What can I do? I can't walk out of the door; I can't breathe; I can't go sign on."'

People at the tribunal also talked a lot about the justification of violence through the 'language of collusion', that is, how the state, the media and liberal institutions construct narratives that 'justify and normalise police killings'.[32] For me, this really hit home when Shirley Sylvester started to give testimony. Shirley is Roger Sylvester's cousin. Roger was a 30-year-old Black man who was restrained outside his home in Tottenham in January 1999 by eight police officers, and killed while being transported to hospital. His official cause of death is recorded as 'positional asphyxiation', which is the sanitised medicalised way to describe when someone is strangled to death by the police.[33] While the jury named Roger's death as an unlawful killing, the police appealed and have been protected by the state in a way completely denied to the family. Roger's family have been fighting for justice since 1999. But Shirley asks: 'what does justice look like? Justice is not another inquiry, I don't want Roger to be a footnote in a police training manual.' When Shirley said this, you can see where my hand shook in the notes that I was furiously writing. Shirley is sick of the police talking about 'lessons learned', because if they wanted to learn lessons they would have learned these from the many other times they've strangled people to death before Roger. Not only have other Black men been killed by police in this way in the UK, but this sits in a global context, in extra-judicial sites, where official cause of death is sanitised, and torture goes unnamed, and seen in tactics used by the Israeli Occupation Force in Palestine.

Gargi Bhattacharyya, another expert witness at the tribunal, and someone whose work on racial capitalism has hugely shaped my thinking about welfare and its colonial roots, also talked about the narrative of 'lessons learned' as 'better ways of hiding – they are learning from us so they change their practice', so they can better disguise their violence. Shirley and Gargi both talked about how people's history of mental health is used as a weapon against families and used by the police to deny accountability. This is something we've consistently encountered in how the welfare system denies accountability in making people's lives unliveable by portraying deaths by suicide as the outcome of individual mental health issues, even when people literally name the DWP in their suicide note. Gargi also said something else – that racialised people who come to be brutalised and killed by police are 'framed as already dying' – that is, that we're made to imagine that there's an inevitability to Black people's deaths. An inevitability that disabled people know too well – and that is central to telling the story of some people's lives as not worth living, or as some people as 'better off dead' (a story that sits at the heart of current UK debates about, and fierce resistance to, assisted suicide).[34]

As I listened throughout the tribunal, the different and sometimes incommensurable ideas of justice flowing through the space felt palpable. Some fought for justice in the system, worked with the police, wanted prosecutions of police, and others want abolition – they want a world where there is no policing, no prisons, no immigration detention, no institutions that can kill people with impunity. One of the organisers of the tribunal, Ken Fero (filmmaker and activist from Migrant Media), feels that 'the system we have in place to support the families is too reformist minded and still believes in the state'. It was Janet Alder's clarity of analysis that summed it all up for me: 'There is no justice, the system is rotten.' Janet is Christopher Alder's sister. Christopher, a Black British father of two, was killed by Humberside Police in April 1998 – left to die on the police station floor as officers made racist remarks. Christopher's family have been fighting for justice since 1998.[35]

The People's Tribunal 'reject any more governmental inquiries', as every one has failed to lead to 'the substantive changes needed for justice as well as prevention'. These inquiries 'have not benefited the families, despite millions of pounds being paid to judges, lawyers, and organisations colluding in these cover-ups'.[36] They also 'reject the inquest system' as 'an archaic distraction from the mechanisms of real justice'; they 'reject the government's "language of liberalism" – "these are not deaths in police custody"', they are sustained and systematic 'police killings'; and they argue that we don't need any more legislation or more police training.

There were times at the tribunal, as people talked about dehumanisation, state gas-lighting, hypocrisy, platitudes about justice and accountability, weaponising mental health and suicide, that I felt like I could easily already be at a tribunal on welfare state violence. As I witnessed people's pain and learned from their analysis and tactics, it confirmed that state violence, in its different forms, connects us all, and we need each other to build something different – something just. Bringing people together at a tribunal then is not only about the analysis and demands, it's also about the process – about the methodology of witnessing.

PERMANENT PEOPLES' TRIBUNAL (PPT) – THE HOSTILE ENVIRONMENT ON TRIAL

Seven years before the People's Tribunal on Police Killings, in 2018, the Permanent Peoples' Tribunal put the hostile environment (the policies, as we saw in Chapter 3, put in place by the UK Home Office through the 2014 and 2016 Immigration Acts and designed to make staying in the UK as difficult as possible for people without leave to remain) 'on trial'. The trial found the UK government, and the European Union and its member states, guilty of 'violence by design' that was not new and had existed long before policy was named 'hostile environment'.[37] The demands formulated at the tribunal understand migrant justice as a global struggle, combining reform of existing immigration law and abolition, closing down immigration detention centres and moving towards a longer-term goal of no borders.

Sociologist Leah Bassel was a juror at the Permanent Peoples' Tribunal and writes about the kind of listening and possibility opened up in the space, enabled through the long-term invisible labour of the organisers, in a context which pits migrants and people with citizenship against each other. Instead of 'mobilising pity' while 'consuming the spectacle of migrant suffering', there was an orientation towards justice and building solidarity.[38] People's tribunals sit outside the state-sanctioned justice system, and this is significant because of the colonial foundations of legal systems, meaning that turning to them for justice can be full of contradiction and heartbreak. In people's tribunals evidence can be heard what doesn't usually count within the confines of the law – that harms are designed into systems, 'policy as a perpetrator of abuse, or the state as a thief'.[39]

That the people's tribunal methodology faces away from the state and holds a non-enforceable relation via the law creates uncertainty in the welfare activism of which I have been part. Some of us have suggested we turn to this methodology to make connections across systems of harm and state violence, and to use this analysis to vision and strategise – what do we want and how can we get there? Others think we need an independent inquiry first (discussed in the next chapter) that has some legal clout in enabling access to government documents, if not necessarily in creating meaningful structures of accountability.

Moving even further away from the legal framing of 'tribunal', people's (movement) assemblies bring people together, synthesising collective analysis to inform action. People's assemblies have a long history and have been an important way of practising resistance to current systems while visioning, and strategising towards building new ones. The Zapatistas, Pan African Congresses, Kurdish Liberation Movement, the Occupy movement[40] have all used movement assemblies as a methodology. In the USA, there have been Assemblies of Formerly Incarcerated Peoples (2011, Montgomery

Alabama); Healing Justice Peoples Movement Assembly (2010, at the US Social Forum) and Poor Peoples Caravan & Movement Assembly (2008, Atlanta). Project South explains that these assemblies support 'long-term vision and strategies for liberation':

> We need to envision alternatives and create new structures to initiate the world that we want and deserve. We need to move from single issues to convergence across frontlines. We need to develop collective strategic plans that create immediate results and also lead to long-term systemic social justice.

The assembly collectively answers: 'What are the problems we face? What are the solutions? What are we going to do about it?'[41] Could this, or as Rick Burgess and others suggest, a Truth and Reconciliation process, be a route we'd like to go down with welfare, as a way to help us not only have a collective sense-making and analysis of what's wrong with the current system but also as a way to imagine what kind of welfare we do want, to strategise together how to get there, and to share (multiple, diverse) tactics and practices? The assembly process could also be a way to bring more people into movements, a methodology to help us understand the connections between different groups who experience welfare as a weapon, and what we can learn from each other about our lineages of resistance and tactics. What we do know though is that there is already analysis born of lived experience that shows the welfare system is violent by design and that means that yes, we oppose cuts *and* we need to think beyond cuts, right down into the roots. We need a space oriented to welfare justice where we 'piss on pity' (as disabled people have been doing for years), a space where we collectively denounce deservingness (with each other, and in the quiet ways we do it to ourselves), and where we affirm our collective dignity and leave no one behind.

6

Justice Within and Beyond the State

> When Seni first died, the first meeting with the lawyer, we talked about justice – 'We want justice!' – and he said, 'What do you think justice is?' (Ajibola Lewis)

CRIMINAL 'JUSTICE'/PUNISHMENT

'I believe that if it wasn't for Iain Duncan Smith, Sheila would still be alive', Sheila's father Ken told the *Mirror*.[1] Iain Duncan Smith was secretary of state for work and pensions from 2010 to 2016 – the years when so many disabled people were killed by 'welfare reform'. Sheila Holt, whose sister describes her as 'gentle and kind-hearted', died in 2015. She hadn't worked for 27 years, and had bipolar disorder linked to childhood trauma, but was placed in the Work-Related Activity Group of Employment and Support Allowance. This meant her benefit payment was conditional on her completing activities set by a work coach, including attending work-focused interviews, where failure to meet requirements could result in a benefit sanction. She became incredibly anxious, 'terrified that her benefits would be cut', and was sectioned. A week later, in the psychiatric unit, she had a heart attack, and went into a coma – during which time she received letters from her work programme provider, asking her if she was 'closer to the job market'. After 15 months Sheila died.

Many disabled people and bereaved families want to see the politicians responsible for welfare reform do prison time. The policies they cooked up have killed so many people, and caused so much fear. We've explored how this harm is not only possible to see in hindsight, there's ample evidence that the harm these policies would cause was known about beforehand. Paula Peters from DPAC sums up this longing:

> We're full of anger, you know? For the first few years of the coalition government, I had Iain Duncan Smith's voice in my head every single day. He haunted my nights. He haunted my days. I faced that man down in parliament. And that man's a nasty piece of work. What I'd love to see for justice: I'd love to see every single one of the ministers going back ten years – The Secretaries of State, Prime Ministers – put in the dock for crimes. Because this is crimes against humanity. And it's ideological and it's deliberate. It's deliberately, intentionally, cruel to wear us down, to stop us claiming. And their attitude is, 'The more of us who die, the better.'

While most politicians probably don't know the names of the people their policies have killed (and we will never know all their names either) – we know the names of the politicians who killed them. The name that most often gets spoken is the same one that Sheila's father named – Iain Duncan Smith. During those years, I walked alongside people holding placards at protests with Iain Duncan Smith's face on them demanding he do prison time, and I watched his effigy burned during the 2013 Bonfire of Austerity protests.

Just two months after Sheila's death, Luke Alexander Loy, who had been claiming Incapacity Benefit for more than 20 years, died three months after being found fit for work following a Work Capability Assessment. A doctor had given advice that he was not currently well enough to work. Luke had been sanctioned by the DWP for failing to attend meetings at Jobcentre Plus. His father helped him appeal and DWP reinstated his benefits but it was too late for Luke. His sister told Disability News Service that 'Iain Duncan Smith's call for disabled people to "work your way out of poverty", something her brother was not able to do, was a "deeply irresponsible simplification of such a complex issue."'[2] Luke's sister, Natalie, joined disabled activists from Disabled People Against Cuts (DPAC) in a protest outside the 2015 Conservative Party Conference to 'raise awareness of the human costs of these policies' and 'to hold Work and Pensions Secretary Iain Duncan Smith "accountable" for his actions'.[3]

These are far from the only people who name Iain Duncan Smith – he's so notorious that many people refer to him by only his initials – IDS. In 2015, DPAC had so much material on him that they created the 'IDS Files'.[4] When disabled activists and bereaved families say they want to see prosecutions – Iain Duncan Smith is pretty high on the hit list. But he doesn't work alone. Sometimes I try to imagine that today is the day, after years of campaigning by disabled people and bereaved families, we gather together as Iain Duncan Smith is sentenced at the Old Bailey. Our cheers of joy echo among the massive crowd outside the courts, holding banners and placards to remember all those killed by his policies, as he is bundled into a police van and taken to prison. Imagine the party we'd have, the grief, the relief. But then something niggles – however long his sentence, how could it be enough for the harm he's caused? And what about all the other people who helped him – the people who wrote the policies, did the research, produced the data, advised him, wrote his speeches, looked the other way, kept quiet? Should they all go to prison? Will a few people going to prison change the system? Will it mean that people's lives are valued?

My worry is that if we pursue prosecutions of politicians, we'll come up against the same barriers as those experienced by families trying to prosecute police who murder people. In the same year (2015) that Sheila Holt and Luke Alexander Loy were killed by welfare policies, Azelle Rodney was killed by an armed police officer – Anthony Long. A public inquiry found the killing was not lawful yet the police officer was found not guilty by a jury later in the same year. In 2024, Chris Kaba's killer, Martyn Blake – a police officer – was charged with murder after shooting Kaba in 2022. Two years later, he was cleared of murder by a jury. When police kill Black people, often Black men, they mostly keep their jobs, sometimes they even get promoted. Even when police have been charged with manslaughter, they have often later been cleared of murder by a jury. Could that mean that even if we get Iain Duncan Smith charged, he would later be cleared?

Disabled people's role in showing the protracted body count of welfare reform provides multiple sites of creative tension around justice. Many people seek justice from within the system that harms them; some fight to see the key architects of welfare reform criminalised, despite how the criminal justice system criminalises many disabled and Mad people, especially Black people and people of colour. Others envision justice beyond the state. Perhaps there is no justice for the magnitude of our loss. Or maybe justice is what we're doing every day, right now, together.

Sometimes we want to see someone suffer like Philippa/Errol/Jodey/Faiza/Sheila/Luke (the list is long) did. Our rage is real and totally justified. *And* we also know from those whose loved ones have been killed by police and in prisons, and from the higher number of people of colour, especially Black people, and disabled and Mad people, incarcerated in prisons and institutions, that punishment is part of the very system that harms us and our loved ones, and that the criminal 'justice' system does not deliver justice. But we've been told for so long, so often, that this is justice, that turning away from the criminal punishment system feels like we're letting people down, like we're giving up, like defeat. If we see it as preventing other people from being killed by the welfare system, then no, we haven't experienced justice, not yet. But if we understand justice in the everyday solidarities stitched together by grief, in mutual aid and collective care, then yes, we're practising justice all the time – it's at the end of a phone, mixed in like sugar to a cup of tea.

A disabled person I spoke to, who prefers to remain anonymous, explained:

> From an abolitionist perspective, justice does not look like carceral solutions to these problems, justice doesn't look like a fine or an imprisonment of a specific individual, which structurally leads to no

> change because a new CEO comes in or you and a new policy comes in with the next different type of violence. It's like a bump in the road for these systems of violence. The system will always sacrifice individuals here and there in terms of who maintains it, to give an impression of progress, to give this aesthetic of liberation and change when really, structurally and systemically, nothing has really changed.

The 'aesthetic of liberation and change' – is that what we've been wading through in the tweaks and reforms (at best) that come from inquests, second inquests, appeals, investigations, Internal Process Reviews? Loads can be learned here from people working on connected areas of state violence – especially police and prison abolition – who show us time and time again that reforms often make it harder in the long term to dismantle state violence and all of its interconnecting tributaries. Prison abolitionist Andrea J. Ritchie talks about coming to abolition after years of turning time and again to the (master's) tools many of us know well – policymaking, litigating, organising. And after all these years, she came to understand that these tools would only move us partially, and sometimes not at all, towards the worlds we long for. She reminds us that 'we can't continue to organise in ways that replicate and legitimise the systems we are seeking to dismantle'.[5] Yet the more pressure we face, the more sedimented we become in our ways and the more likely we are to cling to familiar strategies and old tactics.

CAMPAIGNING TO CHANGE THE SYSTEM THROUGH THE SYSTEM

It wasn't as cold as you'd expect for January. Standing outside the Royal Courts of Justice, I was at a vigil for Jodey Whiting organised by DPAC and WinVisible (a multi-racial grassroots group of women with visible and invisible disabilities, who provide collective self-help, information, support and advocacy, and campaigning). Jodey took her own life because of the way she was treated by the welfare system. Jodey's mother, Joy Dove, who was at the Courts demanding a second inquest into Jodey's death, came to talk to us. She held a photo of Jodey.

People killed by the welfare system often aren't named as deaths from state violence; yet the state is the perpetrator even as it kills people at a distance, through bureaucracy – slowly. I wonder what justice would feel like for those who experience welfare state violence, and those bereaved by it, and if anyone ever feels like they've truly won it. Can we hold the state to account for those it has killed in ways that also centre our collective dignity and our full humanity?

Campaigning to change the system that kills people is a big part of many people's fight for justice. In 2023, for the final episode of the Deaths by Welfare podcast, we brought together families bereaved by the connecting state violence of the welfare system, mental health system, and policing. Imogen Day (whose sister died by suicide because of the welfare system) and I had been talking for a while about creating a space for families to talk about campaigning and grief; solidarity and care; different journeys of healing; and justice, both within and beyond the state. Our hope had always been that these spaces stitch a connecting thread for cross-movement solidarity against state violence; a tapestry that grows, and solidifies our eco-systems of resistance. I felt nervous to be alongside these wonderful women – but I needn't have been. Power was palpable in the (virtual) room, a gentle power, a loving grief, grieving as a form of solidarity.

One of the women who joined us was Alison Burton. Alison is Errol Graham's daughter-in-law. Errol who 'never forgot Christmas, or a birthday' and went everywhere on his bike – 'you would never catch Errol on a bus; taxi? – forget it', died from starvation after having his benefits cut off. When he died he weighed just 4½ stone. Errol was unable to engage with the DWP's processes due to lack of accommodation for his mental health issues. The DWP failed to alert any other service, or his family, to the fact that Errol wasn't engaging despite them holding a red flag against his name on their system.

This cost him his life. Red flags refer to a way the DWP is supposed to alert its staff to vulnerable clients, including people who are suicidal. There was also a red flag against the name of Jodey Whiting, who had, on numerous occasions, told the DWP, and ATOS (later replaced by the US outsourcing giant Maximus), that she was suicidal because she was in so much pain. Alison feels Errol 'was subject to a lot of inequalities; and it was down to his Black heritage and his Rastafarian beliefs'. Alison says:

> I think justice, for me, is just changing the way in which the system treats people. We need to find a long-term solution to these issues; and I think that's built off the back of people like us – you know – who have *lived* that experience.

There are lots of ways to try and change systems. Sometimes we try to achieve system change by using the system itself, that is, seeking justice through state machinery (inquests, appeals, second inquests, inquiries) and by campaigning. For some, the decision about whether or not to campaign is a hard one, and not one that most of us are prepared for or knowledgeable about when it happens. Others, like Joy, talk about finding themselves campaigning without even knowing it at first. Joy Dove has fought tirelessly for her daughter through the 'Justice for Jodey' campaign. Joy laughed when she told me that at first 'I didn't *realise* I was on a campaign, to tell you the truth. I was just doing *me*, and everything seemed to fit together.'

The seeds of campaigning can also be sown before a loved one is killed. Philippa Day had discussed her likely death due to how she was being treated as part of her Personal Independence Payment (PIP) claim and provided instructions for her sister Imogen to campaign. Imogen told me 'before she died, she instructed me that if this was to happen to her, that I had to keep going, and I had to make sure that it wouldn't happen again'. Philippa's death was covered extensively in the media, both due to the length of the inquest (eleven days) and the discovery of a suicide note that directly implicated the

DWP in Philippa's decision to end her life. In the note, Philippa wrote about how having her benefits severely cut had forced her to get payday loans which had 'escalated into a hole I can never get out of'. During Philippa Day's pre-inquest reviews it was strongly *implied* by the DWP's legal team that Imogen (Philippa's sister) had written Philippa's suicide note for political gain.

Imogen also talked to me about her family's struggle to both maintain Philippa's right to privacy and the 'important responsibility that we've got as family members to make sure that this doesn't happen again'. Campaigning may involve publicity surrounding a loved one's death, including the nature of their death, their medical history, their struggles, the ways they were abandoned by the state and demonised. This creates additional tensions in navigating publicity and privacy, and how to hold our loved ones sacred while campaigning. Alison Burton talks about how their search for justice included breaching Errol's privacy. For Alison, this was a necessary sacrifice to ensure others got to live:

> It was a really hard decision to make because you've gotta weigh-up the-pros-and-the-cons, really: you've gotta weigh-up the impact of trying to protect the privacy of your loved-one, who you've lost; your mental capacity to deal with the journey ahead – that ripple-effect is gonna be on everybody else as well. There's a lot of decision-making involved, a lot of important decisions to make, before you start that journey, first-and-foremost. It is a challenge; but I think, ultimately, me-personally was met with, 'It's the right thing to do.' I can face those burdens if it means that somebody else will get to *live* in the future; someone else in Errol's position will get to live. I think it really powers my journey to change the system, to make reasonable adjustments for people with mental-health, that's the utmost-important thing for me.

Going public also opens up those who have been killed and their families to further demonisation – where the public and media repeat the dehumanising 'scrounger' narrative, or question the so-called 'deservingness' of people who have died. Sometimes they blame people's families – claiming they should have done something. And sometimes people say we're 'politicising' people's deaths (as if they're not already political). Is it any wonder then that some families (as we saw in Chapter 3) feel they have to paint their loved one as a 'perfect victim' (a hardworker, not a 'scrounger') to legitimise their grief, for their loved one to be publicly mourned? How do you navigate trying to keep your loved one sacred but without falling into the trap of feeling forced into portraying them as a 'perfect victim' – without talking about them as deserving while suggesting others are not, and without saving them from – but at the same time reproducing – the stories, ideologies and logics that killed them?

Little wonder then that there are sometimes family tensions in campaigning – especially when family members and friends don't always agree about campaigning – some might want to campaign while others feel less keen. Anna Susianta, whose 17-year-old son, Komang Jack Susianta, was killed by police in 2015 while experiencing a mental health crisis, explained that, 'When Jack died, I felt it was really important that (whatever I did, and my response) I would always keep the rest of my family in mind; and what I wanted to do, they didn't really want to go with me on. So I've been careful to also try to look after myself through it.' For Anna, this meant choosing not to campaign specifically for Jack, but to be part of many campaigns for others.

PREVENTING FUTURE DEATHS

One day, over Zoom, I found myself chatting to Imogen Day and John Pring (two people without whom the Deaths by Welfare project wouldn't exist). There was a lot of mutual love and joy on a call where we mostly talked about death and about the reviews that the DWP carry out when it considers there has been what it calls the 'death of a customer' (something we explored in Chapter 1). Imogen talked about how both she and her sister Philippa (Pip) knew that welfare state violence was systemic, not individual, and so after Pip died Imogen 'spent a really long time researching; discovered that Internal Process Reviews existed, but were not published', and she found a lot of this from Disability News Service. We traced in Chapter 1 John Pring's work to find out about the internal investigations carried out by the DWP into people's deaths, and how redacted versions of these Internal Process Reviews contain hundreds of recommendations, including repeated warnings that policies were potentially life-threatening, and yet most families have never seen them. The labour that John, and other disabled people, have put into unearthing this, and the way the government has weaponised delay and bureaucracy, led John and I to think and write together on how welfare state violence is often slow and bureaucratic.[6] John Pring fought alongside Imogen and her family for the Internal Process Review into Philippa's death to be released. Imogen told us:

> I didn't have legal representation for the first Pre-Inquest Review; me and my parents were having a little bit of a disagreement about whether or not it was needed. During the first Pre-Inquest Review with our wonderful coroner, Mr. Clow, I let him know that there were Internal Process Reviews, and that I wanted to see it. And I don't think that the DWP's legal team were expecting: a) me to be aware of it; and b) to be quite so openly hostile.

The pre-inquest review led Imogen and her family to get legal representation (from the firm Leigh Day, who have represented a number of families bereaved to welfare state violence). Imogen describes the whole pre-inquest/inquest process as

> utterly exhausting, because not only do you have the obvious grief, and heartbreak, and turmoil over losing a loved one, there's also this impossible anger at the fact that: a) it was preventable; and b) that it's a systemic issue that the DWP are more than aware of, and have made very small attempts to correct.

It's systemic and it's preventable – what do we do with this impossible anger? It's no wonder that Imogen says perhaps there can be no justice for the magnitude of this anger and grief. As Imogen speaks she says the word 'exhausting' many times:

> It was an incredibly long process: at least nine months of requesting the IPR [Internal Process Review]; asking for it; informing the coroner that we needed it, and that he needed to see it as well. And it was just absolutely fascinating when the coroner would ask for these different reports, these different things: the DWP lawyers would, firstly, deny their existence; and secondly, say that they couldn't release them without express consent from the much-higher-ups. The entire inquest felt like they were trying to gatekeep what information: a) we as a family could have; and b) what the coroner could have, even though of all the legal rights that he has to see everything. It felt like the DWP's legal team was just desperate to keep all of the information themselves, and not distribute it. It felt like a battle from-start-to-finish.

As I listened to Imogen, I could sense the feel of the inquest, its texture – a battle, a withholding. She said, 'It was so emotive; there were so many different feelings that were floating around for, I think, everybody. We all had huge trigger-points of, "This is horrific." And yet, we had to do it; we had to show up for her.'

And they did show up for Philippa. John points out that Imogen and her family 'opened the doors for other families' because they were the first family to get hold of an Internal Process Review into a loved one's death – seven years after it had become public knowledge that these largely secretive reviews even existed. I asked Imogen if it made any difference to see the Internal Process Review. And she said: 'it was painful, but necessary for my own grief-recovery. Because we as a family, we needed to know that there was nothing else we could have done; we needed to know that there were these external forces at play here.'

For Imogen, seeing this review eased ongoing fears that she had failed her sister:

> Having the Internal Process Review silenced my night-time questions, right before I was going to sleep, of, 'Could I have done more?' 'What would have happened if I had done ...?' And I really feel for families that still, obviously, have those going-to-sleep anxieties, and don't have answers ... It made it incredibly clear that we as a family had done everything that we could have done, and that it was a governmental system that had let her down.

This, according to Imogen, isn't justice. But having your nighttime worries, the anxieties that flicker across our eyelids as sleep eludes us, eased is still something, we all need to sleep. Most families never get to see these Internal Process Reviews. During Philippa's inquest, the DWP and Capita (a private sector contractor paid to carry out disability assessments, which we met in Chapter 2) were found to have made 28 'mistakes' in the handling of her Personal Independence Payment claim. These 'mistakes' included losing her application, admin errors and refusal to give her a home assessment (Pip never left the house without support). Imogen says, 'each one of those mistakes took something from my sister, it stole a piece of her every single time. When she received a final letter from the DWP informing her she wasn't entitled to a home assessment and would need to attend the assessment centre, it destroyed her.' Not long after, Imogen went round to Philippa's house and found her unconscious with the DWP letter beside her on the bed. 'She wanted to make it incredibly clear to all of us that it was the DWP and Capita that led her to make that decision.'

To stop other people dying like their loved ones, and to change the system so others get to live, is what drives many families. Errol Graham's daughter-in-law, Alison Burton, talks about being able to face the burden of campaigning 'if someone else in Errol's position will get to live'. Seni Lewis died on 4 September 2010 after being restrained by up to eleven police officers while he was seeking help as a voluntary patient at the Bethlem Royal Hospital in Croydon). His mother, Ajibola Lewis, shared that:

> because I can put all my energy into campaigning, and doing things for others; making life safer for others. And in a way, it's helped me deal with the grief. It does! It keeps me focused – 'I don't want anybody to die the way Seni died.' But others have died after; I thought [in] 2010, *nobody* would die the way he'd died, but there have been *so* many deaths after.

We have all been taught and conditioned to feel validated by state recognition – so we seek it, we campaign for it, we feel the need for it in our bodies, we celebrate it when we get it, and then what happens? Often this recognition and validation doesn't lead to systems changing, it doesn't rip out harmful systems at their roots or slowly defund them to create systems that validate our lives and build worlds we want to live in. The systems carry on, maybe with tiny tweaks, and people continue to die and to be killed, in the same ways. Despite the inquest naming 28 'mistakes' made by Capita in the handling of Philippa's Personal Independence Payment claim, Capita still exists. In 2023, the DWP awarded Capita two five-year contracts to carry out assessments of disabled people, one across Wales and the Midlands (£450 million), and the other in Northern Ireland (£110 million).[7]

If justice is the transformation of the systems that disable and kill us then we've never tasted justice, only felt the yearning for it – the ache. On the blog Psychiatry is Driving me Mad, Wren Aves, who describes themself as an autistic, queer, abuse survivor in the UK, and who has experience of the mental health system, wrote about attending 'the inquest of a friend who died by suicide following negligence and abuse from mental health services', reminding us that 'justice won't be found in the coroner's court'. Wren writes:

> Our friends, our family, our peers, ourselves ... we are worth more than the ruling of an inquest. We deserve more than a line of text which attributes some responsibility for our death to the services commissioned to help keep us alive. For the majority of us, all we might expect is that the coroner points out the lack of a care plan, or a missed opportunity to offer support, but ultimately lays no responsibility at anyone's feet, demands no changes be made. That is not justice, and the fact that so many of us think it is, shows the extent of the disempowerment, humiliation, and dehumanisation we have faced from mental health services over the years. For many of our community who have died, their inquest has been the only forum they have ever had for truth, yet so frequently, it barely scratches the surface ... Justice would be actual changes put in place before the person died. Justice would be our lives being valued over mental health service budgets. All I can think is, if inquests really are forums for justice, if change truly arises from them, why do the same failures keep occurring? Why aren't services listening? Why do we keep dying? It's not good enough. We need something more. We deserve something more.[8]

Can we imagine what more we deserve? Learning from those who know more about inquests than they would like, it seems that inquests are a way for some families to feel they are 'showing up' for their loved ones, and a route to get the DWP named and recognised as contributing to people's deaths. This is huge, and it tends to be achieved through the language of failings and mistakes, which takes us into tweaks to the system, concentrates our energy on reforms rather than the transformation often needed to meet families hopes and demands that no one else dies in the way their loved ones did. Philippa's sister, Imogen, talks about how the inquest brought some healing, while also holding the need for abolition of the DWP through the creation of something different – co-developed with disabled people.

JUSTICE THROUGH PUBLIC INQUIRIES

Disability News Service, alongside many disabled people, bereaved families and some MPs, has been calling for a public (statutory) inquiry into 'DWP deaths'. A statutory inquiry in the UK is an independent investigation established by a government minister under the Inquiries Act 2005 to examine events of major public concern.[9] Unlike non-statutory inquiries, they have legal powers to compel witnesses to give evidence under oath and produce documents; however, they are not able to determine liability – meaning they have no power to determine and rule on people's civil or criminal liability. Inquiries operate around finding facts and fault, and making recommendations to prevent the same harms from happening again.

Joy Dove, Jody Whiting's mother, has been calling for an inquiry for more than five years, telling Disability News Service, 'We need to find out who was responsible for what happened. There have been inquiries into Hillsborough and the Post Office scandal. Now we need an inquiry into the deaths caused by DWP.'[10] Mark Harrison, from the Reclaiming Our Futures Alliance, an alliance of Disabled People and their Organisations (DPOs) in England, says an inquiry is 'essential if we are to understand what has gone so horribly wrong in the DWP that has led to so many unnecessary benefit-related deaths'.[11]

It is important to honour the fight for a public inquiry if that is what many people want. And we can also ask ourselves why we want this – what do we think it will do? Learning from others who have gone through similar processes helps us to prepare ourselves for what an inquiry might feel like, the kind of impact we might expect, what it might enable for us, and the kinds of disappointments we might feel. Many people I've spoken about this with talked about those who died in Grenfell Tower, on the night of 14 June in 2017. Often talked about as a tragedy, we now know that the fire that ravaged the tower and killed 72 people, including many global majority and disabled people, was far from an accident. The person chairing the Grenfell

Tower Inquiry, cited by the BBC, 'concluded that a failure to act on repeated warnings about the dangers of combustible materials was a key cause of the disaster'.[12] And despite this and all the damning evidence, where is justice for those who died and those left displaced? And then there's the parties we now know politicians were having while Covid ravaged and disabled our communities. Has the Covid inquiry brought us justice?

One disabled activist who needs to remain anonymous explained that

> this country loves a good inquiry, but inquiries rarely ever instigate change. We investigate and sometimes the investigations are politically skewed to benefit the hopes and aspirations of the ruling class ... If we turn to the state to have a conscience – we'll be holding our breath for a long time.

We can learn from others that we might not feel a sense of justice through an inquiry but we might get other things from it, such as access to documents currently kept secret. Preparing ourselves for this means we could imagine an inquiry as one way of moving towards justice but possibly not an end in itself, meaning our strategies towards justice need to plan beyond an inquiry. One way to do this together could be for us to ask each other and honestly reflect on what we might want from an inquiry – what are the needs we think an inquiry will meet? Access to documents, yes? Justice? Maybe not. Could we also find what we're longing for elsewhere, in other methods?

DISABILITY RIGHTS, DISABILITY JUSTICE

Many people use the law and legal reform strategically in a context of fighting for deeper transformation beyond the law. Yet this became extremely difficult when legal aid was cut in 2012, which according to the *Guardian* led to a 99 per cent drop (between 2011 and 2017) in disabled people being granted legal aid to challenge welfare decisions, and basically denying them the right to legal representation in many benefits cases.[13] Ellen Clifford (from DPAC) showed us what this can achieve when she faced the DWP in court in December 2024 over the 'consultation' (it needs quote marks because as many disabled people have pointed out it was a sham) it carried out with disabled people in 2023 about the proposed changes to the Work Capability Assessment, first proposed by the Conservatives and continued under Labour. Ellen explains that: 'This is a life-or-death issue. One internal DWP estimate (which we only know about because of my legal challenge) indicates that 100,000 disabled people who are classed as highly vulnerable would be pushed into absolute poverty by 2026/27, as a result of the types of cuts they proposed in this consultation.'[14]

The DWP presented these changes as a way to support disabled people into work, when in fact cost savings were the 'primary rationale' for the proposals. It was this that the High Court ruled was unlawful. For Ellen Clifford, there is a bigger message to the government beyond this ruling – that 'measures to help the economy should not require the impoverishment and suffering of hundreds of thousands of Disabled people'. This is also a false economy – that moves costs of welfare into other areas such as the NHS, and the DWP itself acknowledged that reducing people's incomes would likely result in deterioration of people's health and mental health. Here Ellen is using the law to try to stop reforms that will impoverish and harm disabled people in the here and now. Ellen talked to me about lobbying and how we also need to 'make sure that we still have time and space to reflect upon our wider analysis and keep things in perspective, rather than throw everything in with the idea that we'll get this legislation, and then it's going to be fine, or we need more of us in Parliament, and then disabled people will be less oppressed'. For Ellen, 'radical campaigners' (which for her means having an anti-capitalistic analysis) 'have more of an understanding of the limitations of the current system and how far we are able to create real change through the system that we have now, and so maybe less willing to put all our effort into that'. Ellen talked about issues with 'fighting for rights rather than justice in the sense of rights within the status quo'.

Rights is a sticky subject. Legal interventions and rights can be tactics towards larger transformation but they won't necessarily get us there alone. A big part of this, as I have learned from Dean Spade (founder of the Sylvia Rivera Law Project in New York City), is because rights-based models assume a protective relationship with the nation state, and appeal to that protection. This can overlook the experiences of groups who are regularly subject to state violence, including many of the people we have met throughout this book – disabled, racialised, poor and displaced people. Dean Spade also says something else that has stayed with me, that 'we must stop believing that what the law says about itself is true and that what the law says about us is what matters. Law reform and an investment in winning "rights" has proven to legitimize and shore up the very arrangements that produce the harm we seek to eradicate.'[15] This means that not only are systems designed to be complex and therefore hard to hold to account but the law itself shares the same violent colonial white supremacist ableist foundations as the state. Our very idea of justice (or at least the legal version of justice that we've been told is justice) is built upon, produces and requires the exclusion and abandonment of certain groups.

In the book *States of Injury*, political theorist Wendy Brown shows that in liberal capitalism rights often mean the conversion of 'social problems into matters of individualised, dehistoricised injury and entitlement, into matters in which there is no harm if there is no agent and no tangibly violated subject'.[16] The system sets us up to seek recognition and redress for our specific injuries rather than putting our energies into dismantling harmful systems at their roots. In welfare activism, this translates into putting our limited energies into legal representation or individual cases for tribunal to appeal decisions (all of which can be life-saving) without also embedding this in wider analysis of, and building power against, welfare state violence.

In the USA, Leah Lakshmi Piepzna-Samarasinha (a sick, disabled and autistic Disability Justice writer and educator) points out that alongside many wins, the disability rights movement often has a focus on single issues, a predominantly white male leadership, and tends to centre people who could achieve access through a legal/rights-based framework. A common experience for many disabled Black people, Indigenous people and people of colour in the USA (and for many Black people and people of colour I've spoken with in the UK too) was/is racism – in institutions and also in social movements, including disabled people's movements. It was in this context, in the USA, in 2005, that disabled queers and activists of colour, including Patty Berne and Mia Mingus, two queer disabled women of colour, began discussing a second wave of disability rights. This gave birth to Disability Justice as a 'movement-building framework', and to Sins Invalid, a 'disability justice-based movement building and performance project', both of which centre 'the lives and leadership of disabled Black, Indigenous and people of color and/or queer, trans, Two Spirit and gender non-conforming people'.[17] Disability Justice is led by those most impacted, understands that ableism is deeply entwined with white supremacy, heteropatriarchy, colonial conquest and capitalist domination, and is explicitly anti-capitalist. These make up three of the ten principles guiding Disability Justice, as created by Sins Invalid.[18] The others are a commitment to cross-movement and cross-disability solidarity (e.g., Disability Justice is deeply and explicitly aligned with Palestinian liberation), recognising people's wholeness (that we have worth outside of productivity and work), valuing sustainability and pace and interdependence, and practising collective access and collective liberation – we leave no body-mind behind. Talila A. Lewis, a Black queer disabled abolitionist and community lawyer in the USA, explains that while 'disability rights seeks to change social conditions for some disabled people via law and policy, Disability Justice moves beyond law and policy. It seeks to radically transform social conditions and norms in order to affirm and support all people's inherent right to live and thrive."[19]

Because it comes out of the experiences and analysis of Black people, Indigenous people and people of colour, Disability Justice understands that 'state solutions inevitably extend into further control over lives', and that we need to 'meet each others' needs as we build toward liberation'.[20] Even if we don't always call it by that name, so many disabled people practise disability justice in real time – checking in on each other, cooking meals for each other, lending equipment, sharing knowledge, supporting each other to fill out forms, sharing joy. Despite the current horrors, this is fertile soil still to grow our imaginations and practices together – to imagine and practise justice beyond/away from/despite/against the state.

REPARATIVE JUSTICE

'We talk about reparations in other contexts', a disabled activist who chose to remain anonymous explained to me, 'by recognizing there is a real psychological debt owed to the people experiencing these conditions in just explicitly naming the violence is they've been put on for so long'. The demand for reparations comes from movements led by Black people, Indigenous people and people of colour, and colonised peoples. The National Coalition of Blacks for Reparations in America (N'COBRA) have been demanding reparations for African descendants in the USA since they began in 1987, defining reparations as a process to repair, heal and restore a people injured based on their group identity and in violation of fundamental human rights.[21] Reparations are also recognised in international law (not that this should make it any more legitimate!) as a legal framework for providing relief to people who have experienced gross human rights violations. The United Nations has guidelines (adopted in 2005) for the five stages of reparations: restitution (giving back what was taken), compensation (paying people for the harm done), rehabilitation (providing support for healing), satisfaction (acknowledging harm), and guarantees of non-repetition (making sure the harm doesn't happen again).[22]

This currently feels very far away from where the UK government is at in terms of reparations for its role in the transatlantic slave trade – for which it refuses to pay reparations, despite campaigning and blueprints for what this might look like, from Runnymede Trust (an independent racial justice think tank) and others.[23] Though, in fact, the UK has been paying reparations since the abolition of slavery in 1834 – but to the enslavers, not to the people enslaved. When slavery was abolished, the government paid £20 million (worth around £100 billion today) to enslavers to compensate for the human beings who were considered to be their property. UK taxpayers were paying this off until 2015, while simultaneously being told to feel angry about so-called 'benefit fraud'. Can we even begin to imagine what that £100 billion could have been spent on instead?

Thinking globally also demands reckoning with the true costs of our welfare state to the welfare of those who were forced to fund it through colonial extraction – the people who paid for our welfare with their lives? What would reparations look like for the long lineage of welfare state violence – harm that goes back to the roots of the welfare state and poor relief? And what could reparations, and reparative justice, be like for welfare state violence happening now? This is something that people are fighting for right now. Black Families Love & Unite (who work in the Bronx, New York) reimagine and create alternatives to the family policing system (i.e., the child welfare system) 'that empowers and protects the integrity and sanctity of our families and communities'.[24] We've learned from legal scholar Dorothy Roberts how the family policing system in the USA is designed with the same carceral logic as policing and prisons, and built on the destruction of Black families.[25]

In terms of what reparative justice calls 'satisfaction' and 'guarantees of non-repetition', there is huge demand from disabled people and bereaved families for accountability, which Imogen Day says, for her, means 'an apology, an explanation, and proven change'. Jay Watts, a disabled activist and consultant clinical psychologist, reminds us that justice and healing are deeply connected:

> Healing these wounds requires more than silence or superficial reforms. It begins only when three conditions are met: a firm assurance that this violence ends now, a recognition of the backcloth of ideas and policies that gave rise to it, and a public acknowledgment of the injury and subjugation inflicted.[26]

Black Families Love & Unite see reparations as part of wider 'world-making projects', says Imani Worthy, the co-founder, which means demanding 'commitment to acknowledge and apologize for harms, structural changes to prevent future harms and investment into communities historically impacted'.[27] This also means demanding government divestment from the family policing system and reinvestment in meaningful opportunities to heal trauma, to build 'community – and community power – in the face of a system that depends on families' isolation' and shame.[28] If we divest from and defund the DWP, just think of what we could invest in instead. In a report and zine created with families, Black Families Love & Unite give concrete examples of reparations for those harmed though the family policing system: restitution through family reunification, universal basic income, job support; compensation through direct payments alongside systemic change and neighbourhood investment; rehabilitation through holistic care and trauma-informed services; satisfaction through acknowledging harm and accepting responsibility; and guarantees of non-repetition through community-led harm responses, restoring family autonomy and creating spaces for healing.[29]

We often talk about justice as something we fight for, (never) get, tenuously possess, something that escapes and eludes us, something that doesn't exist. But justice is a practice – something we *do* and not something we have – not a destination, not a possession. What if in those moments where people come together, and realise they are not the only ones, and affirm each other's dignity, safety and belonging, and witness each other in their full messy humanity – what if that is a rehearsal of justice, prefigured in those moments of solidarity and connection? This requires us to learn how to create, craft and cultivate the conditions and capacities for these rehearsals and practices of justice. Because, as a disabled activist friend of mine says, 'justice and liberation go hand in hand'.

7

Abolition

ROOTING RADICAL IMAGINATION

'For us to relax in this country', Rick Burgess (from Manchester DPAC) explained to me, 'we would need to see the end of the Department for Work and Pensions ... For the victims and survivors to feel justice, the ideal would be that the DWP is abolished.' That disabled people need to see the abolition of a government department in order to relax speaks volumes to the fear, surveillance, policing and bureaucratic terror that go under the name of 'welfare', and the energy it takes to navigate and resist. Constant job searches, assessments, appeals, meeting conditions, navigating sanctions, always at the edge of (and sometimes totally submerged by) destitution – our current systems are made to prevent disabled people from being able to relax. This is a system that has been designed to make you so on edge that to relax becomes revolutionary.

Rick is far from the only person who wants to see the abolition of the DWP. Imogen Day, who learned about welfare state violence through her sister Pip's experiences and later her suicide, told me without hesitation that

> for me, accountability means an apology, an explanation, and proven change; and I think they've [the DWP] failed on all three fronts. This issue comes from the top down. And I think it's incredibly unlikely, but I would like to see the entirety of the DWP demolished and built

> back up from scratch using a model of co-production, and involving disabled people, and involving claimants, in what they would like the system to look like.

Abolishing the DWP is on the tip of our tongues. The DWP has destroyed so many people's lives, and now so many people want to see it destroyed. Rick Burgess wants 'a state system that is there to help you not fucking murder you'. See how low the bar has become for many people after years of the psychic toll of routine and systemic dehumanisation. This numbs our imaginations – making it, as one disabled activist explained to me 'so hard to reimagine when we're so surrounded by the current way it works'.

In one of many chats with Farzana Khan, co-founder and director of Healing Justice Ldn, we talked about imagination because she knows I find it hard. Need a critique? I'm your person. Need to dream of a new world? You'll find me hiding under the duvet. But she reminded me that I do imagine and build things all the time, and I needed reminding. We're all imagining and building, prefiguring the world we want, and it's okay if we start small, and it's also okay if we dare to dream big. Farzana says the work of visioning and dreaming is different from fantasy – which can feel disempowering in its impossibility. Rather than starting with 'What do we have now, and how can we make it better?', prison-industrial complex abolitionist Mariame Kaba invites us to ask 'What can we imagine for ourselves and the world?' She knows this is tough:

> When we set about trying to transform society, we must remember that we ourselves will also need to transform. Our imagination of what a different world can be is limited. We are deeply entangled in the very systems we are organizing to change ... White supremacy, misogyny, ableism, classism, homophobia, and transphobia exist everywhere. We have all so thoroughly internalised these logics of oppression that if oppression were to end tomorrow, we would be likely to reproduce previous structures.[1]

If we share Imogen's vision to 'see the entirety of the DWP demolished and built back up from scratch', how can we make sure we wouldn't end up re-building something just as violent as the DWP but with a different name? It's hard to imagine life-affirming welfare if all we've known is deaths by welfare. The current DWP uses up resources, exhausts and distracts us, and pushes out alternatives. We get trapped into campaigning for conditionality and sanctions not to be applied to some groups, rather than for a welfare system with no sanctions. Or for some groups to be seen as deserving, while others are not. When I asked Ellen Clifford about reimagining welfare, she told me:

> I think what worries me, and probably what stops me dreaming so big, is I'm just very aware of level of existential threat to disabled people ... I mean, you've got kind of genetic screening on one end and assisted suicide at the other. I'm not even just talking about support to leave the house ... but also people don't have support to be online or check your emails, then you can't even do remote activism. Goes back to a society where people are talking about us without us, and we're not involved in the conversation because we literally can't be. That frightens me a lot.

Abolition can feel tricky in relation to welfare – especially when successive governments have slowly and systematically destroyed the welfare state. But we can all hold complexity, and many things can be true at once. It can be true that welfare is mobilised as a site of extractive abandonment, situated in a long lineage of welfare state violence, while also being true that some people have benefited from welfare, albeit often at the expense of others. Prison-industrial complex abolition, as Ruth Wilson Gilmore reminds us, is not all about destruction and resistance – it's in the realm of transformation, presence, rehearsal.[2] It's about getting at root causes and cultivating conditions that make things like punitive welfare and prisons obsolete. It's a vision that we translate into strategy – allowing us to explore the kinds of actions that bring us closer to the welfare we want, to life-affirming systems that foster care, community, dignity, justice and freedom. In many ways, the social model of disability is abolitionist, because although it is sometimes confined to disability rights, Ellen Clifford reminds us that it was created in the 1970s as a foundation for collective action towards societal transformation.[3]

I keep returning to prison-industrial complex abolitionists Mariame Kaba and Andrea J. Ritchie when they say, about policing and criminal punishment, 'we can't claim the system must be dismantled because it is a danger to Black lives and at the same time legitimize it by turning to it for justice'.[4] We also need to come to terms with our call to abolish a system that threatens the lives of disabled people, poor people, displaced people, racialised people (and many others) while we also legitimise it by appealing to it for justice. Andrea J. Ritchie puts it another way: 'we can't continue to organise in ways that replicate and legitimise the systems we are seeking to dismantle'.[5]

Yet the more pressure we face, engulfed as we are in polycrisis – climate catastrophe, rising power of the far right, nationalism, fascism, continued attacks on disabled people, escalating poverty and extreme wealth (and so much more) – the more likely we are to cling to familiar strategies and old tactics, to not feel safe enough to experiment. What are we clinging to? We explored this when we thought about our practices of evidencing – documenting dossiers of harms to appeal to a government that is killing people. Perhaps under pressure we sometimes cling to the idea that we need more rules, more oversight, and that this will translate into 'safeguarding'. But we also know that more rules often don't mean fewer deaths – decades of resistance to police murders of Black people show us this. Yes, we can do better at documenting harm, we can require people to log the harm they do, to record it, we can turn that into statistics and compare them every year, but often these things don't stop the violence – they just document it better. The data is better, and people keep dying. We slip into focusing on 'flaws' in a system, which channels our energy into correcting and reforming a system designed to harm disabled (and many other) people. Tweaks and reforms in parts of the system will never be enough when the underlying logic and profitability of these systems create conditions that devalue people and make certain lives unliveable. We cling to a shape of resistance – of being against, not for – and find it painful and almost impossible to unfurl towards something new. We're not the only ones – this is why USA-based author and activist Grace Lee Boggs (2011) invited us to go 'beyond protest organizing' into 'visionary organizing', which 'begins by creating images and stories of the future that help us imagine and create alternatives to the existing system'.[6] Rick Burgess says, 'we need to start drawing up the future – join with other groups for wider liberation for all of our communities'. Imagination and abolition aren't only about the future though, they are often grounded and material. As a disabled activist who needs to remain anonymous told me, 'abolition is a constant enactment of what we want – here and now. A vision of the future, transported to the present.' They explained:

> recognizing all the organizing people are doing around welfare state violence, and other violences, is not just to transform the world in a hypothetical future but that it's materially changing the world in the here and now. We don't speak of abolition as just a horizon but abolition as the land we want to walk on here and now, the homes we want to occupy and share with others, the food we want to break with other people. Abolition is the constant enactment of what we want and how we want this world to be in relationship to each other and to the world itself.

This reminds me of what Nila Gupta talks about as hopeful in the wider surveillant context of the panopticon of the DWP:

> But my one hope is that I see so many grassroots people/groups/organisations/communities doing mutual aid, advocacy, support, skill sharing etc. A lot of it is very informal and grassroots and it's

> amazing. So you get people on random forums putting hours into helpful/detailed/informed responses to questions. You get people sharing often traumatic details of the assessment process because they care about someone else going through the same thing. It's fucking amazing. But we shouldn't fucking be going through this shit in the first place.

@Benclaimant is one of these people. After his experience of being sanctioned, he turned to social media to share his experiences and to support people navigating the brutalities of the welfare system. Ben wants support and recognition for people who have lost their jobs, their benefits, their relationships, their homes,

> because really what they're doing is they're grieving. They've lost their entire lives and they're grieving about it. And I want that to be recognised. That's the sort of justice that I want to see happen … I don't believe in benefit sanctions at all. They should be gotten rid of straightaway. I mean, that would be justice. But really, I want to see places that you can go that support you in a holistic fashion.

This kind of mutual aid describes so much of the labour of disabled people and disabled welfare activists, who in helping people navigate a violent system are also prefiguring and practising the kind of world they want. Sick, disabled and autistic Disability Justice writer and educator, Leah Lakshmi Piepzna-Samarasinha talks about how 'like every kind of oppressed people, disabled people are geniuses of staying alive despite everything' through both formalised and low key mutual aid – dance parties on Zoom, groceries delivered, sharing mobility aids, and noticing, checking in, caring.[7] Ellen Clifford reminds me that in our activism and movement spaces

> it's also important to use humour or creativity. Because it's also a space where we're supporting each other, because we need to keep

> each other going. Peer support is really important, but I think it's also about celebrating who we are. Because society might not value us. We might be written off as benefit scroungers, but actually, we are creative. We've got a lot of resources. And I'm proud to be mad. I think we're brilliant.

Disabled transformative justice educator Mia Mingus calls this 'access intimacy' – when someone 'gets' your access needs, 'the way your body relaxes and opens up with someone when all your access needs are being met'.[8] People can and do leverage resources to create the conditions to cultivate mutual aid. Ellen Clifford talks about how DPAC carefully plans 'strategies of mutual care in advance of its protests', including financial support for transport, physical assistance, British Sign Language (BSL):

> The way that we organise a protest is always collectively and it's very inclusive and accessible. So, we've almost got a microcosm of what future society could look like, because we have to be very interdependent and we work together.[9]

This reminds me of what adrienne maree brown calls 'emergent strategy', that 'what we practice at a small scale sets the patterns for the whole system'.[10] And of Andrea J. Ritchie, who talks about 'creating the future in the present, building the world we long for in every interaction'.[11] This is to prefigure – imagine and practise – ways of being that refuse abandonment, and affirm life. Writing about DPAC's prefigurative politics of protest, Debbie Humphry tracks how

> from the inter-dependent mutual support during street actions to developing user-led organisational practices … DPAC's embodied, messy, undecided small-scale actions thus produce a prefigurative 'worldmaking' politics that opens up and constitutes possibilities for post-capitalist futures at wider scales … that privileges care over

competition, collectivism over individualism and reproduction over production.[12]

When we were designing our Deaths by Welfare online timeline with Arjun Harrison-Mann (from the radical access organisation Access, Power, Visibility collective), he told me about his work, in solidarity with DPAC and rooted in Disability Justice, exploring 'open source and DIY approaches to making protest accessible'. What he calls 'Proxy Protest' is about subverting 'everyday technologies – mobile phones / power banks / video calling software – in order to connect those at protests with people unable to be physically present in protest spaces, allowing protesters to become proxies for those connecting remotely'.[13] This also included livestreaming remote protesters into the space 'to move and protest in tandem with each other', using on the ground British Sign Language, Audio Description and Live Subtitling, provided by the community onsite at the protest – through a network of interconnected mobile devices. This taps into a practice of collective access that disabled people have honed over decades of direct action.

We heard earlier from families bereaved to state violence – how they cultivate practices of grief, witnessing, solidarity, care by finding each other, leaning on each other for strength, feeling understood, having people to call, knowing you're not alone. Their refusal to mourn only in private – and instead to grieve together, publicly, for the people we're told don't matter, would have died anyway, deserved it, had no value – is our rebellion and our healing. This rebellious solidarity-through-grief also prefigures the worlds we want – whose foundations are built on interdependence and care. Rethinking and changing our relationship to dependency and deservingess, then, is key to radically reimagining welfare. It's in this way that DPAC and many other disabled people's organising and direct action practises interdependence, collective access, inherent dignity and worth – the ingredients of the kinds of worlds in which we could all thrive. So, how do we get there?

NON-REFORMIST REFORMS

No one needs to tell disabled people that reforms can be violent – much of the current hellscape of welfare has come cloaked in the words 'welfare reform'. Yet often we fight for tweaks to the system – sometimes because even those tweaks can be life-saving, while they also keep our demands small, and ultimately strengthen a system that is killing us. How do we discern between keeping people alive now through small changes, while also not making it harder for ourselves in the long run? Radical thinker André Gorz's writings are helpful here, and especially the idea of non-reformist reforms – changes that make a practical difference in the short term, while also building grassroots power towards larger radical transformations.[14] These reforms are not an end in themselves but are transitional – moving in the direction of revolution.

Prison-industrial complex abolitionists also have a lot to teach us about this. Mariame Kaba warns us that it's legitimate to be concerned that a given reform might end up reinforcing the system, but she cautions against falling into the trap of thinking 'we can't do anything until we overthrow the state', and instead, we can be strategic, backing 'reforms that don't make it harder for us to dismantle the systems we are trying to abolish ... That don't make it harder to create new things.'[15] If we know the system is unjust, then we shouldn't appeal to it for justice. If we know the system isn't broken, but is violent by design, then we shouldn't try to tinker at its edges to 'fix' it. A welfare system built on ableist and racist classification, deservingness, surveillance, punishment and the criminalisation of poverty can't somehow be reformed to make it anti-racist, anti-ableist, fair. We can also learn a lot here from disabled and chronically ill people who know about managing 'spoons' of energy, and practise pacing. Reformist reforms suck up our energies and give the illusion of change while funnelling more resources into violent systems. Instead, Mariame Kaba teaches us that we could be channelling 'our energies towards collective strategies that are more likely to be successful in delivering healing and transformation and to prevent future harms'.[16] It's not that all reforms are bad, it's that we need to be clear on how they will be used and for what – for example, oriented towards building power and cultivating dignity towards safer, more caring, life-affirming systems.

To be able to evaluate whether reforms are reformist or not, we need a collective vision for welfare that we're moving towards.[17] For prison-industrial complex abolitionists, that means a future free from policing, and that future would mean welfare without policing too. But what kind of welfare do we want? A system a bit like we have now but fairer, where welfare is in the hands of the state? Or a completely different way of doing things – where there is no direct replacement but multiple welfare infrastructures? Whatever form this might take, and we probably won't all agree, we need to practise welfare in ways that affirm dignity, safety and belonging, not dehumanise and shame people; that are abundant, not scarce; that grow connections, not isolation; that believe and affirm people, not distrust and surveil them. Knowing what we want welfare to be grounded in helps us to evaluate what small steps we might take to move towards this. When we can't decide whether to back new policies or not, or create or join campaigns, we can explore what kind of vision they're moving towards, asking: Does this affirm our dignity? Does it play into scripts of deservingness and burden, even in its resistance? Does it assume scarcity? Are people with lived experience at the heart of it? Does anyone get left behind, abandoned? Is it at anyone's expense?

DPAC's strategy, as Debbie Humphry learned from speaking with DPAC activists, is to integrate more 'reformist strategies into a longer-term anti-capitalist agenda'.[18] For Ellen Clifford, who is part of DPAC's steering group, it's DPAC's anti-capitalist grounding, which is also one of Sins Invalid's ten Principles of Disability Justice, that makes it radical. This means, as Ellen explained to Debbie Humphry, that just as with mutual aid, 'disabled people are not simply worthy of inclusion when theorising and constructing anti-capitalist and urban resistance, but are integral to and at the forefront of such struggles'.[19] Ellen explained to me that 'judicial review [where a judge reviews the lawfulness of a decision, action or failure to act] has been one of the only tools where we've managed to get wins against the government over the last ten years'. Yet Ellen also says that 'we know from history that the only way to achieve fundamental change is from the grassroots up. When we collectivise and forcefully demand the change that we want to see. And unfortunately, there aren't any easy or comfortable ways to do that.'

We also need to think about if the reforms we're working towards will ultimately strengthen the DWP, and the state. This is always the risk when sometimes well meaning people from the DWP ask to work with us or meet us. Do these conversations make meaningful change and generate some safety or are they used as a tick box for the government to claim they consulted disabled people? We always need a wide analysis of this work – we need our demands and vision to be bigger than the DWP alone. We've seen the success of activism that targets specific companies, such as DPAC's campaigning around Atos. And we've also seen how the government simply finds another company to outsource to, returning to business as usual. This means that if we target companies, we need to do this as part of a bigger demand to stop outsourcing, and completely rethink eligibility and disability assessments. If we focus our energies on demanding to abolish the DWP, what happens if the government abolishes it but in a way that helps them retain power and replicate violence under a different name?

We need to back reforms that move us away from welfare based on shame, deservingness, conditionality, punishment – we need to build the conditions that make welfare state violence obsolete. One step towards this, learning from prison-industrial complex abolitionists, could be to demand divestment of funds from the DWP and their investment into community-led work that supports people in the here and now, builds safer communities and builds power. If we defund the DWP, then we can channel those funds into community wealth stewardship, learning from lineages of Black- and women-of-colour-led mutual savings societies and solidarity economies.

Don't let anyone dismiss this as idealism. People are doing this right now. The brilliant Northern Police Monitoring Project mobilises around funding communities, not policing – grounding our imaginations in concrete ideas for how we could differently spend tax money currently funnelled to the police.[20] Healing Justice Ldn is part of communities led by global majority people collectively stewarding wealth, redistributing resources and reclaiming land as community owned (such as Baobab Foundation, Project Tallawah and the Good Ancestor Movement).[21] Civic Square is demonstrating this at neighbourhood scale in Birmingham by buying a building and co-building a neighbour public square as a way to democratise access to public space; organising street-based demonstrations, such as a neighbourhood trade school and retrofit house; and co-creating doughnut economics at a neighbourhood scale.[22] And as I write this book, Scotland has just passed a Community Wealth Building Bill to support investment in communities through the generation, circulation and retention of wealth in local and regional economies.[23]

This is about land just as much as it is about economies. That's because economic injustice has always also been about land – from the dividing up of land once collectively held – the commons – through the Enclosures Acts (from the 1600s to the 1900s). Those pushed from the land, whose lives had been tied to it, became the workforce industrial capitalism required, and punishment (including iterations of what we would now call police) enforced this change. And this logic of enclosure and extraction didn't stay at home. The wealth stolen through enslavement and colonial extraction built the UK, including the welfare state.

Ask anyone who navigates the world in a wheelchair; whose energy is limited; who masks in public, desperately trying to suppress a stim – disabled people know incredibly well what it's like to navigate a world not designed by or for their body-minds. Part of the power of the social model of disability has been to shift our understanding of disability from being an individual flaw to a product of ableist society – meaning disability is about social justice and spatial justice. As the industrial infrastructure of the cities we try to make a life in were being built in the 1800s, so were asylums and workhouses, meaning that many disabled people were institutionalised, put 'somewhere else' and excluded by design. That means we can't think about spatial justice without disability justice, and the analysis and wisdom that comes from being disabled by design, for capitalism to thrive. But people are trying to shift this by 'centering the lived knowledges and experiences of disabled people as a creative generator for design, rather than a problem to be solved' (such as DisOrdinary Architecture, based in the UK).[24]

Amahra Spence (founder of Black-led organisation MAIA, organiser of The Black Land & Spatial Justice Project, and of Land Black, a speculative design studio prototyping anti-carceral architectural and land-based strategies – indebted to the Land Back movement led by Indigenous peoples), writes that 'recognising that infrastructures of care, memory, imagination and futures require ground beneath them. From understanding that liberation cannot remain metaphorical. From insisting that repair must be rooted.'[25] Land, financial speculation, extreme wealth – these are things we rarely hear spoken of in welfare or health policies; yet think of how they shape our lives, how they distribute our life chances, how things could be different. Imagine welfare rooted in access to land, wealth and resources stewarded by community, cooperative housing, strong local food systems enabling food sovereignty – this is welfare too. Welfare justice is land justice, economic justice, racial justice, migrant justice, climate justice, disability justice, and on and on.

If our economic systems affirmed life, rather than producing premature death, what might welfare be like? Extending Ruth Wilson Gilmore's teachings on 'life-affirming' institutions and systems, Dark Matter Labs (which explores and builds alternative pathways for organising society and stewarding the shared planetary commons) is shifting towards life-ennobling economics. By this Dark Matter

Labs means that the 'structure and values of the economy must be in service to all forms of life (present, future, human, non-human and machine) providing a scaffold of care and respect'.[26] This rests on the fact that, yes, we need to shift to a new economy but we won't get there by 'using the mental models, tools or value systems of the current one' (remember the 'master's tools'). Dark Matter Labs invites us to dream about an economy 'rooted in the recognition of the full web of life', and not based on 'property, labour, extraction, private contracts, governance and monetary colonisation'.[27] What would 'welfare' be like within this kind of economy? Perhaps an even bigger question lurks here: Would we even need a 'welfare system' if we had an economic system rooted in abundance, not scarcity, not reliant on forcing us into waged labour, and not measuring our worth against work? To move towards these life-affirming economies asks us not only to imagine what we need to get there but also who we need to be to get there. Who would we need to be to embody life-affirming economic and welfare infrastructures, and to build systems that don't come from a place of scarcity and punishment – built on abundance, trust and dignity?

EMBODIED TRANSFORMATION AND OUR COLLECTIVE CAPACITY TO HEAL

Prison abolitionists, such as Andrea J. Ritchie, say that: 'Abolition starts with how you talk to yourself.'[28] How do we talk to ourselves about welfare? What do our inner voices say about eligibility, productivity, deservingness? I only really became properly conscious of how I talk to myself, that nasty inner voice, a few years ago – in doing the work around how I might unknowingly and unwillingly be perpetuating ableism. I realised that while I talk about resisting the obsession with work equalling worth, and with constant productivity, and embracing pace and rest, my inner voice, just at the times I want to relax, at times when I'm shattered or feeling very low, is right there asking: 'Why are you relaxing, you should be working', 'you're wasting time sitting here binge watching trashy shows where people get married having never seen each other before, you should be working/exercising/writing a diary/writing a book (writing this book!!!)/batch cooking kids' dinners for the week/cleaning/sorting out the enormous pile of clothes next to my bed that takes on an evil presence in the dark', blah blah blah.

We've internalised the scripts told to us on loop that some people are undeserving of supposedly scarce public resources. The state tells us this to justify decimating the social safety net, and to divert public resources, wealth and life chances away from certain people (often poor, racialised and/or disabled people). This story lives inside us, it shapes how we feel and perceive. Dean Spade, and others, calls this 'subjection' – how we come to know ourselves as subjects: 'the ways we understand our own bodies, the things we believe about ourselves and our relationships with other people and with institutions, and the ways we imagine change and transformation'.[29] How many times have you come across the word 'scrounger'? Day in, day out, in the headlines, in the by-lines, in between the lines. How many times have you encountered the message that your worth comes from paid work, and if you can't get up in the morning or spend the day feeling like shit, then it's your fault (think positive, do some yoga!) This story is ingrained in our muscle memory, it's a habit like brushing our teeth.

Paying attention to how we talk to ourselves, and to how what we say might reproduce the scripts that aren't part of the world we want to live in, opens up space to understand the connections between our inner voice, our relationships with others, and how our societies are structured. It means, as Andrea J. Ritchie teaches us, that abolition 'requires profound transformation within each of us, in how we see, experience and relate to the world around us, and of the societies we create and perpetuate'.[30] There is no quick fix to this, it'll take a long time – but can you allow yourself to dream of what it could be like to feel we deserve support and care, to live and thrive, whether we work or not, and not at the expense of someone else – just that everyone deserves this, full stop.

Community organiser and criminologist Sarah Lamble says that 'there's no point in dismantling prisons and police if we then act like cops and prison guards in our own communities'.[31] This is true of welfare too. There's no point in getting rid of the DWP if the welfare official, job coach, social worker, DWP, the voice of Iain Duncan Smith, still live in our heads; and no point if we continue to police ourselves and each other around eligibility, spy on our neighbours, report people through a benefits hotline, shame each other, call some people undeserving and feel undeserving ourselves. These forces that kill people – the ideas that some people's lives aren't worth living, that some people are deserving and others aren't, that work equals worth – live deep inside us, wired into our nervous systems. Nkem Ndefo (the founder of Lumos Transforms, who teaches embodied self-awareness for social justice) says, 'you cannot build a liberatory future with a nervous system calibrated for war'.[32] We can trace the calibration of our nervous systems over centuries of ideological warfare against poor people. This means changing the deep codes that have conditioned us as part of our embodied transformation – changing what we embody, what we practise, how we talk to ourselves. Without this deep embodied collective change, how can we refuse shame, refuse the devaluation of anyone's lives, refuse to equate worth with work or reduce a person's inherent value to how much they 'cost' the state? And how do we practise these refusals, with no perfect victims, and without any guarantee of redemption?

In her book *The Politics of Trauma: Somatics, Healing, and Social Justice*, Staci K. Haines (the founder of Generation FIVE, an organisation whose mission is to end the sexual abuse of children within five generations, through survivor leadership, community organising and public action) calls this embodied transformation:

> Embodied transformation enables us to respond instead of react, and supports our ability to organise, to innovate, and to creatively

> meet our times and our moment – individually and collectively. It is not just about 'feeling more' but growing our collective capacity to heal, lead, organise and love. While we are impacted and so often traumatised by the polarising conditions [and] we also have capacity to grow, transform, and cultivate ourselves and each other, on purpose.[33]

Throughout history, people have found and continue to find many beautiful ways to embody transformation. Dolly Sen talks about how 'through creativity I have unlearned my conditioning. I no longer believed the scripture of self-hatred, I turned those pages into canvases to make sense of the world, to protest pain, to uncloak the horrors hiding beneath.' Ellen Clifford experiences this in the collective access of protest: 'it's transformational. It's seeing people so empowered because they're being pushed down their whole lives and here they're kicking back a bit. And for me I especially love it when we're cheeky, when we're being challenging. It's really important for disabled people to feel that they're taking the piss out of the system.'

Embodied healing from trauma and oppression is important for us because, as we document at Healing Justice Ldn, it 'frees up our creativity, helps us hold complexity, and supports us in building relationships that can navigate disagreement, joy, learning, and change'.[34] Farzana Khan (the director of Healing Justice Ldn) also said something else (well, many other things) that reminded me of Rick Burgess, cited at the beginning of this chapter. She talked about what we need to cultivate our capacities to imagine, about generating safety in our bodies to give us the option to suspend over-identifying with our immediate reality, and to relax, play, get curious together, to imagine what we'd need for our communities to be safe, for our bodies to be free. This is part of training ourselves in generating safety to build our capacities to do the big imaginative work of designing new worlds. We need repair in order to reimagine. Farzana is teaching us that we can strategise embodied transformation – craft conditions to cultivate it. An example of how we're doing this at Healing Justice Ldn is through our Movement Medicine programme, which grows the capacities of grassroots movements to become sustainable and adaptive in contexts of oppression that rely on un-survivability. One of the many things that has surfaced in this work is the importance of understanding trauma as both individual and collective, meaning responsibility towards healing needs to be collectively and relationally held. Past and present harms live inside us and are encoded into our systems, seeping into our movement work, communities, activism, relationships, ways of being – we need spaces where we can connect to and transform how we embody harms. One way that Movement Medicine does this is through politicised somatics (working with and building on the work of Staci K. Haines).

In somatics, the body is a site of change, both personal and political. Somatics talks about muscle memory, connective tissue; it asks us to pay attention to the sensations in our bodies (that clenched jaw, the numbness) because they are telling us something. What really resonates with me about the way Healing Justice Ldn use this approach is that it teaches us that it's through personal change, collective practices, and transformation of structures and systems that we can 'grow strong and grounded strategy, to build compelling alternatives and to mend the deep impact of oppression and violence'.[35] Nishma Jethwa (who runs Healing Justice Ldn's Movement Medicine programme) explains it much better than I can:

> The way I was introduced to somatics was really through my work supporting people in conflict or rupture – interpersonal, in groups, across movements. As I practiced using community sustaining frameworks like restorative and transformative justice and community accountability frameworks in order to support people to navigate conflicts in generative ways, it became increasingly clear to me that we simply cannot do that work if we are unable: to sit in the discomfort of disagreement, to hold contradictions and complexity, to extend trust across difference, and to hold that short and long term

> practice. It's the practice of embodiment and somatics that has really allowed me to unlock that in myself and see the potential for this work in my community.[36]

Having a political analysis and an understanding of unequal distribution of power is key to politicised somatics, and without it we miss how we are shaped by, resist and reproduce our wider context, the air we breathe. We need a political analysis to this work because, as many disabled and chronically ill people, including Aurora Levins Morales, teach us, 'every form of social injustice demands that we silence our bodies' – we're taught from when we're young to 'manage our flesh for other people's benefit, to train ourselves to be the workers the system needs'.[37] Somatics asks us: is what we are practising aligned with what we most care about? And it helps us understand why the answer to this, if we're being honest, is often 'no'. The things we want to resist (ableism, capitalism, racism, and on and on) live in our bodies – we embody values we know are violent and we don't always embody what we yearn for. And if that's what we embody, then it's likely the things we build – our movements, new systems – will also embody the things we yearn to abolish.

There is something incredibly sad about how our automatic default responses, especially when we're under stress and pressure, or under attack as many people on welfare always seem to be, reproduce the things we don't want as part of our new worlds. When bereaved families talk about how deserving (not a burden, hard-working) their loved one was as a way to appeal to the government and to have their grief legitimised. When some disabled people paint specific impairments as more deserving of welfare than others because they desperately need support to live. When people who have been sanctioned say they agree with sanctioning but that for them it was wrong. When we are made to feel like the only way the government will listen is to pit ourselves against someone else. Politicised somatics offers ways of understanding and shifting this – gently, with love.

These deeply patterned responses and ways of being – what Staci K. Haines calls 'conditioned tendencies' – came about because we needed them to be able to survive, and belong, and over time we forget and they become who we think we are.[38] We generalise them to new contexts and the things that helped us survive can come to limit our range of options of how we show up and respond. We can shift these conditioned tendencies by attending to what they were taking care of – taking on new practices, on purpose, that align with our values, who we want to be, the kind of world we want to live in. This can open up choices in how we respond to pressure, urgency, attack from the state and the media, conflict in our communities and movements.

If we want to radically re-envision welfare and the economy, what would we need to practise? If we want justice, then 'what does it take to embody justice personally? What does it take for masses of people to embody justice?'[39] We need powerful methods, like politicised and/or anti-oppressive somatics, so that we can align our embodied practices with liberatory values. If we dream of welfare that affirms our dignity, then we need to know what it feels like to have our dignity affirmed. In experiencing this, we can get curious about what we'd need to practise, every day, in order to build deep, enduring and robust communities (relational infrastructures) that affirm dignity, and allow us to access our full humanity. Healing shame is about worthiness as inherent – not something that can be given or taken away.

From talking to so many people about welfare, I have come to think that healing from and composting shame – and the deserving/undeserving binary around welfare – would be huge for personal and structural transformation. If we could embody a different relationship to welfare where everyone is deserving at no one else's expense, and where we make shame, conditionality and punishment obsolete and unimaginable, we could grow our connections to one another instead of being pitted against each other; we could be in our own dignity while recognising the dignity of others all at the same time.

NO SHAME IN WELFARE

> Just as poverty does not simply mean not having enough money, losing social security does not only mean being poor. It fosters a mental state: a fear in the pit of your stomach, a sense of shame that you have found yourself in this position and an aching worry you won't get out of it. The fact that it is the government causing this anguish, instead of providing a safety net for your time of need, keeps you awake at night. (Frances Ryan)

'Justice is State accountability, not personal shame', a disabled activist who needs to stay anonymous told me – 'we've been conditioned to think that some people are undeserving of support and that what's happening to them is their fault'. Instead, he says we need to understand that 'this has been done to us and our loved ones by the state' and 'attribute responsibility, accountability and recognition at the feet of, where it deserves to be'. If we still hold inside us the shame we've been made to feel about welfare, then could we design welfare without shame? Or would shame keep showing up – in our imaginations, in our dreams? We need to resource ourselves and others to hold no shame in naming the conditions of precarity and violence that we're navigating. But it can seem overwhelming to try to unlearn and heal from something that has been on repeat every day for longer than our lifetimes.

Perhaps instead of shaming ourselves for feeling ashamed, and to jump into getting rid of shame, one way to start healing could be to ask how has my shame taken care of me? Staci K. Haines sees shame as signalling a 'break in our innate integrity and worth – from the intimate to the systemic' that often accumulates slowly over time, and needs time, and connections to others, to heal. Healing shame is about 'distinguishing what is and isn't our fault, where we are over and under accountable, and how to forgive – especially ourselves'.[40]

Somatics is big on healing shame. But what about for the majority of us who couldn't afford to work with a somatic practitioner? Is there a way for us to heal shame – can we do it collectively? We might start with how much of the shame we're carrying is ours, and how much actually belongs to those who have harmed us and/or who benefit and profit from us feeling ashamed (including the state and media). What messages and stories that we've been told about ourselves have we come to believe, and how do they shape what is and isn't possible for us? What are the other stories we could tell – anchored in our resilience and dignity? We could start to honour our shame *and* start to practise our agency and choice in feeling it. We can gently ask: How does this or has this shame looked after me? How has it protected me? When doesn't it help me? What does it prevent me from doing? Does this shame belong to me, and/or does it belong to other people? Who/what benefits from me feeling ashamed? Who profits from it? Remember – this has been done to us for years, and to some of us for all of our lives, so we can't just change it overnight. Instead, we can ask: What small things do I already do? What can I start to do?

For Staci K. Haines healing shame is integral to learning new practices and building new systems and worlds. It can deepen our connections to others, allow us to take more risks, be more accountable, and make room for generative conflict – 'conflict that leaves us more connected' that deepens trust rather than rupturing relationships.[41] Just imagine what we could dream and build together if we weren't ashamed.

STIGMA FREE FUTURES

In 2022, I joined a group of ten people to work together on poverty-related stigma, and I felt a flicker of exactly what we can do together if we heal from shame. I never imagined on first meeting this group that we would be writing raps together, meeting each other's babies, and sharing our lives for the years to come. We came to call ourselves and our work Stigma Free Futures – rooted in the belief that 'poverty and poverty stigma are inextricably entangled social problems that reinforce and feed each other', and that 'designing stigma out of systems of welfare and support is integral to the fight for economic justice and economic security'.[42]

We fell into ways of working that we came to define as coalitional – as a group of people all with some form of lived experience in relation to poverty and stigma; we didn't want tokenism or extraction of lived experience, we wanted to create a space for listening across difference and space to lean into tensions. Inspired by having a hip-hop emcee from Hull (shout out to the wonderful Steve Arnott aka Redeyefeenix and Beats Bus) as a member of our group, we came to understand our approach as 'the power of we'. And this 'we' didn't always agree. We tussled and grappled and sometimes hurt each other's feelings – we navigated a lot of edges around reform, abolition, horizons, rights. We tended to meet intensively, bringing people together from all across the UK. We felt exhausted afterwards (and during) and didn't always know what to do with our buzzing brains, and our rage.

One thing we did with our collective rage and love was create a manifesto:

> Poverty and poverty stigma are deeply connected. Poverty stigma makes us all feel like we're to blame for poverty. It tries to take away our dignity and inherent worth. It stops us from seeing each other as human beings. It makes us blame ourselves and each other instead of blaming the systems that create poverty and stigma. Stigma is not inevitable; it is deliberate and by design. It benefits those with power. Stigma can be devastating, debilitating and dangerous, and it can kill.[43]

Our recommendations include reframing poverty as an issue of economic injustice (including in relation to wealth inequality), and taking an intersectional approach to addressing it. But I think the surprise finding for the group was that we came to be transformed individually and collectively through our time together. A big part of this was creating space for processing the harm done to us all and recognising our own (often unwitting) complicity in perpetuating harms. This naming and recognition – of who and what harms us – is an essential practice to resistance, coalition and solidarity against oppression.

Together we worked through something that I have always felt icky about – that, yes, shame is a massive part of poverty, but if we only focus on dealing with shame, we can miss the root causes: poverty, inequality, capitalism, neoliberalism, etc. What I learned from this group is how powerful it is to name stigma as by design, and that to destigmatise poverty is key to mobilising people, to building solidarity, and for imagining new systems.

In the words of our group, people shared that: 'Shame makes people want to hide it, I want to scream that "I'm not ashamed, it's not me, it's not my fault, it's the system, why should I feel shame?"' Someone else said: 'The first step to resisting stigma is to know it's not your fault, that it is caused by things beyond you, that you are not alone and that we can stand up against it.' Another said: 'Stigma divides people, and works like a form of coercive control … working to destigmatise poverty is important to build solidarity and collectively mobilise to tackle poverty.'

The process of coming together, as well as what we learned, helped us to understand that personal and collective transformation are key to designing and building practices and systems free from poverty and stigma. We felt a longing, while also struggling to imagine new systems where work doesn't define worth. And no wonder when we understand the centuries-old repetitions that our only value is through waged work. We can't remember the time before this but there was one. And we navigated an edge in our collective thinking around reforms and abolition – recognising that 'while we can and should attempt to design poverty stigma out of our current systems, we also need to look beyond them to create new systems that don't require stigma to function'.[44]

'AND ARE YOU HOPEFUL?' HOPE AS A DISCIPLINE

Prison and policing abolitionists Kelly Hayes and Mariame Kaba, warn us that 'our movements cannot be echo chambers of doom' – we need them to be spaces that radicalise us, not lead us to despair.[45] People often ask me if I'm hopeful – the question always makes me pause. If I am hopeful, then it's in the way Mariame Kaba talks about hope – not as a metaphor but as a 'lived practice. It isn't a thing I possess. Rather I have to remake it daily. I don't have hope, I do hope. It's an active process that I have to regularly commit to.'[46] Hope is a discipline – a regular practice. The places I feel closest to hope are in deep solidarity and collective action with others. Sometimes I think about the future – what kind of world do I long for, and if I looked back from this future, what role would I want myself, and my research, to have been part of and to have contributed to? I don't think the changes we want to see will come from those in power – they'll come from us all, and I want to be a small part of collectively imagining, building and practising what we want and need.

We know so much of what's wrong with the system we currently have – we're experts in its violence. But what do we want instead? This feels like a hard question to answer. When we're under attack, our energies are limited and the exhaustion is real – it's easy to slip into our old shapes and reach for familiar tools, such as our nostalgia for a time when the welfare state protected (some of) us, or appealing to the imagined humanity of the government. But artist and writer Derica Shields, who we have met throughout this book, asks us to move 'beyond the nostalgia and tepid reformism that dominate discussions about the future of the welfare state'.[47] This invites us to get clear, together, on where we want to focus our energies. What's our bigger collective strategy to move us towards the welfare and world we want? And what resources and conditions do we need to strategise together in these times of polycrisis and extreme violence, to keep each other alive, while also building new futures? Right now, this could mean shrinking the current system (through divestment and defunding of the DWP) while investing in building systems that meet people's needs rather than shaming and punishing them.

Given the role of private companies and the insurance industry in shaping the systems we have now, welfare should not be for profit – it should not be shaped by, connected or outsourced to private contractors. We need resourcing of genuine alternatives, not just replacements for what we already have, and giving people real choices and options, where welfare isn't tied to work, where we recognise people's worth has nothing to do with work, and that also provides meaningful opportunities to work for those who can and want to. Welfare should be about the radical redistribution of wealth. This involves rethinking what work could be outside of capitalism, and exploring, as many disabled people currently are, what universal basic income and living wages mean for disabled people. Resisting capitalist productivity, refusing to equate our worth with paid work, changing the way we talk to, and police, ourselves and each other, healing from shame – this is the work we need to do, together.

In reimagining future welfare, someone who wants to remain anonymous talked about a 'total reconceptualization of what we deem as proof of people's contexts and difficulties … We need to flip the scripts around burden of proof and around people abusing the system', and reposition 'the people who are accessing welfare as having the understanding of their situations and what would benefit them'. We need to design new systems based on the knowledge and analysis of disabled people and others who need welfare, which centre the knowledge of lived experience, and where medical knowledge is in allyship, not as gatekeeping. Centuries of manufactured scarcity, and linking welfare to undeservingness, conditionality, punishment and work make it seem naive to ask, simply, what about if we just believe people? This is a refusal to cooperate in dehumanisation by reclaiming the humanity of people on welfare, recognising and affirming dignity with no 'perfect victims'. Indy Johar at Dark Matter Labs suggests one way to flip the script is to shift from seeing welfare as a 'cost' to be reluctantly paid, into understanding welfare as a social investment, and a mechanism to unlock people's and society's capacities, creating the conditions for people to thrive.[48]

In order to make this kind of shift, we need access to meaningful opportunities to collectively heal from welfare state abuse and dehumanisation, to have our pain witnessed, and to heal from fear and shame. This could be resourced through reparations for welfare state violence – the kind happening now, and the kind that built the foundations of the welfare state. Learning from its colonial history, we need welfare that isn't built on extraction and exclusion; welfare that isn't justified at the expense of someone else, somewhere else, however different, however far away. This means delinking welfare from the nation state that borders and weaponises it. It means recognising that it's never only about welfare, because welfare is an important part of a broader global struggle, in which we all have stakes.

It's horrifying that bureaucratic violence, fear, shame, dehumanisation are designed into welfare systems; we should be angry. But it also means we can design welfare differently – in ways that honour interdependency, dignity and safety. It enables us to spend less of our limited energy on reforms that tinker at the edges of a system that is deadly by design, and instead to resource our movements to imagine beyond the state towards life-affirming infrastructures grounded in collective care. Community comes up so much in disabled people's welfare activism. It means finding or creating your community, nurturing connection across our differences, and being in community with others as a practice that both keeps us alive in the here and now and prefigures the world we dream of, the relationships we long for, in all of our messy realness, where there are no perfect victims, where all we've got is each other. This calls for us to practise knowing our own and each other's inherent worth and dignity – our full humanity, on purpose, every day – creating conditions that make welfare state violence obsolete. Just imagine the kinds of beginnings that might grow from this end.

ACKNOWLEDGEMENTS

It takes an enormous community, mostly of people who live at the sharp edges of the welfare system, to collect evidence of harm and resistance, and to use this for transformational change. Thank you to all those who have shared your experience and your stories of loved ones lost – your wisdom, creative genius, grief, joy, rage, love has broken me and sustained me for so many years.

A few very special thanks are due to: John Pring – without you this book wouldn't exist, and no amount of gluten-free protein bars can show my gratitude. Collaborating with you and learning from you is one of the joys of my life and work, and long may it continue; Imogen Day – your analysis born from grief, your wicked sense of humour, the way you love and honour your sister Pip, your generosity – I will always be dreaming of ways we can continue working together; Rick Burgess – modest to the core, I've heard you say many times that you're one of many and no one special, but you are extremely special to me. I have rarely met anyone who can hold complexity as you do. All the way through writing this book, I thought about how much better you would write it.

To those of you who shared your wisdom, analysis and anger throughout the project, on the Deaths by Welfare podcast series, and in the making of the timeline – many of whom are cited in this book – thank you (in no particular order, and in addition to the people already named): Dolly Sen, Ellen Clifford, Tumu Johnson, Andy Mitchell, Ben Baumberg Geiger, Jamie Redman, Caroline Selman, Sara Lomri, Ajibola Lewis, Joy Dove, Alison Burton, Anna Susianta, Alex Murray, Anita Bellows, Ashar Smith, Ben Scott, Bob Ellard, Hannah Kemp-Welch, Hannah Stockwell, Derica Shields,

Stella Dadzie, Akriti Mehta, Jee, Karen Machin, Linda Burnip, Martha Foulds, Miranda Keast, Mo Stewart, Paula Peters, Rebecca Yeo, Rosanna Thompson, Rosemary Moss, SidebySide Network, Sumayya Si-Tayeb, Toby Chai, Vince Laws and Zita Holbourne. Nick Dilworth died during the time he was working with us on the Deaths by Welfare timeline – his knowledge about the labyrinthine bureaucracies of the welfare system made my head spin, and his dedication filled my heart. We miss you Nick. And to all those who I can't name because welfare state violence keeps you anonymous – you know who you are, and I hold you very dear.

Working with the team at Healing Justice Ldn is one of the joys of my life. I am grateful for you all, daily. Thank you for reminding me that striving for perfection can be immobilising, and encouraging me to think out loud, in draft, in real time. Love and gratitude to our team, past and present: Alex Augustin, Sarah Al-Sarraj, Camille Sapara Barton, Stephanie Davis, Rebekah Delsol, Micha Frazor-Carroll, Aiyana Goodfellow, Inaya Hussain, Ewa Jasiewicz, Nishma Jethwa, Sarah Joynt-Bowe, Bareya Khan, Farzana Khan, Evie Muir, Bella Normark, Ilze Rieba, Oscar Revolledo, Khatija Seedat, A'Ishah Waheed, Tarek Younis and Emily Yue. And to some of the people who have been guiding stars for me in this work – maybe even without knowing it – Marai Larasi, Staci K. Haines and Farzana Khan. Farzana – you helped tend the soil for Deaths by Welfare to grow and nurtured its, and my, growth into accessing not only what we're against but also what we need and long for. At first, I had no idea what you meant when you talked about building capacity for transformation, and now I get it. Thank you for your leadership, patience and belief.

Deaths by Welfare was born when I started to work with Healing Justice Ldn in its very early days on a project that we named 'Litany for Survival' (in homage to Audre Lorde), centring the knowledge and practices of marginalised communities around loss, and wider questions about survival, about what constitutes a liveable life, whose lives are seen to 'count', and whose deaths are framed as grievable.

I will always be grateful to the people who helped develop this work into what it is now: Sara Alsaraf, Jos Bitelli, Joseph Gray, Saara Jaffery-Roberts, Ameen Kamlana, Farzana Khan, Lani Parker, Akeim Toussaint Buck and Rose Ziaei.

I have so much gratitude for those involved in our exhibition 'Defiant and Life-Affirming: Resisting State Violence', co-curated in partnership with the International Curators Forum (ICF), at Block 336 in Brixton, as part of Healing Justice Ldn's Rehearsing Freedoms festival. At the heart of our exhibition were the timeline and art pieces, photography and installations by Dolly Sen, Nnull, Sabba Khan, Paula Peters, Disability Murals, Vince Laws, Zita Holbourne and Project Billinghurst. And thanks to all at the ICF, especially Jessica Taylor and Yewande YoYo Odunubi, for your curatorial care and brilliance.

For teaching me about radical access, by design, and for crafting our online Deaths by Welfare timeline, thank you to the people who make up the Access Power Visibility collective: Arjun Harrison-Mann, Benjamin Redgrove and Kaiya Waerea; and to Tzipporah Johnston at Door in the Wall Arts Access. Thank you to TypeOlogy Co-op for our podcast transcripts. I'd also like to thank archivists at the Black Cultural Archives, the National Archives, and the Ahmed Iqbal Ullah RACE Centre and Education Trust Archive.

To our Stigma Free Futures team (past and current): Nkechi Adeboye, Hal Khanom, Steve Arnott, Alana Avery, Stef Benstead, Sarah Campbell, Heather Coady, Nasrat Tania, Patrick Toland, Sarah Whitehead, Alex, and Imogen Tyler. Our collective grief, rage and joy is beautiful – you mean the world to me.

For those who read parts or the whole of this book, I owe enormous gratitude: Stephanie Davis, Emily Yue, Nishma Jethwa, Jon Burnett, Jamie Redman, John Pring, Ian Cushing, Tarek Younis and Sarah Joynt-Bowe. Of course, all errors remain mine. And thank you to my editor David Castle and the team at Pluto Press – for your patience, and for the feedback when I needed it. I'm not sure this is quite the book you thought you were getting, but I appreciate your open minds.

Trying to write a book with very young kids is almost impossible, and would have been entirely impossible without grandparents: my wonderful mum, Jane (every day I think how lucky we are to have you), and my lovely in-laws, Janet and Mike, and Paul and Mimmo. I am so grateful to you all, and sorry we always give you jobs to do when you come round. River and Opal – my sun and moon – if you ever read this, know it was mostly written, teetering on the edge of the bed, as you slept next to me. River, your joy for life and spirit make you the perfect companion for someone interested in documenting creative resistance and defiance. Opal, my calm amidst the storm, who likes to eat watermelon at 5 am, you have learned to walk, talk and scoot while I have been writing, and your joy for life is beautiful. I hope you both help to collectively shape a world where this book is obsolete – categorised as 'history' and read by people who can't even imagine living in a world like this one. And Ian Cushing, what can I say? Thank you for our daily shared looks of exhaustion, the many cups of coffee, the never-finished conversations. I know I'm messy, and you don't like the clutter, but thank you for holding on.

NOTES

PREFACE: CREATING THE DEATHS BY WELFARE PROJECT

1 The UK government department that administers welfare.

2 Walsh, D., Dundas, R., McCartney, G., Gibson, M. and Seaman, R. (2022). Bearing the burden of austerity: how do changing mortality rates in the UK compare between men and women? *Journal of Epidemiology and Community Health*, 76, 1027–33.

3 See the Deaths by Welfare timeline: https://deathsbywelfare.org/

4 See Access Power Visibility collective: https://accesspowervisibility.com/

5 The exhibition 'Defiant and Life-Affirming: Resisting State Violence' was co-curated in partnership with the International Curators Forum (ICF), at Block 336 in Brixton, as part of Healing Justice Ldn's Rehearsing Freedoms festival. At the heart of our exhibition were the timeline and art pieces, photography and installations by Dolly Sen, Nnull, Sabba Khan, Paula Peters, Disability Murals, Vince Laws, Zita Holbourne and Project Billinghurst.

INTRODUCTION: REMEMBERING THE DEAD AND FIGHTING LIKE HELL FOR THE LIVING

1 For a tribute to Nila Gupta, including some of their work, see www.sisofrida.org/tribute-to-nila-gupta/

2 This was part of an online discussion event 'Social fabrics, material conditions, and practices of resistance', with Vince Laws, Dolly Sen, Adelaida Tamayo, Lumi Centurión and Lucía Guerrero Rivière, on 11 June 2025.

3 Black Triangle Campaign: https://blacktrianglecampaign.org/; and Laws, V. (2015). UK Welfare-Related Deaths: The Black Triangle List,

30 April 2015. https://disabilityarts.online/blog/vince-laws/uk-welfare-related-deaths-black-triangle-list-30-april-2015/

4 Pring, J. (2017). Green Party calls on government to launch benefit deaths inquiry. Disability News Service, 9 February 2017. www.disabilitynewsservice.com/green-party-calls-on-government-to-launch-benefit-deaths-inquiry/

5 Hansard (2020). Social Security Benefits: Claimant Deaths, Volume 672, 24 February 2020. https://hansard.parliament.uk/commons/2020-02-24/debates/87FD9D79-2915-41E2-B2C6-9CC5853D6F19/SocialSecurityBenefitsClaimantDeaths#:~:text=Brian%20Sycamore%20died%20in%20September,failing%20his%20work%20capability%20assessment. And video of Debbie Abrahams: www.youtube.com/watch?v=QplsmeFv5D4

6 Laws, V. (2021). *DWP Deaths Make Me Sick* shrouds in Cambridge. Disability Arts Online, 21 April 2019. https://disabilityarts.online/blog/vince-laws/dwp-deaths-make-me-sick-shrouds-in-cambridge/

7 Laws, V. (2018 – ongoing). *DWP Deaths Make Me Sick.* Shape Arts: www.shapearts.org.uk/news/dwp-deaths-make-me-sick-vince-laws

8 Sen, D. (2022). *Broken Hearts for the DWP.* https://dollysen.com/broken-hearts-for-the-dwp/

9 UK Government (2025). Fraud and error in the benefit system: financial year 2024 to 2025 estimates. www.gov.uk/government/statistics/fraud-and-error-in-the-benefit-system-financial-year-2024-to-2025-estimates

10 Tax Justice Network (2024). A quarter of global tax dodging is enabled by the UK and British Overseas Territories. https://taxjustice.uk/blog/a-third-of-global-tax-dodging-is-enabled-by-the-uk-and-british-overseas-territories/

11 Kim, J.B. (2021). Cripping the welfare queen: the radical potential of disability politics. *Social Text*, 148(39), 79–101 (p. 81).

12 Kitchen, R. (2003). Investigating benefit fraud and illness deception in the United Kingdom. In Halligan, P., Bass, C. and Oakley, D. (Eds), *Malingering and Illness Deception.* Oxford: Oxford University Press, p. 313.

13 Report to Prevent Future Deaths (2021). Phillipa Day. www.judiciary.uk/wp-content/uploads/2021/02/Phillipa-Day-2021-0043.pdf

14 Pring, J. (2021). Philippa Day: flawed PIP system led to young mum's death, says coroner. Disability News Service. www.disabilitynewsservice.com/philippa-day-flawed-pip-system-led-to-young-mums-death-says-coroner/

15 Pring, J. (2022). The Department for Work and Pensions: Deaths, cover-up, and a toxic 30-year legacy. Disability News Service. www.disabilitynewsservice.com/the-department-for-work-and-pensions-deaths-cover-up-and-a-toxic-30-year-legacy/

1. EVIDENCE OF VIOLENCE, AND THE VIOLENCE OF EVIDENCE

1 BBC (2013). Stephanie Bottrill suicide note blames government. BBC, 13 May 2013. www.bbc.co.uk/news/uk-england-birmingham-22500009
2 Napier, A. (2011). Jobseeker took own life. *Southern Daily Echo*, 21 June 2011.
3 Allen, G. (2019). Tragic tenant left suicide note sarcastically 'thanking' Universal Credit bosses. Derbyshire Live, 12 April 2019. www.derbytelegraph.co.uk/news/local-news/universal-credit-suicide-brian-sycamore-2749062
4 Pring, J. (2020). Disabled woman left note implicating DWP and its PIP failings in her death. Disability News Service, 12 November 2020. www.disabilitynewsservice.com/philippa-day-disabled-woman-left-note-implicating-dwp-and-its-pip-failings-in-her-death/
5 Pring, J. (2021). Coroner silent on why DWP was not questioned at inquest, despite 'nightmare' messages. Disability News Service, 16 December 2021. www.disabilitynewsservice.com/coroner-silent-on-why-dwp-was-not-questioned-at-inquest-despite-nightmare-messages
6 Ryan, F. (2020). Britain's brutal benefits system is driving people to despair. *Guardian*, 4 March 2020. www.theguardian.com/commentisfree/2020/mar/04/britain-benefit-system-generating-mental-distress-errol-graham
7 Hunt, H. (2013). Get-tough tests face the sick on benefit. *Liverpool Echo*, 8 May 2013. www.liverpoolecho.co.uk/news/liverpool-news/get-tough-tests-face-sick-benefit-3488200
8 Osborne, G. (2012). *New Statesman*, 8 October 2012. www.newstatesman.com/business/economics/2012/10/george-osbornes-speech-conservative-conference-full-text
9 Hall, M. (2011). 75% on sick are skiving. *Daily Express*, 26 January 2011.
10 Quarashi, N. (2025). Britain is becoming a nation of dishonest scroungers who openly steal from supermarkets and defraud the benefits system. *Daily Mail*, 18 January 2025.

11 Briant, E., Watson, N. and Philo, G. (2011). Bad News for Disabled People: How the Newspapers are Reporting Disability. Project Report. Strathclyde Centre for Disability Research and Glasgow Media Unit, University of Glasgow, Glasgow, UK, p. 4.

12 Riley-Smith, B. (2012). Disability hate crime: is 'benefit scrounger' abuse to blame? *Guardian*, 14 August 2012. www.theguardian.com/society/2012/aug/14/disability-hate-crime-benefit-scrounger-abuse

13 Cameron, D. (2011). We Are All in This Together. Speech in Witney, 20 August 2011. www.ipswichconservatives.com/news/david-cameron-we-are-all-together

14 Quarmby, K. (2015). Disability hate crime motivation survey – results, 22 July 2015. https://katharinequarmby.com/2015/07/22/disability-hate-crime-motivation-survey-results/

15 Garthwaite, K. (2014). Fear of the brown envelope: exploring welfare reform with long-term sickness benefits recipients. *Social Policy & Administration*, 48(7), 782–98.

16 Shields, M. (2012). Norwich man killed himself 'over back-to-work fears'. *Norwich Evening News*, 24 April 2012.

17 DPAC website: https://dpac.uk.net/

18 Pring, J. (2014). DWP contradicts its own position on benefit-related deaths … again. Disability News Service, 17 October 2014. www.disabilitynewsservice.com/dwp-contradicts-its-own-position-on-benefit-related-deaths-again/

19 Chakelian, A. (2015). Disabled man killed himself over benefit cut, coroner rules. *New Statesman*, 21 September 2015.

20 Pring, J. (2016). DWP secrecy over benefit-related suicides. Disability News Service, 10 March 2016.

21 Johnson, T. (2023). Panel discussion. Welfare State Violence: A Feature Not a Bug, with Tumu Johnson, Derica Shields, Stella Dadzie and China Mills. Rehearsing Freedoms Festival, Healing Justice Ldn. www.youtube.com/watch?v=6nJNJzm53pg

22 Fricker, M. (2007). *Epistemic Injustice: Power and the Ethics of Knowing*. Oxford: Oxford University Press.

23 McDonald, C. (2013). Heartbroken dad blames benefits axemen for driving his ill son to commit suicide. *Daily Record*, 22 September 2013.

24 Armstrong, J. (2014). More than 80 suicide cases directly linked to Coalition cuts claim disability campaigners. *The Mirror*, 4 May 2015.

25 Armstrong, More than 80 suicide cases.
26 Pring, J. (2025). Call for public inquiry into deaths after coroner rules suicide was 'triggered' by DWP. Disability News Service, 5 June 2025. www.disabilitynewsservice.com/call-for-public-inquiry-into-deaths-after-coroner-rules-suicide-was-triggered-by-dwp/
27 McVeigh, K. (2015). DWP urged to publish inquiries on benefit claimant suicides. *Guardian*, 14 December 2015.
28 Chakelian, Disabled man killed himself over benefit cut.
29 Pring, J. (2015). WCA death scandal: 'DWP and Atos killed my son'. Disability News Service, 9 November 2015. www.disabilitynewsservice.com/wca-death-scandal-dwp-and-atos-killed-my-son/
30 Pring, J. (2015). Coroner's 'ground-breaking' verdict: suicide was 'triggered' by 'fit for work' test. Disability News Service. 18 September 2015.
31 Traynor, L. (2013). Benefit cuts blind man committed suicide after Atos ruled him fit to work. *Mirror*, 28 December 2013.
32 Hansard (2020). Social Security Benefits: Claimant Deaths, Volume 672: debated on Monday 24 February 2020. https://hansard.parliament.uk/commons/2020-02-24/debates/87FD9D79-2915-41E2-B2C6-9CC5853D6F19/SocialSecurityBenefitsClaimantDeaths
33 Museum of homelessness (2024). The Dying Homeless project 2024 findings. https://shorturl.at/Dlai3
34 Pring, J. (2016). DWP dismissed coroner's concerns over WCA suicide link, document reveals. Disability News Service, 17 March 2016. www.disabilitynewsservice.com/dwp-dismissed-coroners-concerns-over-wca-suicide-link-document-reveals/; and Pring, Coroner's 'ground-breaking' verdict.
35 Black Triangle Campaign: https://blacktrianglecampaign.org/2013/10/09/disabled-nottingham-man-killed-himself-after-his-benefits-were-stopped-by-dwp-atos-h-m-coroner/
36 Black Triangle Campaign.
37 Pring, J. (2019). Lobby aims to persuade MPs that DWP must First Do No Harm on assessments. Disability News Service, 24 January 2019. www.disabilitynewsservice.com/lobby-aims-to-persuade-mps-that-dwp-must-first-do-no-harm-on-assessments/
38 Millward, G. (2022). *Sick Note: A History of the British Welfare State.* Oxford: Oxford Academic.
39 Gregory, J. and McKiernan, J. (2024). Rishi Sunak sets out plans to tackle 'sick note culture'. BBC, 19 April 2024.

40 National Audit Office (NAO) (2020). Information held by the Department for Work & Pensions on deaths by suicide of benefit claimants. www.nao.org.uk/wp-content/uploads/2020/02/Information-held-by-the-DWP-on-deaths-by suicide-of-benefit-claimants.pdf

41 Deaths by Welfare timeline: https://deathsbywelfare.org/

42 Nixon, R. (2011). *Slow Violence and the Environmentalism of the Poor*. Cambridge, MA: Harvard University Press, p. 2

43 Carson, R. (1962 [2000]). *Silent Spring*. London: Penguin.

44 Pring, J. (2022). The Department for Work and Pensions: deaths, cover-up, and a toxic 30-year legacy. Disability News Service, 27 March 2022. www.disabilitynewsservice.com/the-department-for-work-and-pensions-deaths-cover up-and-a-toxic-30-year-legacy/

45 Nixon, *Slow Violence*, p. 41.

46 Barr, B., Taylor-Robinson, D., Stuckler, D. et al. (2015). 'First, do no harm': are disability assessments associated with adverse trends in mental health? A longitudinal ecological study. *Journal of Epidemiology and Community Health*, 70(4), 339–45.

47 UN Committee on the Rights of Persons with Disabilities (2016). Inquiry concerning the United Kingdom of Great Britain and Northern Ireland carried out by the Committee under Article 6 of the Optional Protocol to the Convention; and UN Committee on the Rights of Persons with Disabilities (2024). Report on follow-up to the inquiry concerning the United Kingdom of Great Britain and Northern Ireland conducted under Article 6 of the Optional Protocol to the Convention. Geneva.

48 Knight, T., Dickens, S., Mitchell, M. et al. (2005). Incapacity Benefit reforms – the personal adviser role and practices: Stage Two. Research Report No. 278. https://webarchive.nationalarchives.gov.uk/20091222172300/http:// research.dwp.gov.uk/asd/asd5/rrs-index.asp

49 Pring, J. (2015). 'Ruthless' DWP 'forced through WCA despite knowing of harm'. Disability News Service, 11 December 2015. www.disabilitynewsservice.com/ruthless-dwp-forced-through-wca-despite-knowing-of-harm/

50 Ravetz, A. (2006). Green Paper: A New Deal for Welfare: empowering people to work. An independent assessment of the arguments for proposed Incapacity Benefit reform, pp. 1–26 (p. 25).

51 Mills, C. (2023). How the DWP fought to withhold evidence its policies kill disabled people. Open Democracy. www.opendemocracy.net/en/dwp-disability-benefits-jeremy-hunt-autumn-statement/

52 Pring, J. (2021). DWP figures reveal sharp rise in secret benefit death reviews. Disability News Service, 12 August 2021. www.disabilitynewsservice.com/dwp-figures-reveal-sharp-rise-in-secret-benefit-death-reviews/

53 Pring, J. (2024). *The Department: How a Violent Government Bureaucracy Killed Hundreds and Hid the Evidence*. London: Pluto Press.

54 National Audit Office (2020). Information held by the Department for Work and Pensions on deaths by suicide of benefit claimants. www.nao.org.uk/wp-content/uploads/2020/02/Information-held-by-the-DWP-on-deaths-by-suicide-of-benefit-claimants.pdf

55 Rummel, R.J. (1994). *Death by Government*. London: Routledge. Online. www.hawaii.edu/powerkills/NOTE1.HTM

56 Rummel, *Death by Government*.

57 El Kurd, M. (2025). *Perfect Victims and the Politics of Appeal*. Chicago, IL: Haymarket Books, p. 157.

58 Spade, D. (2015). *Normal Life: Administrative Violence, Critical Trans Politics, and the Limits of Law*. Durham, NC: Duke University Press, p. 10.

59 Symonds, T. (2021). Grenfell cladding email: keep poor test 'confidential'. BBC, 18 February 2021. www.bbc.co.uk/news/uk-56115167#:~:text=Tom%20Symonds,Lower%20safety%20rules

60 Symonds, Grenfell cladding email.

61 Mingus, M. (2022). You are not entitled to our deaths: COVID, abled supremacy & interdependence. Leaving Evidence blog, 16 January 2022. https://leavingevidence.wordpress.com/

62 Herman, J. (1992). *Trauma and Recovery: The Aftermath of Violence – from Domestic Abuse to Political Terror*. New York: Basic Books, p. 8.

2. WORK DOES NOT DEFINE OUR WORTH

1 Pring, J. (2015). Government hides information on death of Michael O'Sullivan. Disability News Service, 16 October 2015. www.disabilitynewsservice

2 Spartacus Network (2022). The People's Review of the Work Capability Assessment. Citizen Network. https://citizen-network.org/uploads/attachment/409/the-peoples-review-of-the-wca.pdf

3 Barr, B., Taylor-Robinson, D., Stuckler, D. et al. (2015). 'First, do no harm': are disability assessments associated with adverse trends in mental

health? A longitudinal ecological study. *Journal of Epidemiology and Community Health*, 70(4), 339–45.

4 Mind (2016). One in two people with mental health problems have felt suicidal because of money, housing or benefits issues. Mind.

5 Mind (2020). People, not tick boxes: a call to rebuild the disability benefits system. Mind. www.mind.org.uk/media/6483/people-not-tick-boxes-october2020.pdf

6 Burgess, R., Duffy, S., Dilworth, N., Bence, J., Blackburn, W. and Thomas, M. (2013). Assessing the Assessors. https://citizen-network.org/uploads/attachment/433/assessing-the-assessors.pdf

7 House of Commons Work and Pensions Committee (2014). Employment and Support Allowance and Work Capability Assessments First Report of Session 2014–15. House of Commons Work and Pensions Committee. www.mind.org.uk/media/4290/mental-health-sector-response-fifth-independent-review-wca.pdf

8 Dwyer, P., Scullion, L., Jones, K., McNeill, J. and Stewart, A.B.R. (2020), 'Work, welfare, and wellbeing: the impacts of welfare conditionality on people with mental health impairments in the UK'. *Social Policy and Administration*, 54(2), 311–26 (p. 317).

9 Baumberg Geiger, B. (2018). A Better Work Capability Assessment Is Possible. Demos. https://demos.co.uk/wp-content/uploads/2018/12/2018_A_Better_WCA_is_possible_FULL-4.pdf

10 Spartacus Network, The People's Review.

11 Hale, C. (2018). Reclaiming 'chronic illness': an introduction to the Chronic Illness Inclusion Project. A discussion paper from the Centre for Welfare Reform. https://chronicillnessinclusion.org.uk/wp-content/uploads/2021/04/reclaiming-chronic-illness-discussion-paper.pdf

12 Rutherford, J. (2007). New Labour, the market state, and the end of welfare. *Soundings*, 36, 40–55.

13 Aylward, M. and Locascio, J.J. (1995). Problems in the assessment of psychosomatic conditions in social security benefits and related commercial schemes. *Journal of Psychosomatic Research*, 39(6), 755–65.

14 Stewart, M. (2016). *Cash Not Care: The Planned Demolition of the UK Welfare State*. London: New Generation Publishing.

15 Hansard (1999). Welfare Reform and Pensions Bill, Volume 601: debated on Thursday 10 June 1999. https://hansard.parliament.uk/lords/1999-06-10/debates/c366417d-d490-4ce6-9e08-b2ee9e05212a/WelfareReformAndPensionsBill

16 Harris, J., Sapey, B. and Stewart, J. (1999). 'Blairface: third-way disability and dependency in Britain'. *Disability Studies Quarterly*, 19(4), 365.
17 Waugh, P. and Schaefer, S. (2000). 'Disabled told to seek work or lose 226 benefits'. *Independent*, 27 November 2000.
18 George W. Bush. New Freedom Initiative: http://washingtonpost.com/wpsrv/onpolitics/elections/bushtext020101.html
19 Halligan, P.W., Bass, C. and Oakley, D.A. (2003). *Malingering and Illness Deception.* New York: Oxford University Press.
20 Aylward, M. and Sawney, P. (1999). Disability assessment medicine. *BMJ,* 318, S2–7186.
21 Rutherford, New Labour.
22 Wikeley, N. (1995). The Social Security (Incapacity for Work) Act. *The Modern Law Review*, 58(4), 523–33.
23 Hansard (2006). Benefit Fraud, Volume 442: debated on Thursday 9 February 2006. https://hansard.parliament.uk/Commons/2006-02-09/debates/66d94eec-8df6-4cd0-8ad4-2b0d30932762/BenefitFraud
24 Schram, S. (2000). In the clinic: the medicalization of welfare. *Social Text*, 62(1), 62–81.
25 WPSC (2006). Work and Pensions Select Committee: Supplementary memorandum submitted by UnumProvident following the publication of the Welfare Reform Green Paper. www.publications.parliament.uk/pa/cm200506/cmselect/cmworpen/616/616we37.htm
26 Private Eye (2011). Unum, the American insurance company, and income protection cover. 11 November 2011. The ME Association. https://meassociation.org.uk/2011/11/private-eye-piece-on-unum-the-american-insurance-company-and-income-protection-cover-11-november-2011/
27 Freud, D. (2007). Reducing Dependency, Increasing Opportunity: Options for the Future of Welfare to Work. An independent report to the Department for Work and Pensions.
28 Jolly, D. (2013). Getting rich on disability denial. *Red Pepper*, February/March. https://ocean.exacteditions.com/issues/34541/page/19
29 Disability News Service (2012). Paralympics protest aims to strike 'major blow' against Atos. Disability News Service, 29 August 2012. www.disabilitynewsservice.com/paralympics-protest-aims-to-strike-major-blow-against-atos/
30 Humphry, D. (2023). 'I've always felt these spaces were ours': disability activism and austerity capitalism: reflections on *City*'s interview with DPAC. *City*, 27(1–2), 162–89 (p. 179).

31 www.theguardian.com/society/2015/jan/18/after-hated-atos-quits-will-maximus-make-work-assessments-less-arduous

32 McMillan, T. (2019). How one company is making millions off Trump's war on the poor. *Mother Jones*, January/February 2019. www.motherjones.com/politics/2018/12/how-one-company-is-making-millions-off-trumps-war-on-the-poor/)

33 Mcmillan, How one company.

34 Maximus UK website: www.maximusuk.co.uk/

35 Maximus US website: https://maximus.com/federal-government/fed-defense

36 See DPAC files on Maximus: https://dpac.uk.net/tag/maximus/; and Pring, J. (2014). Incompetence, discrimination and 'fraud': the US company that could take over from Atos. Disability News Service, 17 October 2014. www.disabilitynewsservice.com/incompetence-discrimination-and-fraud-the-us-company-that-could-take-over-from-atos/

37 Almeida, L. (2025). US firm that tests eligibility for UK disability benefits reports 23% rise in profits. *Guardian*, 29 May 2025. www.theguardian.com/society/2025/may/29/us-firm-maximus-that-tests-eligibility-for-uk-disability-benefits-pays-out-10m-in-dividends

38 Almeida, US firm that tests eligibility for UK.

39 Pursglove, T. (2023). Health Transformation Programme update. Statement made on 25 May 2023, Statement UIN HCWS807. https://questions-statements.parliament.uk/written-statements/detail/2023-05-25/hcws807

40 Pring, J. (2025). Tory minister chose Capita director to carry out secret review of DWP deaths. Disability News Service, 7 August 2025. www.disabilitynewsservice.com/tory-minister-chose-capita-director-to-carry-out-secret-review-of-dwp-deaths/

41 Pring, J. (2016). Capita faces fresh calls to be stripped of PIP contracts after documentary. Disability News Service, 14 April 2016. www.disabilitynewsservice.com/capita-faces-fresh-calls-to-be-stripped-of-pip-contracts-after-documentary/

42 Serco website: www.serco.com/about

43 Gallagher, P. (2024). Morning Mail: Serco's secret algorithm, abuse claims over Gaza raid, Greens' demand on offshore gas. *Guardian*, 12 March 2024. www.theguardian.com/australia-news/2024/mar/13/morning-mail-sercos-secret-algorithm-abuse-claims-over-gaza-raid-greens-demand-on-offshore-gas

44 McRae, I. (2023). Disabled people are 'set up to fail' by the DWP in target-driven disability benefits system, whistleblowers reveal. *Big Issue*, 6 July 2023. www.bigissue.com/news/social-justice/dwp-disability-benefits-claimants-fail-whistleblowers/

45 Ramesh, R. (2013). Atos benefit claimants face biased medical assessments, doctor alleges. *Guardian*, 16 May 2013. www.theguardian.com/society/2013/may/16/atos-doctor-claimants-biased-medical-assessments

46 Burgess, R., Duffy, S., Dilworth, N., Bence, J., Blackburn, W. and Thomas, M. (2013). Assessing the Assessors. https://citizen-network.org/uploads/attachment/433/assessing-the-assessors.pdf

47 McRae, Disabled people are 'set up to fail'.

48 McMillan, How one company.

49 Death Panel: www.deathpanel.net/transcripts/organized-abandonment-with-ruth-wilson-gilmore

50 Wilson Gilmore, R. (2007). *Golden Gulag: Prisons, Surplus, Crisis and Opposition in Globalizing California*. Berkeley, CA: University of California Press, p. 247.

51 Adler-Bolton, B. and Vierkant, A. (2025). *Health Communism*. London: Verso, pp. 23–4.

52 Nielsen, M. (2025). Ensuring genocide: the insurance industry and Israel's war machine. Boycott Bloody Insurance. www.palestine-studies.org/en/node/1657136

53 Puar, J.K. (2017). *The Right to Maim*. Durham, NC: Duke University Press, p. xviii.

54 Russel, M. and Malhotra, R. (2002). Capitalism and disability. In Panitch, L. (Ed.), *A World of Contradictions*. Socialist Register, p. 223. https://socialistregister.com/index.php/srv/article/view/5784

55 See Katz, M.B. (1989). *The Undeserving Poor: America's Enduring Confrontation with Poverty*. New York: Oxford University Press.

56 Fox-Piven, F. and Cloward, R. (1972). *Regulating the Poor: The Functions of Public Welfare*. New York: Vintage Books, p. 3.

57 Poor Law Commissioners' Report of 1834, by the Commissioners for Inquiring into the Administration and Practical Operation of the Poor Laws. Presented to both Houses of Parliament by Command of His Majesty. London: Darling and Son, p. 228.

58 Poor Law Commissioners' Report, p. 264.

59 Driver, F. (1993). *Power and Pauperism: The Workhouse System 1834–1884*. Cambridge: Cambridge University Press, p. 59.

60 Adler-Bolton and Vierkant, *Health Communism*, p. 48.
61 Burnett, J. (2022). *Work and the Carceral State*. London: Pluto Press.
62 It was through Rebecca Yeo and the Disability and Migration Network that I learned about this tension.
63 Byrne, P. (2014). Tragic youngster killed himself because he couldn't get a job – but was too proud to claim benefits. *Mirror*, 20 May 2014.
64 Pring, J. (2023). Watchdog tells DWP to release secret assessment of decision to scrap WCA. Disability News Service, 9 November 2023. www.disabilitynewsservice.com/watchdog-tells-dwp-to-release-secret-assessment-of-decision-to-scrap-wca/
65 Pring, Watchdog tells DWP.
66 Swann, C. (undated). The future of the Work Capability Assessment. Child Poverty Action Group. https://cpag.org.uk/news/future-work-capability-assessment
67 Baumberg, B., Warren, J., Garthwaite, K. and Bambra, C. (2015). Rethinking the Work Capability Assessment. Demos, p. 14. https://demos.co.uk/wp-content/uploads/2015/03/Rethinking_-_web_1_.pdf
68 Russell, M. and Malhotra, R. (2002). Capitalism and disability. In Panitch, L. (Ed.), *A World of Contradictions*. Socialist Register, pp. 211–28 (pp. 219–20). https://socialistregister.com/index.php/srv/article/view/5784

3. NO 'BURDENS' AND NO PERFECT VICTIMS

1 Shields, M. (2012). Norwich man killed himself 'over back-to-work fears'. *Norwich Evening News*, 24 April 2012.
2 Armstrong, J. (2014). More than 80 suicide cases directly linked to Coalition cuts claim disability campaigners. *Mirror*, 4 May 2015.
3 Lyons, J. (2014). Killed by benefits cuts: starving soldier died as result of Iain Duncan Smith's welfare reform. *Daily Mirro*r, 27 July 2014.
4 Schalk, S. (2022). *Black Disability Politics*. Durham, NC: Duke University Press; and Clare, E. (2017). *Brilliant Imperfections: Grappling with Cur*e. Durham, NC: Duke University Press.
5 Mills, C. (2018). 'Dead people don't claim': a psychopolitical autopsy of UK austerity suicides. *Critical Social Policy*, 38(2), 302–22; and Mills, C. (2022). Burden and benefits-related suicides: 'misperception' or state crafted reality? *Journal of Public Mental Health*, 21(1), 46–56. doi:0.1108/jpmh-09-2021-0124

6 Vargas, J.C., and James, J.A. (2013). Refusing Blackness as victimization: Trayvon Martin and the Black Cyborgs. In Yancy, G. and Jones, J. (Eds), *Pursuing Trayvon Martin: Historical Concepts and Contemporary Manifestations of Racial Dynamics*. Lanham, MD: Lexington Books, pp. 193–204 (p. 193).
7 El Kurd, M. (2025). *Perfect Victims and the Politics of Appeal*. Chicago, IL: Haymarket Books, p. 25.
8 Lorde, A. (1979 [2007]). The master's tools will never dismantle the master's house. In *Sister Outsider: Essays and Speeches*. Berkeley, CA: Crossing Press, pp. 110–14 (p. 113).
9 Kaba, M. (2021). *We Do This til We Free Us: Abolitionist Organising and Transforming Justice*. Haymarket books: Chicago, IL, pp. 37–8.
10 Adler-Bolton, B. and Vierkant, A. (2025). *Health Communism*. London: Verso, p. 5.
11 Bhambra, G.K. (2022). Relations of extraction, relations of redistribution: empire, nation, and the construction of the British welfare state. *The British Journal of Sociology*, 73, 4–15.
12 Fieldhouse, D.K. (1984). The Labour governments and the Empire-Commonwealth, 1945–51. In Ovendale, R. (Ed.), *The Foreign Policy of the British Labour Governments, 1945–1951*. Leicester: Leicester University Press, pp. 83–120.
13 See Semmel, B. (1960). *Imperialism and Social Reform: English Social Imperial Thought, 1895–1914*. London: Allen and Unwin.
14 Beveridge, W. (1942). *Social Insurance and Allied Services* (Cmd. 6404). London: His Majesty's Stationery Office (HMSO).
15 Hayes, D. (2002). From aliens to asylum-seekers: a history of immigration controls and welfare in Britain. In Cohen, S., Humphries, B. and Mynott, E. (Eds), *From Immigration Controls to Welfare Controls*. London and New York: Routledge, pp. 11–29.
16 El-Enany, N. (2020). *(B)ordering Britain: Law, Race and Empire*. Manchester: Manchester University Press.
17 Bryan, B., Dadzie, S. and Scafe, S. (1985 [2018]). *Heart of the Race: Black Women's Lives in Britain*. London: Verso, p. 111.
18 Bryan et al. Heart of the Race, p. 111.
19 Miller, M. (Ed.) (2023). *Speak Out: The Brixton Black Women's group*. London: Verso.
20 Ritchie, A.J. (2017). The violent policing of Black motherhood: how and why cops target mothers of color. Salon. www.salon.com/2017/08/01/

the-violent-policing-of-black-motherhood-how-and-why-cops-target-mothers-of-color/

21 Daguerre, A. (2008). The second phase of US welfare weform, 2000–2006: blaming the poor again? *Social Policy and Administration*, 42(4), 362–78.

22 Roberts, D. (2017). *Killing the Black Body: Race, Reproduction, and the Meaning of Liberty*. New York: Vintage Books, Random House; and Gordon, L. (1995). *Pitied But Not Entitled: Single Mothers and the History of Welfare*. Cambridge, MA: Harvard University Press.

23 Levins Morales, A. (1998 [2019]). *Medicine Stories: Essays for Radicals*. Durham, NC: Duke University Press.

24 Kim, J.B. (2021). Cripping the welfare queen: the radical potential of disability politics. *Social Text*, 148(39), 79–101 (p. 79).

25 Kaba, M. and Ritchie, A.J. (2022). *No More Police: A Case for Abolition*. New York: New Press, p. 146.

26 Shilliam, R. (2018). *Race and the Undeserving Poor: From Abolition to Brexit*. Newcastle-Upon-Tyne: Agenda Publishing.

27 Open letter by Elizabeth I to the mayors of England, 11 July 1596 (National Archives, PC 2/21 f.304). www.nationalarchives.gov.uk/education/resources/elizabeth-monarchy/open-letter-by-elizabeth-i/#:~:text=They%20served%20in%20wealthy%20households,black%20people%20from%20her%20realm

28 Jones, H., Gunaratnam, Y., Bhattacharyya, G., Davies, W., Dhaliwal, S., Forkert, K., Gleadhill, E. and Saltus, R. (2017). *Go Home: The Politics of Immigration Controversies*. Manchester: Manchester University Press, p. 125.

29 Gordon, P. and Newnham, A. (1985). *Passport to Benefits: Racism in Social Security*. London: Child Poverty Action Group (CPAG) and Runnymede Trust.

30 *Morning Telegraph*, Sheffield, 4 March 1983 (Black Cultural Archives).

31 *Bedford Record*, 4 May 1982 (Black Cultural Archives).

32 *Oldham Evening Chronicle*, 24 September 1982 (Black Cultural Archives).

33 WI World (1984). Black claimants getting a raw deal. WI World, 3 August 1984 (Black Cultural Archives).

34 *Morning Star* (1984). Black families denied benefits during checks, 23 July 1984 (Black Cultural Archives).

35 *New Statesman*, 14 September 1984 (Black Cultural Archives).

36 Smith, R. (1988). Black claimants targeted, 5 May 1988 (Black Cultural Archives).

37 Siddiqui, S. (2024). The attack on welfare: from disability benefits to asylum support. Institute of Race Relations. https://irr.org.uk/article/the-attack-on-welfare-from-disability-benefits-to-asylum-support/#:~:text=Sophia%20Siddiqui%20analyses%20the%20outgoing,asylum%20welfare%20in%20the%201990s.

38 Southall Black Sisters: https://southallblacksisters.org.uk/our-services/sbs-no-recourse-fund/

39 Cohen, S. (2002). In and against the state of immigration controls: strategies for resistance. In Cohen, S., Humphries, B. and Mynott, E. (Eds), *From Immigration Controls to Welfare Controls*. London and New York: Routledge, p. 222.

40 Webbe, C. (2020). Mercy Baguma's tragic death should mark a turning point for the Home Office. *Guardian*, 26 August 2020. www.theguardian.com/commentisfree/2020/aug/26/mercy-beguma-death-home-office-asylum-seeker

41 Ryan, F. (2018). The hostile environment? Britain's disabled people live there too. *Guardian*, 26 April 2018. www.theguardian.com/commentisfree/2018/apr/26/hostile-environment-britain-disabled-people-windrush-benefits

42 Migrants Rights Network: https://migrantsrights.org.uk/projects/hostile-office/deprivation-of-citizenship/

43 Cohen, In and against the state, p. 225.

44 Kim, Cripping the welfare queen; and Cohen, C.J. (1997). Punks, bulldaggers, and welfare queens: the radical potential of queer politics? *GLQ: A Journal of Lesbian and Gay Studies*, 3(4), 437–65 (p. 438).

45 *Manchester Evening News* (1982). Race fury picket hits dole office, 16 August 1982 (Black Cultural Archives).

46 *Spare Rib* (1982). 30 women and children occupied the DHSS office in Longsight Manchester in support of Parveen Khan and Manjit Kaur, 29 November 1982 (Black Cultural Archives).

47 *Spare Rib*, 30 women and children.

48 Gordon and Newnham, *Passport to Benefits*, p. 21.

49 Gordon and Newnham, *Passport to Benefits*, p. 21.

50 Joint Council for the Welfare of Immigrants (JCWI) (1982/3). Annual report.

51 Gordon and Newnham, *Passport to Benefits*, p. 46.

52 Queen, D. (2020). A tribute to Manjeet Kaur. Greater Manchester Coalition of Disabled People. https://gmcdp.com/tribute-manjeet-kaur

53 Free Osime Brown: lessons of the campaign (2022). Labour campaign for free movement. www.labourfreemovement.org/free-osime-brown-lessons-of-the-campaign/

54 Kids of Colour (2026). Joint enterprise continues to devastate our communities: verdicts from Manchester Crown Court. https://docs.google.com/document/d/1j2Rm-bECloNPxwevA5aAiYvmZyWR4dOjUsnGEi_QIgs/edit?tab=t.0

55 Cohen, In and against the state, p. 222.

56 Cohen, In and against the state, p. 231.

57 Cohen, In and against the state, p. 231.

58 Disability Murals: www.disabilitymurals.org.uk/bristol.php#mural; Disability and Migration Network.

59 Yeo, R. (2025). *Disabling Migration Controls: Shared Learning, Solidarity, and Collective Resistance*. London: Routledge. Rebecca has played a central role in creating the Disability and Migration Network – a space organised to build solidarity among disabled people and disabled migrants, including asylum seekers and refugees.

60 Mingus, M. (2011). Moving Toward the Ugly: A Politic Beyond Desirability. *Femmes of Color Symposium Keynote Speech,* Oakland, CA. https://leavingevidence.wordpress.com/2011/08/

61 Kim, Cripping the welfare queen, p. 85.

62 Kim, Cripping the welfare queen, p. 96.

4. POLICING WELFARE

1 Pring, J. (2015). Government hides information on death of Michael O'Sullivan. Disability News Service, 16 October 2015. www.disabilitynewsservice

2 Wacquant, L. (2009). *Prisons of Poverty*. Minneapolis, MN: University of Minnesota Press.

3 Cummins, I. (2022). W*elfare and Punishment: From Thatcherism to Austerity*. Bristol: Bristol University Press.

4 Pring, J. (2017). Tory conference: activists criticise 'heavy-handed' police action at tram protest. Disability News Service, 5 October 2017. www.disabilitynewsservice.com/tory-conference-activists-criticise-heavy-handed-police-action-at-tram-protest/

5 Pring, J. (2019). Police force admits agreement to share information

about protesters with DWP. Disability News Service, 25 July 2019. www.disabilitynewsservice.com/police-force-admits-agreement-to-share-information-about-protesters-with-dwp/

6 Pring, Police force admits.

7 Humphry, D. (2023). 'I've always felt these spaces were ours': disability activism and austerity capitalism: reflections on *City*'s interview with DPAC. *City*, 27(1–2), 162–89 (p. 171). https://doi.org/10.1080/13604813.2023.2172907

8 Humphry, 'I've always felt these spaces were ours', p. 171.

9 Home Office (2016). Data sharing in enforcement cases: standards of operational practice. https://assets.publishing.service.gov.uk/media/5a80322c40f0b6230269213e/Data-sharing-standards-of-op-practice-v1.pdf

10 Joint Council for the Welfare of Immigrants (JCWI) (1982/3). Annual report.

11 Redman, J., Fletcher, D.R., White, R. and Mccarthy, L. (2024). 'You had to be the detective': implementing workfare in British employment services. *Journal of Social Policy*, 53(4), 897–915.

12 Redman, J. et al. 'You had to be the detective', p. 898.

13 Kaba, M. and Ritchie, A.J. (2022). *No More Police: A Case for Abolition*. New York: New Press, p. 147.

14 Wright, S., Johnsen, S. and Scullion, L. (2018). Why benefit sanctions are both ineffective and harmful. Welfare Conditionality blog, 17 September 2018. www.welfareconditionality.ac.uk/2018/09/why-benefit-sanctions-are-both-ineffective-and-harmful/

15 Wang, J. (2018). *Carceral Capitalism*. South Pasadena, CA: Semiotext(e). Distributed by MIT Press Direct.

16 Cameron, D. (2011). We Are All in This Together. Speech in Witney, 20 August 2011. www.ipswichconservatives.com/news/david-cameron-we-are-all-together

17 See Tyler, I. (2020) *Stigma: The Machinery of Inequality*. London: Zed Books.

18 Shields, D. (2021). A heavy nonpresence. Canopy, p. 11. https://tc3.canopycanopycanopy.com/contents/a-heavy-nonpresence

19 Roberts, D. (2022). *Torn Apart: How the Child Welfare System Destroys Black Families – and How Abolition Can Build a Safer World*. New York: Basic Books, p. 303.

20 Lewis, T.A. (2020). Disability Justice is an essential part of abolishing

police and prisons. Medium, 7 October 2020. https://level.medium.com/disability-justice-is-an-essential-part-of-abolishing-police-and-prisons-2b4a019b5730

21 O'Hara, M. (2016). Up to half of people killed by US police are disabled. *Guardian*, 29 March 2016. www.theguardian.com/society/2016/mar/29/media-must-report-police-violence-towards-disabled-people

22 Ben-Moshe, L. (2020). *Decarcerating Disability: Deinstitutionalization and Prison Abolition.* Minneapolis, MN: University of Minnesota Press.

23 Millward, G. (2022). *Sick Note: A History of the British Welfare State.* Oxford: Oxford Academic, p. 185.

24 Neocleous, M. (2000). *The Fabrication of Social Order: A Critical Theory of Police Power.* London: Pluto Press.

25 Gupta, N. (2019). The invisible prison – panopticon of the DWP. Recovery in the Bin. https://recoveryinthebin.org/2019/07/27/the-invisible-prison/

26 Bentham, J. (1812). *Pauper management improved: particularly by means of an application of the panopticon principle of construction.* London. Independent pamphlet.

27 Thanks to Jon Burnett for helping me understand the significance of Bentham's privatisation of poor relief.

28 Watts, J. (2018). No wonder people on benefits live in fear. Supermarkets spy on them now. *Guardian*, 3 May 2018.

29 Public Authorities (Fraud, Error and Recovery) Act 2025. https://bills.parliament.uk/bills/3921

30 Disability Rights UK (2024). DWP plans for bank account surveillance likely to breach privacy law and could amount to 'unlawful discrimination'. www.disabilityrightsuk.org/news/dwp-plans-bank-account-surveillance-likely-breach-privacy-law-and-could-amount-unlawful?srsltid=AfmBOoq4ov3qHC6UgNj5lvLk0X_XQYnwM_fmwYnxHSjLx0TL12j3Inwf

31 Evans, A. (2024). DWP hires 3,400 benefits police to check Universal Credit claimant bank accounts. *Express*, 15 May 2024. www.express.co.uk/finance/personalfinance/1899692/DWP-hires-3400-benefits-police

32 Hansard (2025). Public Authorities (Fraud, Error and Recovery) Bill, Volume 761: debated on Monday 3 February 2025. https://hansard.parliament.uk/commons/2025-02-03/debates/77054A7F-DE22-4477-

9E06-2E33B6125D5C/PublicAuthorities(FraudErrorAndRecovery)Bill#contribution-A9470C3F-D591-45AE-80B1-1868584AF33B

33 Roberts, D. (2017). *Killing the Black Body: Race, Reproduction, and the Meaning of Liberty*. New York: Vintage Books, Random House.

34 McDonnell, J. (2025). John McDonnell's contribution to the Public Authorities (Fraud, Error and Recovery) Bill. www.john-mcdonnell.net/news/2025/02/12/john-mcdonnells-contribution-to-the-public-authorities-fraud-error-and-recovery-bill/

35 Hansard (2025). Public Authorities (Fraud, Error and Recovery) Bill, Volume 761: debated on Monday 3 February 2025. https://hansard.parliament.uk/commons/2025-02-03/debates/77054A7F-DE22-4477-9E06-2E33B6125D5C/PublicAuthorities(FraudErrorAndRecovery)Bill#contribution-4C36CA3B-CF66-4708-8A9F-F1011949F14A

36 DWP video: https://twitter.com/DWPgovuk/status/1649846712578473985

37 UK Parliament (2025). Public Authorities (Fraud, Error and Recovery) Act 2025. https://bills.parliament.uk/bills/3921; also see Pring, J. (2025). Peers derail government plans to hand some DWP staff powers to use force against benefit claimants. Disability News Service, 23 October 2025. www.disabilitynewsservice.com/peers-derail-government-plans-to-hand-some-dwp-staff-powers-to-use-force-against-benefit-claimants/

38 GfK NOP Social Research (undated). Targeting Benefit Thieves Campaign Tracking Research Report on the launch and first burst of the new 'And they thought they'd never be caught' campaign. A research report for the Department for Work and Pensions. https://assets.publishing.service.gov.uk/media/5a7f5d5ce5274a2e8ab4bbc2/foi-905-2011-reprtc.pdf

39 Pring, J. (2017). Sister launches judicial review claim in bid for sanctions death inquest. Disabiltiy News Service, 16 February 2017. www.disabilitynewsservice.com/sister-launches-judicial-review-claim-in-bid-for-sanctions-death-inquest/

40 Hattenstone, S. (2016). Faiza Ahmed: how one woman's cries for help were missed by every authority. *Guardian*, 6 February 2016. www.theguardian.com/uk-news/2016/feb/06/faiza-ahmed-cries-for-help-missed-every-authority-simon-hattenstone

41 Wright, S. and Patrick, R. (2019). Welfare conditionality in lived experience: aggregating qualitative longitudinal research. *Social Policy*

and Society, 18(4), 597–613 (p. 605); and Dwyer, P., Scullion, L., Jones, K., McNeill, J. and Stewart, A.B.R. (2020). Work, welfare, and wellbeing: the impacts of welfare conditionality on people with mental health impairments in the UK. *Social Policy and Administration*, 54(2), 311–26.

42 Mehta, J., Taggart, D., Clifford, E. and Speed, E. (2018). Where your mental health disappears overnight: disabled people's experiences of the employment and support allowance work related activity group. Inclusion London and the University of Essex, London. www.inclusionlondon.org.uk/wp-content/uploads/2018/10/ESA-WRAG-Report.pdf

43 Redman, J. (2019). The benefit sanction: a correctional device or a weapon of disgust? *Sociological Research Online*, 25(1), 84–100. https://doi.org/10.1177/1360780419851132

44 Travellers Times (2017). Gypsy, Roma and Traveller children in care – a TT investigation. www.travellerstimes.org.uk/features/gypsy-roma-and-traveller-children-care-tt-investigation

45 de Vries, R., Reeves, A. and Geiger, B. (2017). Inequalities in the application of welfare sanctions in Britain. Working paper, London School of Economics,15, August 2017. https://eprints.lse.ac.uk/101853/1/de_Vries_Reeves_Geiger_inequalities_in_the_application_of_welfare_wp15.pdf

46 Disability Rights UK (2018). DWP should immediately stop benefit sanctions imposed on disabled people or those with a health condition say MPs. www.disabilityrightsuk.org/news/2018/november/dwp-should-immediately-stop-benefit-sanctions-imposed-disabled-people-or-those

47 Fletcher, D.R. and Redman, J. (2022). 'The sanctions are good for some people but not for someone like me who actually genuinely does their job search.' British Jobseeker's Allowance claimant views on punitive welfare reform: hegemony in action? *Capital and Class*, 47(3), 429–49 (p. 430).

48 Fletcher and Redman, The sanctions are good for some, p. 429.

49 DWP (2023) The Impact of Benefit Sanctions on Employment Outcomes: draft report. www.gov.uk/government/publications/the-impact-of-benefit-sanctions-on-employment-outcomes-draft-report; and Disability Rights UK (2023). Sanctions ineffective as a way of getting people into jobs or to work more hours, finds suppressed DWP report. www.disabilityrightsuk.org/news/sanctions-ineffective-way-getting-people-jobs-or-work-more-hours-finds-suppressed-dwp-report?srsltid=AfmBOop_5tkCY3kwO36oI1irRF5ZhEPQ47qhAyoPsATR0Rko1ESuaW50

50 DWP, The Impact of Benefit Sanctions.

51 Wintour, P. (2008). Purnell orders review into sanctions in benefits system. *Guardian*, 7 August 2008. www.theguardian.com/politics/2008/aug/07/welfare.socialexclusion

52 Waddell, G. and Aylward, M. (2005). *The Scientific and Conceptual Basis of Incapacity Benefits*. London: The Stationery Office, pp. 47, 166.

53 Jones, K.S. (2015). Nudging conformity and benefit sanctions: a state experiment in behaviour modification. Politics and Insight blog. https://politicsandinsights.org/2015/11/14/nudging-benefit-sanctions/

54 Project NIA: https://project-nia.org/mission-history

55 Kaba and Ritchie, *No More Police*, p. 147.

56 Schenwar, M. and Law, V. (2020). *Prison by Any Other Name: The Harmful Consequences of Popular Reforms*. New York: New Press.

57 Davis, A.Y. (1998). Masked racism: reflections on the prison industrial complex. www.historyisaweapon.com/defcon1/davisprison.html

58 Kaba and Ritchie, *No More Police*, p. 140.

59 Gupta, The invisible prison.

60 Michel Foucault elaborated on the panopticon as a metaphor for modern disciplinary societies in Foucault, M. (1975 [2020]). *Discipline and Punish: The Birth of the Prison*. London: Penguin.

61 Pring, J. (2023). Disability minister faces resignation calls after posting 'dangerous' and hostile video. Disability News Service, 27 April2023. www.disabilitynewsservice.com/disability-minister-faces-resignation-calls-after-posting-dangerous-and-hostile-video/

62 Boal, A. and Epstein, S. (1990). The cop in the head: three hypotheses. *TDR* (1988–), 34(3), 35–42 (p. 35).

63 Boal and Epstein, The cop in the head, p. 35.

64 Mills, C. (2022). Burden and benefits-related suicides: 'misperception' or state crafted reality? *Journal of Public Mental Health*, 21(1), 46–56.

5. DEADLY BY DESIGN: BUILDING POWER AGAINST WELFARE STATE VIOLENCE

1 I am indebted to the questions about policing in Kaba, M. and Ritchie, A.J. (2022). *No More Police: A Case for Abolition*. New York: New Press.

2 DPAC Leeds (2025). No more welfare deaths. https://dpac.uk.net/2025/06/leeds-dpac-action-no-more-welfare-deaths/

3 Miller, M. (Ed.) (2023). *Speak Out: The Brixton Black Women's group.* London: Verso.

4 Emejulu, A. and Bassel, L. (2019). Women of colour's anti-austerity activism. In Cooper, V. and Whyte, D. (Eds), *The Violence of Austerity.* London: Pluto Press, pp. 117–18.

5 Bhattacharyya, G. (2015). *Crisis, Austerity, and Everyday Life: Living in a Time of Diminishing Expectations.* Basingstoke, UK: Palgrave Macmillan.

6 Davis, S. (2026). Breathing spaces: crisis, denial, and building collective care in the age of pandemics. Healing Justice Ldn. https://healingjusticeldn.org/wp-content/uploads/2026/04/HJL_BS_Digital-Report_Final.pdf

7 Piepzna-Samarasinha, L.L. (2021). How disabled mutual aid is different than abled mutual aid. Disability Visibility project. https://disabilityvisibilityproject.com/2021/10/03/how-disabled-mutual-aid-is-different-than-abled-mutual-aid/

8 Shields, D. (2021). A heavy nonpresence. Canopy, p. 10. https://tc3.canopycanopycanopy.com/contents/a-heavy-nonpresence

9 Shields, A heavy nonpresence, p. 10

10 Bryan, B., Dadzie, S. and Scafe, S. (1985 [2018]). *Heart of the Race: Black Women's Lives in Britain.* London: Verso, p. 109.

11 Bryan et al., *Heart of the Race,* pp. 110–11.

12 Roberts, D. (2017). *Killing the Black Body: Race, Reproduction, and the Meaning of Liberty.* New York: Vintage Books, Random House, p. 203.

13 Shields, A heavy nonpresence, p. 15.

14 Cooper, V. and Whyte, D. (Eds) (2017). The Violence of Austerity. London: Pluto Press; and Redman, J. and Fletcher, D.R. (2022). Violent bureaucracy: a critical analysis of the British public employment service. *Critical Social Policy*, 42(2), 306–26.

15 Johnson, T. (2023). Panel discussion on Welfare State Violence: A Feature Not a Bug, with Tumu Johnson, Derica Shields, Stella Dadzie and China Mills. Rehearsing Freedoms Festival, Healing Justice Ldn. www.youtube.com/watch?v=6nJNJzm53pg

16 Deaths by Welfare (2023). Resisting welfare state violence and documenting evidence for justice: sharing learnings from the Deaths by Welfare project, with China Mills, Monica Sharman and Rick Burgess. The Centre for Cultures and Environments of Health (CCEH)

at the University of Exeter, 24 January 2023. www.youtube.com/watch?v=StQlcWXs6nI

17 Pring, J. (2025). Racist responses to disability hate crime campaign signal 'deeply worrying' trend'. Disability News Service, 11 September 2025. www.disabilitynewsservice.com/racist-responses-to-disability-hate-crime-campaign-signal-deeply-worrying-trend/

18 Voting intention amongst disabled people. https://x.com/LeftieStats/status/1906102440157405325

19 Kim, J.B. (2021). Cripping the welfare queen: the radical potential of disability politics. *Social Text,* 148(39), 79–101 (p. 80).

20 Mingus, M. (2010). Interdependence. https://leavingevidence.wordpress.com/2010/01/22/interdependency-exerpts-from-several-talks/

21 The People's Assembly (2025). Welfare not warfare. https://thepeoplesassembly.org.uk/2025/09/19/welfare-not-warfare-stop-the-genocide-end-austerity-fight-for-justice/

22 Levins Morales, A. (1998 [2019]). *Medicine Stories: Essays for Radicals.* Durham, NC: Duke University Press, p. 67.

23 Hayes, K. and Kaba, M. (2023). *Let This Radicalize You: Organizing and the Revolution of Reciprocal Care.* Chicago, IL: Haymarket Books, p. 178.

24 Hayes and Kaba, *Let This Radicalize You*, p. 152.

25 Hayes and Kaba, *Let This Radicalize You*, p. 151.

26 Barton, C.S. (2024). *Tending Grief: Embodied Rituals for Holding Our Sorrow and Growing Cultures of Care in Community.* Berkeley, CA: North Atlantic Books.

27 Healing Justice Ldn (2025). What it takes to heal. A panel discussion with Prentis Hemphill, Marai Larasi and Farzana Khan. March 2025. https://healingjusticeldn.org/methodology/what-it-takes-to-heal/#:~:text=What%20It%20Takes%20To%20Heal%20is%20an%20exploratory%20conversation%20with,of%20embodiment%20for%20collective%20transformation

28 https://peoplestribunal.info/wp-content/uploads/2025/03/PTPK-Tribunal-Document.pdf

29 Elliot-Cooper, A. and Yonucu, D. (2023). Racism, policing, and the Black resistance in Britain: A conversation with Adam Elliot-Cooper. *Polar Journal.* https://polarjournal.org/2023/11/08/racism-policing-and-the-black-resistance-in-britain-a-conversation-with-adam-elliot-cooper/

30 People's Tribunal on Police Killings website: https://peoples-tribunal.org/

31 People's Tribunal on Police Killings (2025). Tribunal document, 5–6 April 2025, p. 4. https://peoplestribunal.info/wp-content/uploads/2025/03/PTPK-Tribunal-Document.pdf

32 People's Tribunal, Tribunal document, p. 10.

33 People's Tribunal, Tribunal document, p. 25.

34 See *Better Off Dead?* Directed by Liz Carr, BBC One, May 2024.

35 Alder, J. (2024). *Defiance: Racial Injustice, Police Brutality, a Sister's Fight for the Truth*. London: Dialogue Books.

36 People's Tribunal, tribunal document, pp. 3–4.

37 Permanent Peoples' Tribunal, Final Deliberation, Session on the violations with impunity of the human rights of migrant and refugee peoples (2017-2019), hostile environment on trial, London hearing 3-4 November 2018. London: Pemanent Peoples' Tribunal London Steering Group, 2018. https://static1.squarespace.com/static/5ef1ea802f151722ebb7bb43/t/5efa0362 195b1f4a833b97f2/1593443176894/PPT-London-Deliberation_FINAL.pdf

38 Bassel, L. (2022). A promise of listening: migrant justice and the London Permanent Peoples' Tribunal. *Race and Class*, 63(4), 35–55 (p. 38).

39 Bassel, A promise of listening, pp. 48–9.

40 Project South (2019). https://meyerfoundation.org/wp-content/uploads/2019/12/Peoples-Movement-Assembly-Organizing-Handbook.pdf

41 Project South, pp. 8–9.

6. JUSTICE WITHIN AND BEYOND THE STATE

1 Wynne-Jones, R. (2015). Sheila Holt: woman ordered to find work while lying in coma dies aged 48. *Mirror*, 17 March 2015. www.mirror.co.uk/news/uk-news/ros-wynne-jones-sheila-hounded-death-5353202

2 Pring, J. (2015). Fitness for work test and sanctions helped kill my brother. Disability News Service, 9 October 2015. www.disabilitynewsservice.com/fitness-for-work-test-and-sanctions-helped-kill-my-brother/

3 Pring, Fitness for work test.

4 DPAC (2015). IDS files: Iain Duncan Smith vs reality. https://dpac.uk.net/2015/08/the-ids-files-iain-duncan-smith-vs-reality-idsfiles/

5 Ritchie, A.J. (2024). *Practicing New Worlds: Abolition and Emergent Strategies*. Chico, CA: AK Press, p. 4.

6 Mills, C. and Pring, J. (2024). Weaponising time in the war on welfare: slow violence and deaths of disabled people within the UK's social security system. *Critical Social Policy*, 44(1), 129–49.

7 UK Parliament (2023). Health Transformation Programme update. Statement made on 25 May 2023. Statement UIN HCWS807. https://questions-statements.parliament.uk/written-statements/detail/2023-05-25/hcws807

8 Aves, W. (2023). Justice won't be found in the coroner's court. Psychiatry is Driving Me Mad blog. www.psychiatryisdrivingmemad.co.uk/post/justice-won-t-be-found-in-the-coroner-s-court

9 Inquiries Act 2005. www.legislation.gov.uk/ukpga/2005/12/contents

10 Pring, J. (2012). MPs join activists and families in call for public inquiry into years of DWP deaths. Disability News Service, 12 December 2024. www.disabilitynewsservice.com/mps-join-activists-and-families-in-call-for-public-inquiry-into-years-of-dwp-deaths/

11 Reclaiming Our Futures Alliance (ROFA) website: www.rofa.org.uk/ ; and Pring, MPs join activists.

12 Casciani, D. (2024). Grenfell Report: key findings from the inquiry. BBC, 4 September 2024. www.bbc.co.uk/news/articles/c049yvrd5qxo

13 Helm, T. (2018). Disabled people lose legal aid in 99% of benefits disputes. *Guardian*, 14 April 2018. www.theguardian.com/society/2018/apr/14/disabled-people-lose-legal-aid-99-per-cent-benefits-disputes

14 Public Law Project (2025). High Court victory for PLP client over DWP consultation on disability benefit reforms. https://publiclawproject.org.uk/latest/high-court-victory-for-plp-client-over-dwp-consultation-on-disability-benefit-reforms/ and full judgment here: https://publiclawproject.org.uk/content/uploads/2025/01/Clifford-v-SSWP-Judgment-16-January-2025-1.pdf

15 Spade, D. (2015). *Normal Life: Administrative Violence, Critical Trans Politics, and the Limits of Law.* Durham, NC: Duke University Press, p. 71.

16 Brown, W. (1995). *States of Injury: Power and Freedom in Late Modernity.* Princeton, NJ: Princeton University Press, p. 124.

17 Piepzna-Samarasinha, L.L. (undated). Disability Justice: an audit tool. https://static1.squarespace.com/static/5ed94da22956b942e1d51e12/t/625877951e18163c703bd0f4/1649964964772/DJ+Audit+Tool.pdf; Sins Invalid: https://sinsinvalid.org/about-sins/

18 Sins Invalid (2019). Skin, tooth and bone: the basis of movement is our people. A Disability Justice Primer. Sins Invalid.

19 Lewis, T.A. (2020). Disability Justice is an essential part of abolishing police and prisons. https://level.medium.com/disability-justice-is-an-essential-part-of-abolishing-police-and-prisons-2b4a019b5730

20 Sins Invalid (undated). 10 principles of Disability Justice. https://sinsinvalid.org/10-principles-of-disability-justice/

21 National Coalition of Blacks for Reparations in America: https://ncobraphl.org/about-ncobra/

22 UN (2005). Basic Principles and Guidelines on the Right to a Remedy and Reparation for Victims of Gross Violations of International Human Rights Law and Serious Violations of International Humanitarian Law: draft resolution. https://digitallibrary.un.org/record/545961?ln=en&v=pdf

23 Runnymede Trust. (2025). *Reparations*. London: Runnymede Trust.

24 Black Families Love & Unite: https://blackfamiliesloveandunite.org/

25 Roberts, D. (2022). *Torn Apart: How the Child Welfare System Destroys Black Families – and How Abolition Can Build a Safer World*. New York: Basic Books, p. 303.

26 Pring, J. (2024). Deaths, lies and cover-ups: the case for a public inquiry into the 'unthinkable cost' of DWP's systemic violence. Disability News Service, 20 December 2024. www.disabilitynewsservice.com/deaths-lies-and-cover-ups-the-case-for-a-public-inquiry-into-the-unthinkable-cost-of-dwps-systemic-violence/

27 Worthy, I. (2025). Why Aren't we talking about family policing when we talk about reparations? https://imprintnews.org/opinion/why-arent-we-talking-about-family-policing-when-we-talk-about-reparations/260100#:~:text=Reparations%20for%20family%20policing%20also,stop%20terrorizing%20communities%20of%20color

28 Worthy, Why aren't we talking about.

29 BLU (2024). Repairing harms from family policing. https://issuu.com/blackfamiliesloveandunite/docs/reparationsinchildwelfare; and BLU (2025). Families belong together, families demand repair. https://issuu.com/blackfamiliesloveandunite/docs/2025_blu_report_draft_final_pages

7. ABOLITION

1 Kaba, M. (2021). *We Do This til We Free Us: Abolitionist Organising and Transforming Justice*. Chicago, IL: Haymarket Books, p. 4.

2 Wilson Gilmore, R. (2020). Abolition is presence, which means abolition is life in rehearsal. Cited in Hayes, K. and Kaba, M. (2023). *Let This Radicalize You: Organizing and the Revolution of Reciprocal Care*. Chicago, IL: Haymarket Books, p. 236.

3 Clifford, E. (2020). *The War on Disabled People: Capitalism, Welfare and the Making of a Human Catastrophe*. London: Zed Books, p. 309.

4 Kaba, *We Do This til We Free Us*, p. 65.

5 Ritchie, A.J. (2024). *Practicing New Worlds: Abolition and Emergent Strategies*. Chico, CA: AK Press, pp. 5–6.

6 Boggs, G.L. (2011). *The Next American Revolution: Sustainable Activism for the Twenty-First Century*. Oakland, CA: University of California Press, p. 53.

7 Piepzna-Samarasinha, L.L. (2021). How disabled mutual aid is different than abled mutual aid. Disability Visibility project. https://disabilityvisibilityproject.com/2021/10/03/how-disabled-mutual-aid-is-different-than-abled-mutual-aid/

8 Mingus, M. (2011). Access intimacy: The missing link. Leaving Evidence blog. https://leavingevidence.wordpress.com/2011/05/05/access-intimacy-the-missing-link/

9 Humphry, D. (2023). 'I've always felt these spaces were ours': disability activism and austerity capitalism: reflections on *City*'s interview with DPAC. *City*, 27(1–2), 162–89 (p. 181).

10 brown, a.m. (2019). Fractals: the relationship between small and large [Fractales: la relación entre lo pequeño y lo grande]. https://earthlingopinion.wordpress.com/2019/03/01/fractals-the-relationship-between-small-and-large/

11 Ritchie, *Practicing New Worlds*, pp. 24, 17.

12 Humphry, 'I've always felt these spaces were ours'.

13 Proxy Protest: www.arjunhm.co.uk/projects/proxy-protest/

14 Gorz, A. (1987). Strategy for labor. In Nissen, B. and Larson, S. (Eds), *Theories of the Labor Movement*. Detroit, MI: Wayne State University Press.

15 Kaba, *We Do This til We Free Us*, p. 149.

16 Kaba, *We Do This til We Free Us*, p. 65.

17 See Up End Movement's Framework for evaluating reforms to the family policing system. https://upendmovement.org/wp-content/uploads/2023/01/upEND-abolitionist-framework-01-2023.pdf

18 Humphry, 'I've always felt these spaces were ours'.

19 Humphry, 'I've always felt these spaces were ours'.
20 Northern Police Monitoring Project (NPMP) (2026). Fund communities not policing. https://npolicemonitor.co.uk/wp-content/uploads/2026/01/a4-fund-communities-booklet-3-2.pdf
21 See Baobab Foundation: www.baobabfoundation.org.uk/ and Project Tallawah: https://www.projecttallawah.org/
22 Civic Square Neighbourhood Doughnut: https://drive.google.com/file/d/1xB9Do11juIIdruD11xBQ3wHEH9gMk9cY/view
23 Scottish Parliament Community Wealth Building Bill (2026): www.gov.scot/news/investing-in-local-economies/
24 DisOrdinary Architecture: https://disordinaryarchitecture.co.uk
25 Spence, A. (2026). Land is the question: on racial capitalism, spatial justice and the urgency of a Land B(l)ack movement. https://amahraspence.substack.com/p/land-is-the-question?utm_source=share&utm_medium=android&r=62xmcv&triedRedirect=true
26 Dark Matter Labs (2024). Life-ennobling economics. https://provocations.darkmatterlabs.org/introducing-life-ennobling-economics-part-1-d950ae770ef2
27 Dark Matter Labs, Life-ennobling economics.
28 Ritchie, *Practicing New Worlds*, p. 95.
29 Spade, D. (2015). *Normal Life: Administrative Violence, Critical Trans Politics, and the Limits of Law.* Durham, NC: Duke University Press, p. 6.
30 Ritchie, *Practicing New Worlds*, p. 45.
31 Lamble, S. (2022). Resisting the cop in our head. *New Internationalist*, 14 April 2022. https://newint.org/features/2022/02/07/everyday-abolition-resisting-cop-our-heads
32 Ndefo, N. (2025). Rootwork: rallying together for these times. A series of workshops with Nkem Ndefo and Healing Justice Ldn, November 2025.
33 Haines, S.K., cited in Healing Justice Ldn (2025). Movement Medicine Handbook. Internal document. Also see Haines, S.K. (2019). *The Politics of Trauma: Somatics, Healing, and Social Justice.* Berkeley, CA: North Atlantic Books.
34 Healing Justice Ldn (2025). Movement Medicine Handbook. Internal document.
35 Healing Justice Ldn, Movement Medicine Handbook.
36 Jethwa, N. (2025). 'What it takes to heal', with Prentis Hemphill, Marai Larasi and Farzana Khan. https://healingjusticeldn.org/methodology/what-it-takes-to-heal/

37 Levins Morales, A. (2019). *Medicine Stories: Essays for Radicals*. Durham, NC: Duke University Press, pp. 48–9.
38 Haines, *The Politics of Trauma*.
39 Haines, S.K. (2020). The politics of trauma. Open Democracy, 11 August 2020. www.opendemocracy.net/en/transformation/politics-trauma/
40 Haines, *Politics of Trauma*, p. 298.
41 Haines, *Politics of Trauma*, p. 298.
42 Tyler, I. and Campbell, S. (2024). Poverty stigma: a glue that holds poverty in place. Joseph Rowntree Foundation. www.jrf.org.uk/power-and-participation/poverty-stigma-a-glue-that-holds-poverty-in-place
43 Stigma Free Futures manifesto.
44 Stigma Free Futures manifesto.
45 Kaba, M. (2023). Beyond doom, toward collective action. In Hayes, K. and Kaba, M. (2023). *Let This Radicalize You: Organizing and the Revolution of Reciprocal Care*. Chicago, IL: Haymarket Books, pp. 178, 149.
46 Hayes, K. and Kaba, M. (2023). *Let This Radicalize You: Organizing and the Revolution of Reciprocal Care*. Chicago, IL: Haymarket Books, p. 232.
47 Shields, D. (2021). A heavy nonpresence. Canopy, p. 19. https://tc3.canopycanopycanopy.com/contents/a-heavy-nonpresence
48 Johar, I. (2015). From welfare as cost to collective investment (draft). Dark Matter Labs. https://provocations.darkmatterlabs.org/from-welfare-as-cost-to-collective-investment-draft-d605efb05039

INDEX